Beyond the Sound of Cannon

Beyond the Sound of Cannon
Military Strategy in the 1990s

by

Richard J. Meinhold

McFarland & Company, Inc., Publishers
Jefferson, North Carolina, and London

355.033
M51b

British Library Cataloguing-in-Publication data are available

Library of Congress Cataloguing-in-Publication Data

Meinhold, Richard J., 1935–
    Beyond the sound of cannon : military strategy in the 1990s / by
Richard J. Meinhold.
      p.   cm.
    Includes bibliographical references (p. 175) and
index.
    ISBN 0-89950-697-6 (library bdg. : 50# alkaline paper) ∞
    1. United States — Military policy. 2. United States — National
security. I. Title.
UA23.M44 1992
355'.0335'73 — dc20   91-50943
                                                   CIP

Manufactured in the United States of America

McFarland & Company, Inc., Publishers
  Box 611, Jefferson, North Carolina 28640

For all my shipmates,
past and present,
wherever they may be

Contents

Introduction

Ever since humans first appeared on the earth they have been in continuous conflict with nature and, frequently, with other people as first, tribes fought tribes, then communities fought communities, city-states fought city-states, and finally, nation-states fought nation-states. Man the warrior is both an historic and contemporary figure.

In times when primitive transportation, communications, and weapons limited a group's effectiveness, the planning of battle structure, force movement, and concentration of forces were minimal because clashes were constrained in scope, time, and the damage wrought. As technological progress removed these limitations, the payoff for developing and executing strategy increased markedly.

The Importance of Strategy

Nearly everyone has some sense of what strategy is. Heinrich von Bülow, a German man-about-many-things writing in the early 1800s, defined strategy as "the science of the movements of war outside the field of vision of the enemy, tactics being within their vision."[1] The word strategy is derived from the Greek "strategia," meaning generalship,[2] and until the recent past, has been used almost exclusively in relation to military matters.[3]

Military strategy is now officially defined as "the art and science of employing the armed forces of a nation to secure the objectives of national policy by the application of force or the threat of force."[4] A military strategist is a laborer in the field of military strategy. He or she develops a strategy or several strategies that are, quite basically, designs for the employment of resources to fulfill certain objectives that will assist in reaching established strategic goals. Strategic goals in a military context relate to a war rather than to a battle, the latter being merely a constituent part of the former.[5]

In our time strategies must marshal all of the wealth, manpower, and

1

will of a nation and employ them with purpose so that a government may carry out its responsibilities, including the physical protection of its citizens and the conservation of the society it serves. To fulfill these security needs, most nations have created and maintained an armed military force. But establishing and sustaining such a force is not enough; it must be employed in ways that enhance the security of the nation—a challenging task in today's environment. The employment process generally begins with planning, and this element is the subject of the pages which follow.

National security is the term used to describe the product of efforts to ensure that a nation's territory, institutions, and freedom to interact with other nations are protected from outside intervention. While the term itself is relatively new, the concept can be traced to the early stages of human development. Subjected to ongoing physical, economic, and social threats, prehistoric peoples began grouping together into communities as a way of coping with these threats and achieving some level of security.

The nation-state that eventually emerged represented a higher level of group response to these same dangers. Nationhood was not a panacea, however, because threats to nations developed as well. A strong state was subject to pressure from the outside; that is, from other states. Weak ones not only faced danger from the outside, but could be challenged from the inside whenever reform-minded groups struggled for power. These threats continue to challenge countries today; a modern nation needs to devote as much attention to security in its mature years as it did in its growing ones.

Techniques employed to establish the security of a nation would, in a perfect world, reflect careful, reasoned identification of its vital interests and the best alternatives for protecting them. The specific activities undertaken on the basis of such study would probably represent an amalgamation of interests and prevalent views on the subject. However, in this imperfect world decisions are often based on other criteria. Here in the United States, national security policy fluctuates with the perspective of the political party currently in power and is sometimes only discernible indirectly through careful study of the matters that typically dominate headlines and thus occupy attention —the defense budget and the procurement of weapon systems. Although this focus on budgetary and procurement matters in the United States is not new—expenditures on or for the military have drawn a critical audience except during wartime—the level of attention it currently receives says much about the contemporary role of the military.

U.S. Strategy in the World Arena

Emphasis on the armed forces as the primary instrument in maintaining national security developed in the immediate post–World War II years.

Before that war, the nation's security was largely a product of more than a century and a half of geographic and political isolation from the world's other power centers. By 1939, however, advances in transportation communications and weapon technology were making the world smaller. Therefore, when nearly six years of fighting Nazi Germany had left most of the countries in Europe powerless and thus vulnerable to infiltration, if not invasion, by the forces of anticapitalism, leadership in the United States saw no alternative to ending the country's isolation and assuming a leadership role.

This role reversal, whatever its positive effects, soon resulted in the division of much of the world into two opposing ideological camps. The leaders of these groups, the United States and the Soviet Union, had emerged from the war militarily much stronger than other countries because the raw power of nuclear energy as a weapon had been demonstrated; military capability assumed greater importance and eventually overshadowed all other considerations. An actual war between these heavily armed adversaries seemed likely to destroy the world, so a conflict of a different sort was joined. Not a war of bullets, but of influence and ideology, a zero-sum game with uncommitted nations as the markers. Unfortunately, because the wartime bipartisanship in American foreign policy had foundered on political rocks, maneuvers in this non-shooting contest were not to be planned by those experienced in the give and take of diplomacy, but by those who wore uniforms.

The State Department, full of experienced professional Foreign Service officers and very much in charge of policy, was politicized in 1952 when the Republican Party regained power for the first time in 20 years. Gradually, much of the expertise in the State Department was diluted to such an extent that the foreign policy of the administrations that followed, irrespective of political persuasion, seemed awash in shifting and poorly defined objectives. During this time the nuclear threat represented by the Soviet Union became more stark and more immediate when ballistic missiles were added to the list of vehicles capable of delivering a nuclear attack. Under these conditions, the national security apparatus came to be dominated by the Department of Defense.

This perception of an increased threat to the nation propelled security issues to the forefront of the electoral process. From the presidential campaign in 1948 on, a candidate's attitude toward military preparedness, communism, and relations with the Soviet Union became matters to be weighed heavily in assessing his fitness for office. More recently, in addition to these general matters, candidates' positions on the advisability of building or procuring particular weapon systems have become specific campaign issues.

Unfortunately, such national security litmus tests have not produced a particularly enlightened, or even *consistent*, approach to security problems. Rather, they have resulted only in an "undifferentiated and excessively abstract view of U.S. vital interests and of Soviet threats to them, crisis-born fluctuations in perception of the threat, spasmodic responses to uninterrupted crisis and the [growing] disparity between interests and power."[6]

In the beginning, deliberate decisions were made. When Stalin refused to withdraw the Red Army from eastern European countries, supported communist guerrillas in Greece, and began pressuring Turkey over the Dardanelles in the late 1940s, the fear that communism would spread throughout Europe provoked a U.S. strategy of containing "aggression" of the Soviet Union, almost without regard to its location. This decision begat commitments in all corners of the globe, many of which called for (and still do) U.S. military force deployments or employments, some simultaneously, and potentially on opposite sides of the world. Forces were structured, equipped and rationalized on the basis of the bi- and multilateral agreements forged in support of the strategy.

Now, many years later, most of the conditions that necessitated those promises of military support no longer exist; the world has changed in dramatic ways. Whereas 51 nations allied to the United Nations organization in 1945, there are more than 159 member nations today.[7] While the Soviet Union and the United States remain the only superpower states from a military perspective, the Soviet Union is an economic disaster area; the United States no longer dominates the world economy as it once did because the countries of Western Europe, Japan, and other Asian nations have recovered from the devastation of war and returned to economic viability. Evidence is accumulating that there may be as many as five world powers instead of just two in the not too distant future.

The extent of the change in relations between the United States and the Soviet Union can be seen when considering that, despite decades of tension and sometimes outright hostility, agreements have been reached on a number of issues of contention. Further, a reduction, if not elimination, of any likelihood of a military clash between opposing alliances in Europe has occurred with the dissolution of the Warsaw Pact in the wake of the loosening of the grip of the Communist Party in countries it has dominated. Commercial contact is growing.

Although war between the superpowers has thus far been averted, the frequency of conflict has not declined since World War II; rather, the number of "smaller" conflicts has increased, particularly where nationalistic feelings, often exacerbated by deep-seated religious, economic, or cultural differences, have boiled to the surface. Revolution and violence have often resulted.

At the same time, nonmilitary threats to world peace and security have proliferated to the extent that economic instability, environmental destruction (acid rain), life-threatening diseases such as Acquired Immune Deficiency Syndrome (AIDS), and substance abuse (particularly drugs) may, if left unchecked, produce social outcomes at least as devastating as war. The recognition that grappling with these issues is an integral part of national security is only now dawning.

Reassessing U.S. Strategic Planning

In light of all this change, the U.S. faces a strategic dilemma. The designs for achieving national scurity objectives, i.e., its strategies, have remained, for all practical purposes, the same as when they were formulated some 40 years ago. However, a national security strategy designed to counter a particular enemy in a less sophisticated and bipolar world is not likely to be adequate and appropriate for the technologically advanced and multipolar one that seems to be emerging.

The same is true in the area of military strategy. Since, as noted earlier, military considerations have dominated foreign policy areas for years, a relaxation of military tensions should result in a return to a balanced approach of statesmanship and military muscle in national security affairs. Translating that into military strategy will not necessarily be easy, however, because as Richard Stubbing says in *The Defense Game*,

> The formation of U.S. Defense policy is at once a debate — concerning extremely complex judgments as to military threats, requirements, strategies and technologies — and a tug of war between powerful and often unseen interests in the defense establishment. Thus the defense program is in no way a rational blueprint leading from clearly identified threats to coherent military plans and efficient defense expenditures.[8]

The type of intramural struggle referred to above is typical of conflict resolution in U.S. society; in this case it reflects the more than two centuries of experience, real and imagined, that has fostered particular views regarding the makeup and exercise of American military power. Alas, in the contemporary world this problem-solving methodology may be dysfunctional, if not downright dangerous, because it tends to focus attention inward on the arguments rather than outward on the problem.

The specific future, of course, is unknown. It is certain, however, that the environment of the years ahead will to a large degree be shaped by decisions made today. Because wars have often started when one side miscalculated the intentions, commitment, or value system of the other, decisions to exercise military (or any sort of national) power must be made wisely. How a leader might use the power available to him will depend on his relationship with his followers, his strategic vision, his predilections regarding the use of the military, the character of the forces to be employed, and the extent to which the specific problem has been analyzed, all matters of interest when developing schemes of military action—that is, military strategy. The extent to which each of these elements is "in play" will greatly influence the magnitude and direction of force application. If decisions neglect current realities and are made without regard to the interests of the nation and its direction, the future is likely to be rife with crisis and conflict, conditions that have all too often given rise to the use (or abuse) of national military power.

In this book I have sought to illuminate important features of these critical planning elements and portray the current state of the process for developing military strategy here in the United States—with all its warts—in the hope that attention will be directed to making the necessary improvements. Specific strategies will not be explicated in any depth here; to the extent that they exist, they are well detailed elsewhere.

Chapter I contains an assessment of the impact of critical political, economic, and technological environmental elements on the development of military strategy. In earlier times, the use of force and the manner of engagement were more clearly understood. The development of atomic and nuclear weapons and the proliferation of conventional weapons, as well as the squeeze of political, social, and economic pressures, have added new dimensions to the traditional craft of warfare. The expanded spectrum of conflict that has emerged runs the gamut from terrorist acts to general nuclear war. Each class is described and the readiness of U.S. forces to participate in them is discussed. The picture is not bright.

The reasons for this pessimism are detailed in the next several chapters. First, the development of strategy and strategic thought in the United States, including its historical roots, is briefly traced. Chapter II documents strategy in American history through the end of World War II, a period that revealed the two faces of the United States, isolationist and internationalist. Prior to World War II, the United States had spent most of its recognized existence avoiding, as much as possible, political contact with other power centers of the world. To be sure, many (but certainly a small minority) had recognized that responsible participation in the affairs of the world would be necessary. When that participation was finally forced on the country in the aftermath of World War II, it was ill prepared to accept the burden.

Chapter III tells that part of the story. As the sole possessor of atomic weapons in the immediate postwar period, the United States was unquestionably the most powerful country in the world. When the choice was made to remain globally engaged, changes were needed to ensure that any call could be answered. A national security apparatus was erected, which included the National Security Council to advise the President, the Central Intelligence Agency to better coordinate intelligence collection and interpretation, and a National Military Establishment (the name was changed to the Department of Defense later) to provide military forces.

This structure was designed to aid in containing Soviet Union adventurism and to protect the United States. When the Soviets exploded an atomic weapon in 1949, it became clear that the future of the United States was to be nothing like its past. The popular notion that atomic weapons alone could ensure peace was seriously undermined when North Korea ignored their potential and attacked South Korea, although the implications of this act were not well recognized at the time.

The attraction of the relatively small and less expensive military force required to operate a nuclear deterrent force proved irresistible to the U.S. military establishment, and a proclamation was made to the effect that nuclear weapons would be used in "massive retaliation" for any transgression. Not surprisingly, this concept quickly proved inadequate and was replaced in the 1960s by the doctrine of flexible response, according to which force was to be met with like force—nuclear with nuclear, conventional weapons and forces with conventional. In a very real sense, all of these strategies have been successful vis-à-vis the Soviet Union, but less so in other parts of the world. The fruits of this history culminate, for good or ill, in the U.S. defense establishment of today, which will, unless some intervention occurs, continue to be part of tomorrow.

Chapter IV is devoted to describing today's dynamic environment, where political, economic, and intramural forces exert pressure on the military, while the threat against which most of the defense establishment was erected is melting away. Demands for a smaller defense budget and, consequently, a smaller military force have followed. These appeals are both philosophical and pragmatic. Throughout United States history, whenever no immediate threat was in sight, pressures to dismantle the existing military establishment have mounted because its maintenance is seen as a diversion of resources better spent in the business arena. Pragmatically, there is a disinclination to pay the cost of maintaining a large force structure.

Currently, the perception of a diminished threat emanating from the Soviet Union is based largely on the assessment that the intention to do the United States harm is no longer present even though the capability to do damage remains. Of utmost importance in the calculus, however, is the incontrovertible fact that while intentions may rapidly change (in a few months, days, or even hours or minutes), rebuilding a capability, if destroyed or otherwise not present, can literally take years. It is for this reason that striking a balance among the elements of national power, foreign and military policy, and the forces to execute them is mandatory.

Reducing the military establishment by very much may also have unwelcome consequences in the economic arena. Since World War II, the military-industrial complex has become, quite apart from its contribution in making the country secure, an integral part of both the political and economic landscape. The defense establishment (industry, and the Department of Defense, which includes civilians and military) is estimated to employ some 6.7 million people[9] and contributes to the economy of all 50 states to some degree. Companies and corporations involved in military production are large contributors to political action committees and to the campaigns of individual politicians.

The task of reconciling the diverse views on this subject is complicated by the fact that most of the players thrusting and parrying have been conditioned to accept a set of beliefs about how a nation should use its military power. This American strategic culture has evolved through the interaction of elements that will be treated in the next three chapters. Its geopolitical derivations make up the substance of Chapter V. The geographic location of the United States provided a sufficient level of security during the early, particularly vulnerable, years. Ensuring that security in the long run, however, prompted other actions that included significant acquisitions of land, by purchase and other means, and the establishment of some sort of protective force. Because the drafters of the Constitution were determined to forge a nation different from those in the Old World, the military element created was unlike those of other nations. It was to be controlled by civilians and sized only as needed. In the long run, the country was to be defended by its citizens.

The results of that approach are reviewed in Chapter VI, where the actions of the U.S. military forces in their major engagements through the years are chronicled. This path has not been particularly long in relation to the military histories of many other nations, but it has featured involvement in a variety of types of conflict.

The predilection to reduce military forces to almost nothing in the wake of these wars ensured that little planning for a military confrontation of nearly any sort was in evidence until after World War II. When some preparation was undertaken, it was focused on a single enemy.

The last element shaping the strategic culture is the perspective offered by the larger American culture and its embedded value set — to the extent that this polyglot society can be said to have a dominant one. It seems to be true that in this relatively populous nation the majority of people have little interest in much beyond their own backyard, with the result that a small group of citizens defines the values and the larger issues of international intercourse for the rest. The communications revolution, which has provided nearly unlimited access to information, has not ameliorated this condition to any great extent, particularly given an environment where the majority of people seem not to care.

Chapter VII analyzes how the discernible value set shared by most Americans appears to be less a definition, but rather an aspiration.

Concepts of morality, technological achievement, pragmatism, and competition are important to Americans and thus influence their interactions in the world.

The strategic culture that emerges from the melding of the geopolitical, military, and social elements infects all, including the developers of military strategy. If planning for a future is to be more than simply planning for a new past, the developer and the decision maker must recognize and account for the confining elements of that culture.

This focus on the strategic heritage and culture of the United States can provide a framework for understanding the problems that exist in the development of military strategy. Chapter VIII contains a description of the strategic framework that represents the whole. One dimension of that structure is hierarchical in nature; at the highest level is the strategy that is to guide the nation in pursuit of its interests. A clear statement of this "national strategy" is absolutely critical since all others, in a sense, flow from it. Next are the organizational strategies formulated by the governmental departments, such as Defense and State, to employ their "forces" in support of the national strategy. At the third level are operational strategies. These are carried out by the major divisions within the departments; in the Department of Defense, for example, the unified commanders command forces in the various theaters and mission areas of interest. The lowest level discussed here is the level at which execution strategies are formed. These provide for direct unit maneuver just above the tactical action level.

Those who develop these strategies find themselves working in three dimensions because the framework has the additional elements of geographical location and the political state of the world. When viewed in its totality, then, the "body" of military strategy accommodates all contingencies, with strategies formulated for all areas of interest under all likely conditions at all appropriate levels.

Because the grand or national strategy of the United States has been so stable for the past 45 years, little creative development has occurred at any level. That which has been undertaken has exercised organizations at the unified commander (operational strategy) and component commander (execution strategy) levels. The most recent example is that developed for allied forces in the war with Iraq (Operation Desert Storm) by the Commander-in-Chief, Central Command. Given the anticipated shape of the world that is now emerging, new strategies will be needed at all levels in the last years of the twentieth century—a significant challenge!

Unfortunately, the system may not be up to producing useful innovations. Chapter IX enumerates some institutional problems as well as all-too-human failings, like cognitive blocks and biases of various types, which are likely to inhibit the flexibility and responsiveness needed. It is not the developmental process alone that is of concern, but the evaluation and decision processes as well. Having developed candidate strategies, an evaluation of each one relative to its chances of achieving the desired objectives and choosing of one (or several) to be employed must be made.

Unfortunately, as is addressed in Chapter X, obstacles exist here as well. High-level strategies are difficult to evaluate both because of their size and scope and because a good methodology for doing so is not yet at hand. Those at lower levels can be evaluated to a degree by "capturing" reality through exercises, simulations, games, and analytic models. Each of these "tools" has its strengths and its deficiencies.

Whatever the process employed in assessing the viability of a strategy, a decision to use it, or the selection of one from among an array of alternatives, is necessary. It is difficult to have much confidence in the outcome of the current process for choosing. Decision systems have been largely ignored by the military until recently, although this is the arena where help is desperately needed. The most effective defensive system in the world is useless if deployed in the wrong place or at the wrong time. There are techniques that could aid decision makers, such as decision diagrams, but the time and talent for humans to develop alternatives using them is probably excessive.

This review of the tools at hand does not bolster confidence in the ability of the establishment to develop, evaluate, and put in place military strategies appropriate to locations and conditions in the years ahead. Almost nothing in the American experience prepares us for coping with what the future seems likely to bring. Significant attitudinal changes in the doer and process changes in the doing are necessary. They are neither unimaginable nor impossible. Suggestions as to how the changes might be brought about are detailed in Chapter XI, while Chapter XII summarizes the work.

So long as thousands of nuclear warheads and millions of conventional ones remain at hand amid rising expectations, dwindling resources, ideological differences, and a widening gap between the rich and the poor, it is unlikely that the danger of all war can be ended permanently. However, as a country and a people, we can, with courage and wisdom, continue to minimize the chances of the occurrence of a cataclysmic one, as well as manage lesser conflicts that might break out by preparing and executing comprehensive strategies. But an effort to do so must be undertaken, an effort that focuses around the energies of the citizenry, for "a well-informed public is the best ally of a rational national security policy."[10]

While engaging the public is never an easy task, it is extremely important that all affected participate in the national security process. As Rear Admiral J. C. Wylie has stated, "Strategy is everybody's business. Too many lives are at stake for us not to recognize [it] as a legitimate and important public concern."[11] It is my hope that this book will provoke some to interest themselves more directly in their own and the nation's future.

CHAPTER I

Living in an Uncertain World

The Evolution of Conflict

Human history is filled with the sounds of battle — a musical score influenced in every era by the prevailing political, economic, and technological environment.[1] In the prehistoric period, early peoples could be said to have been in "violent motion" everywhere, moving across the land, killing, destroying, and occasionally building. Warfare was often a way of life for all able-bodied men; weak tribes simply disappeared, either destroyed or assimilated by their more powerful neighbors. Tribes gave their allegiance to the strong. When there was no one to fight, restless young men sought out a leader who provided them with food, shelter and weapons in exchange for their services.

In some areas, enough people gathered and worked together to build a community; other groups developed a nomadic way of life; and still others became traders and explorers on land and sea. Communities grew into small city-states that survived only until overrun and destroyed by invaders, who would then build a new civilization on the ruins. This group would in turn be overwhelmed, and yet another civilization would take its place. Where conditions were right, permanent settlements devoted to agriculture, animal husbandry, and mining took root; goverments proliferated, armies were formed, battles fought, and empires created.

Gradually, the concept of service to the governmental entity became widespread. Free men were expected to serve when called, and to bring their own food and equipment. Early empires like those of Mesopotamia, Egypt, Greece, China, and Rome fielded relatively large armies made up of "regulars" and "militia" to acquire territory and protect their borders.

However, countless battles against external enemies, civil wars, revolts, and the death toll attributable to disease eventually weakened most empires and left them vulnerable to determined attack. The cost of expanding or defending, in both human and economic terms, undermined governmental structures to the extent that by the ninth century, the locus of power in European states was shifting from the king to the wealthy land owner. This became even more pronounced as feudalism took hold in Europe.

Powerful men gathered peasants around them to work the land and to populate their private armies. When between-settlement trading of products gathered momentum and a market economy was revitalized, it had both a civilizing and a locally demilitarizing effect. Townspeople grew less inclined to leave their businesses or farms to fight; they often chose, instead, to hire soldiers to fight for them. This largely selfish act had a particularly salutary effect in that it eliminated plundering by "unemployed" soldiers — paid a living wage, those worthies no longer had to turn to that particular form of military art.

With the protection offered by the mercenaries the economy was free to grow, thus raising more tax revenue. This surplus, in turn, could be used to hire more, or more competent, soldiers and to obtain better weapons for them, ensuring a high standard of protection. Since the soldiers were likely to spend much of their pay in the town, the economy was further stimulated; the cycle benefited all as the quality of life improved. By the fifteenth century European city-states were recruiting and organizing substantial mercenary armies. From the soldier's perspective, it was a business; soldiers moved easily from army to army.

The capabilities and size of the armies maintained depended on the wealth of the sponsoring individual or organization. Superiority was often determined by the number of armed men fielded and the sophistication and extent of supply, communications, and weapon capabilities.

The size of armies could be increased by a variety of techniques, including the most direct method of hiring or conscripting more men. Alliances with other tribes, city-states, or nations could also be entered into, which could effectively increase the size of a force and might enhance total fighting capability as well. Such alliances might deter larger and more powerful enemies from attempting to dominate either the individual unit or the resultant union.

Supplying food for the soldiers and fodder for the horses was critical to any military operation. Early armies were expected to live off the land by foraging, an activity that took time and energy from the business at hand and could be dangerous in unfriendly territory. Later, when supplies were transported along with the army, the number of days of operation were determined by the amount carried; continual replenishment was required for extended operations.

Communications and weapon capabilities became more critical as battle threatened. The greater the distance between communicating elements, the more fragile the link. Initially the means of communication were restricted to visual or aural signals like smoke signals, flags, or bugle calls. The receiver had to have a sight line to the sender or be within hearing. To guarantee communication of information, a prior understanding of the meaning of each signal was mandatory. Moreover, an agreement on meaning had to be reached before any attempt; consequently, the types of information likely to be communicated had to be anticipated.

These conditions tended to bound the information exchange fairly narrowly. When the receiver was out of sight or hearing, messengers carrying written or verbal communiques had to be employed. This was a time-consuming, not to mention uncertain, method; if harm befell the messenger in or near an actual fight, an important message might go undelivered. The communication techniques and their reliability dictated, to a large extent, the ability to deploy, maneuver, and react.

Finally, if all else were equal, the quality of arms carried by each side could make the difference. Wealthy governments or organizations could buy the most modern arms to increase their chance of victory. As economic conditions improved, the introduction of new technology produced more effective weapons. Improvements in two areas in particular provided significant enhancements in capability: increasing the range and the rate of application of weapons.

In the earliest days, when the weapon was little more than a sharpened stick, the "range" of application was dependent on the wielder's reach and thus was measured in feet — until some imaginative (or perhaps desperate) warrior threw his, increasing the effective range to yards. In the one-man, one-stick situation, a warrior could be counted on to engage only a handful of enemies during a finite period of time, regardless of his fighting fervor and strength. Compounding the problem of range and number of applications was the requirement to hold on to the stick, or, alternately to maintain a large supply of them very close at hand, which limited mobility.

Increasing the range of weapons and improving the rate of use made each soldier much more effective because he could deliver a greater number of weapons during a fixed period of time. Probably the first significant increase was provided by the bow and arrow. Because of the standoff provided, the archer could deliver numbers of arrows at the enemy as it approached. From a strategy standpoint, this added firepower made more maneuver options possible. Artillery made the range of engagement even greater, since it could be fired at targets out of the gunner's sight. The addition of gunpowder to shells added a capacity to do much greater damage, by exploding and killing many of the enemy at once.

The state of the art and the state of an individual army with respect to size, supply, communications, and weaponry determined the breadth of employment options available to the commander.[2] However, the selection of a particular option by him would have been based on considerations peculiar to the time and place of the contemplated action.

Raymond Aron, a distinguished interpreter of the field, observed that "strategic thought draws its inspiration ... at every moment of history from problems which events themselves pose."[3] In other words, events took place in a particular environment, a context that varied considerably in response to socioeconomic and political (governmental) conditions as civilization matured.

By the sixteenth and seventeenth centuries in Europe, the confluence of economic and social activity, occasioned by the developing markets for goods and the intercourse among groups with differing languages, religions, and customs, had fostered the centralization of political authority in areas that soon emerged as nation-states. The economic strength of these entities helped develop the weapons and other trappings of military power that, along with geographical factors, defined borders and provided the means for maintaining the integrity of the newly formed state.

Up to this point in time, wars continued to be frequent and not necessarily unpopular. They could stimulate economic growth to a degree because governments had to increase expenditures for soldiers and weaponry; this in turn primed the economy. Under the "rules" of the day, moreover, the victor in a war expected to recover his "investment" by requiring the losing side to pay reparations.

This was a double-edged sword, however, since lengthy wars were enormously expensive. Maintaining armed forces could consume as much as half of a government's total expenditures in peacetime, and nearly all of them during war. As the network of nations grew and technological advances produced more sophisticated weaponry, the costs continued to escalate.[4]

By the early nineteenth century, the political turmoil and financial drain of almost continual warfare were exacting a toll, particularly in Europe. At the same time, enhanced communications and improvements in transportation and manufacturing output were fostering the development of world trade, which, in turn, made peace and stability desirable. Consequently, after Napoleon's defeat early in the century a sort of peace settled in. Only small, limited conflicts took place for some time after.

Near midcentury, this relative quiet was shattered by a monstrous conflict in the United States, a harbinger of the wars to come—huge armies locked in struggles that would consume enormous financial, material, and human resources. Progress over the next hundred or so years, both scientific and technical, made matters worse by enabling armies to be more efficient killing machines in the world wars of the twentieth century. Finally, at the end of World War II, technological advances brought humanity face to face with the potential agent of its destruction.

The world was changed forever by the power of the atom. The specter of conflict between or among nations that possess weapons based on that elemental power provided a powerful impetus to ensure that such an event never occurred. Deterring aggression through the maintenance of substantial military strength became the sine qua non of military strategy. Acquiring and maintaining the wherewithal to deter meant that technologies were pushed, arsenals expanded, and the count of nuclear weapons doubled, and doubled again and again until, in 1990, there were more than 40,000 warheads available to the superpower states.

Deterrence has ensured that the much-feared general war has, up until now, been staved off. However, the disinclination of the superpowers and their clients to become involved in fighting each other directly has not eliminated conflict altogether; it has simply created new dimensions for it.

The Modern Spectrum of Conflict

A warrior resurrected from the Middle Ages would find the variety of today's conflicts confusing. In his day, wars were clearly defined and bounded affairs, aimed at achieving specific and relatively narrow objectives. His counterpart from the nineteenth or early twentieth century would feel somewhat more at home; veterans of those years would have participated in more widespread and "modern" conflicts, including some between alliances of nations where the major partners committed their economies and their populations to total war, to the destruction of the enemy's political infrastructure. In contrast, today's fighting man is likely to find himself battling a wide array of antagonists, including terrorists, guerrillas, and soldiers of a technologically advanced and well-equipped army.

Figure 1 is a depiction of this contemporary spectrum of conflict. Any particular type may be defined by the degree of violence, the number of participants (i.e., the numbers of nations or individuals affected), and an estimation of the likelihood of its occurrence. The possibilities range from isolated and locally damaging acts by a few individuals, to more traditional wars between nations, to conflicts of great and widespread destruction, the type likely to develop between opposing superpower alliances. While they are easily separated here, distinctions between and among classes are not always clear and categorization of a particular outburst must be—and often is—made after the fact.

General Nuclear War

The class of conflict most likely to produce a high level of violence by a large number of belligerent nations or forces is that of all-out or general

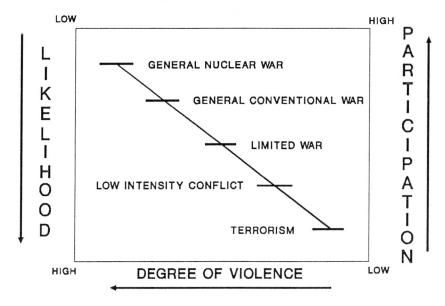

Figure 1. Spectrum of Conflict

nuclear war. Such a conflict would see the superpowers launch thousands upon thousands of nuclear-tipped missiles and bombs. While efforts to "limit" damage might well be attempted, the total numbers of weapons likely to be employed would ensure casualties numbering in the millions on both sides.

Moreover, should such an exchange take place between the United States and the Soviet Union, the devastation would most probably not be confined solely to the main belligerents. As part of their respective plans, it is almost certain that the United States would find it necessary to strike selected targets in countries allied to the Soviet Union, while the Soviets would find it prudent to eliminate complexes in western Europe, in the People's Republic of China, and perhaps Japan. Great Britain, France, and China, all possessors of nuclear missile forces, would retaliate with their supply (if they had not already fired preemptively). Other nations who have hidden the fact that they possess nuclear weapons might well decide to take advantage of the general mayhem and "nuke" a perennial enemy.

Happily, the chance of such a catastrophic conflict being initiated by one or the other of the superpowers or their allies does not seem high. For some time now, informed and unbiased observers have admitted the difficulty involved in constructing a believable set of conditions in which such freewheeling exchanges might occur. The fear of retaliation in kind, together with uncertainties about the effects of large-scale nuclear attacks, is still holding the line.

Further, the dramatic changes in the political atmosphere between the United States and the Soviet Union in the past year make it even more implausible. Decades of chilly and, more often, frigid relations have given way to what could be constructive ones in the wake of major political changes in the USSR. Despite these developments, large numbers of nuclear weapons will remain. If they exist, they can be used.

Even small numbers of detonations may bring about a catastrophe because of the cumulative effects of nuclear weapon explosions on the earth's environment. This possibility, popularly called "nuclear winter," was originally raised in a study completed by a group of distinguished and concerned scientists. In general, the authors concluded that the planet's ecological system might not survive nuclear warfare, whatever the immediate fate of the population.[5] According to this theory, smoke and dust from the weapon detonations and the resulting firestorm might block out the sun for a lengthy period of time, resulting in drastically lower ground temperatures and severe damage to the food chain.[6]

The issue is controversial. Clearly, the actual effects would be very much dependent on the specific number, location, size, type of burst (air or ground), and frequency of detonations, but the possibility certainly exists that the environmental effects of a nuclear exchange might far outweigh the physical damage done.[7]

General Conventional War

The next lower level of violent confrontation—and one judged only a little more likely to occur—is a general war between groups of nations, where each side employs only nonnuclear (conventional) weapons. The hypothetical scenario for this type of conflict has typically been a Warsaw Pact attack across the North Atlantic Treaty Organization (NATO) front in Germany, with hostilities breaking out elsewhere soon after. This hypothesis proposes that the two alliances do battle on land, at sea, and in the air across a global stage, much in the manner of the previous world wars. It is difficult even to speculate about the level of destruction that might be wrought in this type of war. The sophistication and capability of current weapon systems would suggest that at least the amount of devastation wreaked in World War II would be achieved.

An important unknown here, as in any conflict where one or both sides possess nuclear weapons, is the willingness and the ability of the combatants to restrict weapon employment to the conventional level. This is particularly true if one side perceives itself to be "losing." If the survival of the political and economic systems integral to a nation were a matter of indifference, winning or losing in a conflict would be unimportant. Indeed, the likelihood of conflict would be low. However, since this condition ordinarily does not exist and is unlikely to in the future, then winning is important.[8]

This being the case, if one side or the other abstains from using nuclear weapons early on, perhaps during inconclusive phases of the conflict, the compulsion to use them when the possibility of defeat looms could be irresistible. Even if one side maintains tight control over its own inclinations, it cannot control those of the adversary. After all, there are two playing. Control of the escalation process, while devoutly sought after, is probably illusory at best.

It is important to note here that it would not be necessary to employ what are called "strategic" weapons;[9] tactical nuclear weapons could be enough. The difference between weapons labeled strategic and those labeled tactical has nothing to do with the explosive power (yield) of the weapon. The distinction has to do with the intended employment, including location, and the delivery vehicle.

The effects on targets, of course, are determined solely by the power and location of the burst and the numbers of weapons, not how the devices got there. While it is generally true that current tactical weapons produce smaller yields, there is no technical reason for this. With state-of-the-art weapon technology, small weapons with very large yields could be commonplace. Exchanging tactical weapons in any number would in all likelihood raise the stakes considerably, risking escalation to general nuclear war.

Again, we may well question the likelihood of such a contest given the disintegration of the Warsaw Pact, the pronouncements that the Cold War has ended, the pull-back of Soviet forces, and the diminution, if not dissolution, of military capabilities in many eastern European countries. While all of these changes are underway or already a reality, it is worth noting that the breakdown of the Warsaw Pact and NATO alliance structures and the consequent loss of the political cohesion and discipline they wrought will leave a vacuum, one that could produce chaos and uncertainty—a situation ripe for autocratic intervention. A European war between the current alliances may not be likely, but it does not take much time to choose up sides. Weapons will continue to exist and be available for use by the most powerful.

Limited War

The next stop moving down the scale of conflict is at limited war. While this class has much in common with traditional warfare of the nineteenth century and earlier, its "popularity" results from the view that direct confrontations between superpowers pose extremely hazardous situations. Instead, these "little" wars at points of tangency between ideologically opposed countries or between nation-states on opposing paths can be substituted.

A limited war is one between two nation-states, or groups of nation-states, which is circumscribed by agreement, either tacit or explicit, in terms of political objectives, military aims, weapons used, size of force commitments, or geographical areas. It is a government-against-government scrap. While certain dimensions of the war will be proscribed, the amount of damage and destruction may still be high. Levels will be determined, in part, by the type and numbers of weapons on each side as well as where they are used. For example, battles fought in cities between forces supported by tanks, artillery, and aircraft are likely to be very destructive of property and result in numerous casualties, including many noncombatants. Battles fought in the countryside, on the other hand, would probably involve fewer civilians, although the effect on agricultural production might be pronounced.

The Korean War, where North Korea attacked its immediate neighbor, but ideological enemy, South Korea, was the best known of this class in the nuclear era. Both nations quickly gained support from others, but the fighting was confined to the Korean Peninsula (indeed, when it appeared that it might break out of that arena, China intervened militarily), the status quo ante became the objective, and nuclear weapons were not employed. Other examples of this class include the three Arab-Israeli clashes, the Iran-Iraq war and, most recently in the same area of the world, the 1991 U.N.-Iraq war.

This last conflict (called by some Operation Desert Storm) meets all of the criteria for the limited war category. Iraq's invasion and occupation of neighboring Kuwait precipitated responses from around the world. The United States organized diplomatic and economic pressure in an attempt to coerce a withdrawal and rushed troops to Saudi Arabia to prevent further Iraqi adventurism, while the United Nations Security Council passed resolutions condemning the invasion and demanding withdrawal, encouraging economic sanctions against Iraq, and finally authorizing the use of force to achieve the removal of Iraqi troops.

Twenty-eight nations provided military forces to a coalition, led by the United States, which initiated combat activities against Iraq on January 16, 1991, with the objectives of achieving complete withdrawal of Iraqi forces and the return of the Kuwaiti government to its rightful position.[10] Victory was declared some six weeks later; when Iraq agreed to all conditions of a cease-fire, operations were suspended on February 28.

The likelihood of other similar wars in our day is at least moderate. Although there is an onus attached to the violation of a neighbor's border, ancient antagonisms fired by economic and social pressures, real and imagined, persist and are likely to be the cause of more limited wars, especially in the Third World. The ten-year-long Iran-Iraq war mentioned above may be an example of what may be expected — two historic enemies slugging it out with arms and ammunition obtained from other parties.

Low-Intensity Conflict

The technological and social changes occurring over the last 40 years have enhanced the status of the next class, the low-intensity conflict (LIC). From the participant's point of view it is clearly misnamed since, as far as he is concerned, the intensity is seldom low. Moreover, it is not the intensity or the numbers of the forces involved which distinguish this type of conflict from the others; rather it is its character. That is, unlike the previously described classes, this type of war is not waged to destroy a sociopolitical system, but to seize control of one. With this as an objective, psychological weapons are every bit as — if not more — important as firearms. Revolutionary and counterrevolutionary struggles where the armed forces of a government (irrespective of its legitimacy) face guerrilla or irregular forces populate this category. The protagonists are locked in a battle of political as well as physical survival.

The Vietnam War began as a low-intensity conflict but became a limited war when the North Vietnamese Army became actively involved. Early operations of the communist opposition (the Viet Cong) were aimed at seizing control of the government from within. When they were unsuccessful, North Vietnam openly entered the fray with the apparent objective of unifying the country by force.

Third parties may and do supply one side or the other; occasionally they may become an active participant in the limited wars or low-intensity conflicts generally for their own reasons, which are probably not the same as those of the indigenous groups. In Vietnam (and Korea), for example, local forces were fighting to maintain control of their country. The United States intervened to "counter communism" and to impress the Soviets with the nation's resolve.

The areas in the world where revolutionary or counterrevolutionary bouts may erupt are already legion, and it seems likely that the numbers will only increase.

Terrorism

The final category of conflict, terrorism, is typically lumped together with low-intensity conflict (and often with some questionable "military" activities like drug enforcement, as well), but it is deliberately discussed separately here because its objective is different. Terrorism typically seeks to bring about change of some sort (policy, action, etc.) rather than to seize power. The distinction is sometimes difficult to see in practice since terrorist acts by both sides are often part of a low-intensity conflict (and other classes of conflict as well).

Terrorism is defined here as the carrying out of an undeclared war on one or several states or nations by small groups. It can be a low-risk, low-cost method of attacking established entities and is particularly attractive to groups that lack armed forces. Terrorist organizations may, like revolutionary groups involved in low-intensity conflicts, receive support from third parties in the form of training, weapons, or havens.

It should be added here that nuclear (or chemical, for that matter) weapons could be employed by one of the combatant sides in a limited war, a low-intensity conflict, or even by terrorists. Many nations have or are attempting to develop such weapons, and "suitcase" bombs have been a concern for some time. It is not at all clear what might deter the possessors, particularly if the enemy has no comparable weapons. Use would probably change the entire complexion of any conflict.

Planning and Response to Classes of Conflict

As defined here, this spectrum spans participation from the involvement of small groups to alliances of nations and encompasses violence from small, isolated acts to nuclear conflagrations. One need only peruse daily newspapers to ascertain that at any given time, a conflict of some sort is going on somewhere in the world. Many nations are vulnerable to attack from both within and outside, and resulting conflicts often drag in neighbors, whether geographical or ideological, as well.

Given this situation, a prudent nation prepares itself for eventualities across the entire spectrum because concentrating preparations for only one class of conflict can mean unpreparedness for the others. The objectives in each case are different, as are the specific approaches and resource requirements.

For example, "general" conflicts, as they have been defined here, involve many participants, are fought on a global scale, and have specific characteristics. Although the exact unfolding of a general nuclear conflict is not known, it may be surmised. It seems likely that if one were to occur it would begin after a period of extreme tension or conflict (perhaps a general or limited conventional war) with an initial massive strike from one side provoking a counterstrike from the other.

Since in nuclear conflict weapon considerations tend to predominate because of the relative destructive power of even one of them, a period of little or no action would probably follow the initial exchange as the enormity of the damage is assessed and options reviewed by surviving command authorities. Another spasm of fire-counterfire may very well ensue. After the second exchange, it seems likely that the casualty and damage levels suffered will begin to affect the cohesion of the respective armed forces and their bosses, the decision makers, with unknown results. In a nuclear war the only real "players" are those in the military on both sides who fight the strategic weapon systems and the decision makers who order their use. Everyone else is, for all practical purposes, only a target.

The weapons used in this scenario — long-range and highly destructive — could conceivably be employed in a general conventional or even a limited war where there are targets of high value to be lost by both sides, such as military installations and manufacturing and population centers. Using such weapons, even sparingly, may well result in rapid escalation to a general nuclear conflict. If first use occurred in a limited war involving superpowers, the same result could also occur.

Whereas weapons are king in the nuclear war, in general conventional conflict manpower increases in importance. Where the power of destruction of individual weapons is less, presenting a larger mass on the theory that the weapons can be overwhelmed before all of the force has been eliminated becomes a viable option. Furthermore, some sort of offensive action on the part of the side interested in a particular outcome (generally the initiator of the conflict) will be required because forcing a conclusion will be difficult using only conventional weapons from a distance.

Weapons, training, and plans for this type of conflict are designed to impose conditions on the enemy by force of arms — that is, by maneuver and attrition. Mobility and firepower are desirable attributes for weapon systems designed for conventional wars. Since such a war would be widespread, operating environments must be considered in weapon design; the gun may be, for example, needed in Norway, in the Sahara, and in the jungles of Southeast Asia. Strategic weapon systems, which numerically comprise only a minuscule part of the arsenal, do contribute in lesser-order conflicts by deterring escalation to the nuclear threshold but have no direct role in fighting.[11]

The personnel and their equipment gathered for a general conventional war can be useful in a limited war as well. Since by definition there will be at least two structured armies facing one another, such a conflict is, in some respects, a general conventional war in miniature. There may well be differences in the sophistication of both weapons and maneuver schemes depending on the belligerents and the geographic location but, basically, the fighting will be traditional.

Only some of the resources acquired for the above conflict categories will be useful in the low-intensity one. In this case "regular" and "irregular" forces face off. Pitched battles in the open, or on terrain amenable to mass maneuver, where the destructive potential and agility of arms typical of conventional forces such as artillery, tanks, and close air support aircraft would be useful, are not likely to occur. The irregular forces would continuously seek to fight only at locations and on terms favorable to them. It is not necessary for them to "win" in battle(s) because the objective is not territory but the heart and soul of a country. Unless the irregulars are poorly led, foolish, or decidedly unlucky, the climactic battle or series of them devoutly hoped for in general or limited conventional wars are not likely to occur.

Opposing terrorism is also different. Police personnel and methods are much better suited to combating terrorism than the military, although there certainly is a utility for military intelligence systems. A terrorist group is generally much smaller, even more "irregular," and better hidden. Often it will be operating on friendly, if not native, territory where a facility and its personnel, such as an embassy and its diplomats, of the United States are the outsiders. If military forces are to be used, they must be specially trained and equipped if they are to be effective. *Equipping* here means more than just weapons and clothing; it means they must be given specific legal empowerment, including police powers, if necessary.

Clearly, there are qualitative differences among the types of conflicts, not just quantitative ones. Given the differing objectives of belligerents and the character of actual conflicts, strategies designed for one are not likely to be applicable to all. Neither, then, are force structure or weapon systems, since procurement policies for them are (or should be) derived from the strategy selected for the conditions and type of conflict.

In general, American forces have been organized and equipped for unlimited general and traditional limited war. While most are prepared for warfare using only conventional weapons, some units are assigned nuclear missions. This military posture suits the rather simplistic American conception of war that tends to identify an "evil" enemy that is then called out and defeated in a contest of arms. This style of warfare tends to be successful when the "enemy" has something tangible to lose—an asset to be bombed, shelled, sunk, or captured. Typically guerrillas, revolutionaries, and terrorists have few, if any, of these.

Unfortunately, with only these forces at hand, engaging in low-intensity conflicts and counterterrorist activities tends to be frustrating since clear-cut, decisive action is seldom possible; the weight of U.S. manpower and material, strengths in more traditional and conventional wars, is largely irrelevant. This requirements-to-capabilities mismatch is exacerbated by a disturbing tendency on the part of the U.S. military to conduct "standard" operations without regard for what might be needed. That is to say, the

U.S. military tends to choose to do what it can do, rather than what should be done.

Restraining military efforts in small-scale conflict poses some very real problems for the United States. First and perhaps foremost, gaining and maintaining popular support for such conflicts, which are likely to be drawn out and tend to be fought in foreign lands for philosophical rather than survival (from the standpoint of the United States) reasons, is difficult because the national attention span for events outside the country is extremely short.

Yet in a country dependent on mobilizing civilians for its soldiery, that support is critical. When this fundamental fact has been forgotten — particularly in limited wars like Korea and Vietnam — the results have been unpleasant. In the latter case, both the military and the civilians in government worked diligently to keep the escalation of the war from the public, thus forfeiting any public support which would have been helpful if (in this case, when) the adventure went sour.[12]

During the "phony war" period prior to combat operations in the recent UN-Iraq War there was much public wringing of hands in the United States over the country's willingness to stay the course when the body count started piling up, a legacy of the Vietnam experience. In anticipation of a need for persistence, statements by both civilian and military officials connected with the Defense Department were cautious regarding prospects, effectively setting the stage for a protracted conflict. At the same time, considerable effort was expended in shaping public opinion about the rightness of the cause. In the end, the war was so short and, from the coalition's standpoint, so bloodless, support was never in doubt.[13]

Second, since action in these affairs tends to be in the service of political rather than military ends, a new sophistication is required of civilian and military leaders, as well as of the public. Achieving this enlightened position is made difficult by the prevailing American view that it is only when political methods have failed that military ones begin. This either-or orientation comes from a seemingly native distrust of politics in general and a dislike, if not fear, of ambiguity.

Much of the blame for this lack of sensitivity to the elements of conflict management can be laid at the feet of successive administrations who have taken pains to manipulate, not inform, and placate, not involve, the public. The result of this noninvolvement is a tendency to judge success (or failure) in terms of participation — in terms of investment in men, materials, or time — and not on moral, legal, constitutional, or policy grounds.

From the perspective of the military, it has traditionally eschewed political considerations and been concerned only with beating the enemy. Unfortunately, in many situations it may not be clear exactly who is the enemy, let alone what it means to "beat" him. The current environment will require close cooperation and coordination between the military and the politicians, rather than the antagonism that took over in both Korea and Vietnam.

Actions at this limited end of the spectrum tend to be waged not so much for the bodies of men as for their minds, a kind of warfare much more psychological than physical. Major powers have not fared particularly well in these types of conflicts. One reason may be that the size of their bureaucracies, both governmental and military, precludes paying sufficient attention to the nuances of ideological conflict. Since large nations have been "successful" in general (otherwise they would not be large), they tend to believe that their way is not just the right one, but the only one.

In at least a tip of the hat to the possibility of participation in conflicts other than general war, the U.S. Army has established highly mobile "light" divisions, has maintained the Special Forces, and has trained a special group to participate in hostage rescue. The Navy's Special Warfare group can also be employed in lower-level conflicts, while the Air Force provides an airlift and clandestine insertion capability. Most of these special groups, however, would be employed in unconventional warfare operations[14] that support regular forces engaged in mid- to high-intensity conflicts.

What is more, these units are made up of crack troops who tend to operate and remain outside the mainstream of the service organization. In this country, where military service is a profession within which success is dependent on following certain paths — paths more aligned with the organizational requirements for major conflicts — becoming an expert in restricted kinds of warfare may not be very rewarding.

Finally, preparing for participation in conflict across the entire spectrum runs full tilt against a philosophy of preferring weapons and machines over men as fighting instruments, a reflection of the high value placed on human life by American society. Unfortunately, technologically advanced devices, even the very smart ones, have limited utility at the more "restrained" end of the spectrum; they require extensive planning and preparation prior to their use to maximize their effectiveness whatever the venue.

In the past, preparation for and participation in what are surely the most likely levels of confrontation for the United States — combating terrorism, low intensity conflict, and limited war — have been very uneven. The experiences in Korea, Vietnam, and the Iranian desert are rife with lessons to be learned.[15] In the recent UN-Iraq War, by contrast, where most of the forces were from the United States, nearly every military move of the coalition was successful, in some cases beyond anything imagined. Every class of weapon, whether being used for the first or the umpteenth time, seemed to work exactly as desired. The planning for military operations seemed faultless and the execution, flawless.

Anticipating the need for operations is another story. Typically, crises seem to pop up full blown. Whatever indications there may have been go unheeded, which results, in the absence of any preplanning, in a fair amount of dithering. Getting organized takes much time and, in some cases, costs unnecessary lives.

In this day and age, all that most of the world asks is to be free of all conflict, to be at peace. Unfortunately, peace is only one of a number of possible states that exist in the world. In the years between 1945 and 1983, years many would consider peaceful ones, there were 11 conflicts between nations, 23 "liberation" movements, and 37 civil wars.[16] Each day many nations face crises and even combat.

In such a world, even if the rapprochement between the Soviet Union and the United States continues, other dangers are afoot, as the Middle East once again demonstrated in 1990 and 1991. They may not directly threaten the United States, but may be aimed at our interests abroad. A country that has been taken by surprise almost continuously should take steps to ensure that it will never be unprepared again, no matter what the challenge. Unfortunately, strategic planning has not been one of this country's long suits.

CHAPTER II

The Strategic Heritage
of the United States
from the Beginning to 1945

Military strategy provides the blueprint for applying or threatening to apply force in the pursuit of some objective(s).[1] In order to be effective, the strategy must account for the environment and the capabilities of the forces to be used. In the beginning the designs were simple. Individuals ruled kingdoms, principalities, and territories of uncertain borders. Most often the head of state who held political power also led the army, a warrior-king. Disputes were largely with neighboring groups over specific issues such as territorial boundaries. If military actions were necessary, the king rode at the head of a relatively small army raised specifically for the contemplated conflict. The objective was to bring the enemy army, configured, armed and led much as his, to a decisive battle. Unfortunately (or, perhaps, fortunately), this seldom occurred.

Because of poor roads, inadequate maps, primitive communication methods, and inaccurate means to measure time, the joining of opposing forces in combat often necessitated prior agreement over time and place. When a meeting did occur, each side maneuvered so as to avoid pitched battles, which were expensive in terms of manpower. Because positional advantage was often accepted by the military "community" of the time as tantamount to victory, the side best situated occasionally gained the decision without fighting when the opposition, recognizing the inevitability of defeat, retired instead.

Similar difficulties in engaging enemies plagued navies. Fleets had to locate each other at sea, an almost impossible task unless a meeting were arranged in advance. Even if this were accomplished, other challenges remained. Admirals had to not only select formations that maximized the firepower available, but, most difficult of all, remain engaged long enough for the firepower to make a difference. Under these conditions, the line between strategy and tactics was barely distinguishable.

This environment existed until the end of the fourteenth century, when the range and rate of firepower increased as muskets and cannon replaced the bow and catapult. Several nation-states had been formed by this time, and others were soon to follow. Territorial disputes and in some cases religious intolerance provided the occasions for conflict. By the end of the next century, the battlefield had changed markedly. The much-increased firepower of infantry and artillery provoked an avid interest in the building of fortifications. As armies grew larger, the ability and inclination to maneuver them declined, and fortifications multiplied. Battles were fought in the daylight and generally only during good weather. Armies typically retired to winter quarters.

During this period, the exercise of military power became increasingly more conservative. The mercenaries making up most armies were, like other military equipment, expensive and not to be wasted. The military literature of the time advocated the standardization of fighting technique. War became more and more like a game of chess, so stylized that it scarcely disturbed the civilian population.

Early in the seventeenth century, a major change was noticeable. By this time, nearly all the major nation-states of Europe had been formed; the mercenary was being replaced by the citizen soldier conscripted as a protection against the potential tyranny of the "hired gun." This was a way to reduce the cost of maintaining armed forces and an economic stimulus used to assimilate the un- and underemployed.[2]

The Birth of American
Military Policy During the Revolution

These issues were of little moment to the colonists in the New World, who had only limited knowledge and experience of, and less interest in, military matters. What military presence there was existed only because the English crown had included soldiers among the settlers on the theory that the colonies should provide for their own defense. Local militia units comprised of volunteers and others "drafted" under a universal military obligation for able-bodied males were formed in each colony to protect settlements against Indian attacks.[3]

Many of the colonists were hunters, but few had been in any kind of formal battle line. Militia training, therefore, tended to be concerned with improving individual skills as opposed to learning old-world tactics of massed infantry. Militia organizations were particularly satisfying to townspeople who required occasional protection but distrusted a standing or professional force in the first place, and did not want to pay for maintaining one in any case. Militia provided the security of "... local people under local leadership meeting local needs."[4]

The almost constant wars in Europe had left Great Britain's treasury feeling the strain. George III decided that the colonies should foot the bill for that portion of the British Army stationed in North America to prevent war. Following through, the British Parliament passed a series of taxation and related acts between 1765 and 1774. Most of these were designed to raise revenue for the Crown, but one, which the colonists particularly resented, sought to save money by forcing citizens to provide quarters for soldiers. These measures all lapsed into disuse or were repealed after specific acts of defiance by the colonists, particularly in Massachusetts.

The winds of discontent had been blowing in that colony since 1765 when a patriot (or rebel, depending upon your point of view) political organization coalesced to resist perceived oppression. With this organization continuously fanning the flame of any crisis, almost every parliamentary act and action was viewed as infringing on the colonists' rights as Englishmen. In response to what was generally seen as increasing British recklessness, each colony sent representatives to a first Continental Congress, which met in Philadelphia in September 1774 to discuss redress. At the same time, colonies increased the importation of powder and arms, which were stowed out of reach of British troops.

As the tension grew, the British Army in Massachusetts Colony was pulled back to Boston. From there, on a fateful day in April 1775, a detachment of British soldiers set out for Concord to confiscate powder and other military equipment that had been collected by the militia. En route, "the shot heard round the world" rang out, and the rebellion that would become a successful war for independence was underway.

In the wake of these spontaneous actions, the Massachusetts Provincial Congress, which had met as a "shadow" government in late 1774, assumed direction of activities, including formation of a volunteer army. The governing bodies of Connecticut, Rhode Island, and New Hampshire, upon hearing of the situation, dispatched volunteer militia units for support.[5]

As these reinforcements moved toward Boston and potential battle, delegates were again gathering in Philadelphia for a second Congress to consider alternative methods for gaining British assurance of respect for colonist rights. In an astute political move orchestrated by the faction seeking independence from Great Britain, the representatives of the Massachusetts and New York colonies requested that the Congress assembled provide "advice" to those colonies respecting the countering of British troop movements.

George Washington, a delegate from Virginia, was a member of a committee to study what might be required for defending New York, and the Congress declared itself a Committee of the Whole to consider the general situation. It was agreed that reconciliation with the Crown was to be hoped for, but that defense of the colonies was also necessary. Several days later, the Committee of the Whole decided to raise an army.

It was clear from the beginning that Congress, able to wield only those powers permitted by the colonies,[6] was interested in having a commander-in-chief for the army who would remain subject to their direction. The members were convinced that George Washington would do so, and thus named him commander of the newly created Continental Army.

The prospect could not have entirely pleased the new commander-in-chief. His army was comprised of generally poorly trained volunteers who had signed on for relatively short periods of time. The only arms readily available were those the recruits had brought with them. The army would be required to move over the few bad roads that connected the isolated population centers of the colonies and to fight in the heavily forested land in between, environmental conditions that made both movement and maneuver difficult.

Employment of the British and Continental armies was based on the objectives of each side. The British government vacillated between a coercive and a conciliatory position, the first requiring punitive actions and forced obedience, the second, negotiations. The British were also ambivalent about force levels. With precious little warning, the redcoats had seen their relatively short supply line, drawing on settlements in the colonies, lengthen over 2000 miles to their homeland across the sea. Further, since there was no real "center" in this new world, seizing or even blockading a particular location was unlikely to be decisive. The army would need to occupy many areas in order to exert control and thus would require sizable numbers of troops. The anticipated uprising by loyalists to the King that, it was hoped, would add to troop strength never did transpire; thus British generals were continuously requesting more troops.

Early colonial thinking favored reconciliation, although certainly not as vassal states. Spurred on by Samuel Adams and other pro-independence delegates, however, the objective rapidly changed; in a narrow vote by the Continental Congress in 1776, the decision was taken and a committee formed to declare independence.[7]

In the early months of the war, the Continental Congress had formulated and even ordered the execution of strategy in parallel with the commander-in-chief. It was finally realized that such a system was not efficient, and the chore of strategy was left to General Washington. Congress continued on with its main functions of authorizing troops, accumulating material, attempting to finance the operations, and conducting foreign relations.

General Washington soon realized that the Continental Army was much more than just a fighting force; it was a symbol of independence. It was incumbent on him, therefore, to keep the army together and avoid risk. As a consequence, the strategy he pursued required deliberate actions (including numerous tactical retreats) to avoid a climactic battle, which, it seemed almost certain, the Continental Army would lose. The army was used in an offensive mode sparingly, and then only at times when activity and success were necessary to maintain cohesiveness. [8]

From a strategic perspective, this produced two benefits. First, the army remained a viable force, and, second, time to collect allies and to better train and equip the fighting men was gained. In the end, this strategy was successful. The French, enlisted as an ally against their historical nemesis Great Britain, provided funds and forces (particularly naval) that helped tip the balance. While British forces (and Parliament) might ultimately have tired of chasing the Continental Army and so "forfeited" the war, without the supplies and money from France and Holland, the colonies would probably never have survived long enough to take advantage of it.

The combined French and Continental armies cornered the British after years of maneuver and, by siege, forced the surrender of an entire British army at Yorktown, Virginia, in October 1781. Although it was several years before the war formally ended, the starch had been taken out of the British; and this was the last action of any consequence in the colonies.

The settlement came none too soon, since the colonies had stopped paying their soldiers, France had quit the scene, and the colonial economy was collapsing. With the conclusion of the war Congress tried to release its soldiers, but the Continental Army, which had been so difficult to raise, was even harder to disband when due back pay. The intervention of their retiring commander-in-chief calmed the situation, and the soldiers finally melted back into the society from which they had come.

The question of the sort of military establishment the new government should have at hand remained. Washington was asked for his recommendations. He proposed a small standing army and navy backed up by a well-trained militia, the continuing manufacture of military equipment, the laying up of ordnance and firearms in arsenals, and the establishment of military academies.

Although received politely, Washington's recommendations were, in general, ignored. The government was broke, and there was no visible threat to the security of the colonies. The military men who understood the requirements of waging war were mustered out, and no organization existed to keep the files (or the faith, for that matter).

Neither national security nor strategy was a matter given much thought in the years immediately following the war. It was not until conflict with France seemed likely near the turn of the century that the thoughts turned to how the country might be defended. The Secretary of the Navy, Benjamin Stoddert, ventured a strategy by suggesting that a fleet of ships of the line (12 ships with 74 guns each) should counter any invasion attempt by intercepting the enemy at sea. This not only would deter any enemy, he felt, but would provide the wherewithal to destroy one foolhardy enough to try. Congress at first agreed, appropriating money to build six of the ships. However, the troubles with France were settled and plans for the ships (and the strategy) were abandoned.[9]

It was at about this time that an "aggressive, mobile combative strategy replaced the slow strategy of siegecraft" in a Europe aflame with conflict.[10] Napoleon Bonaparte's Army of France epitomized these changes. Where armies had heretofore fought as much for position as to inflict damage on the enemy, his was maneuvered solely with the thought of annihilating the opposition. This technique, documented in the writings of Henri-Antoine Jomini, one of the first theorists of modern warfare, soon became the model for militaries throughout the world, and was still in vogue some 100 years later.

Jomini began studying Napoleon's early campaigns in 1798, when he was only 19 years old. From these observations he concluded that strategy amounted to a fixed set of techniques that culminated in the massing of great numbers of troops at a specific point so as to attack the enemy with overwhelming force and quickly win a decisive victory. His exposition of these "principles" of war was so widely read that, according to John Shay, "...simplifying, reducing, prescribing ... had become the dominant realities of Western military thought by the turn of the [nineteenth] century."[11]

Carl von Clausewitz, a soldier himself and often called the first major theoretician of strategy, was also studying Napoleon about the same time. Clausewitz, however, did not formulate recipes for successful warfare; his view of war was somewhat more abstract. In his treatise *On War*, published after his death, war was, perhaps for the first time, captured as the complex set of motivations, natures, emotions, and causes and effects that it had become.[12] Clausewitz characterized war as a potpourri of violence and passion, uncertainty, chance, probability, and political purpose. Singling out this latter element was probably Clausewitz's best-known and most lasting contribution to the strategic arena. He stated, "War is not merely a political act but also a real political instrument, a continuation of political commerce, a carrying out of the same by other means."[13] Both of these writers were to impact strategic thought over the next century; Jomini in the near term, Clausewitz much later.

Military matters were not given much thought in a United States still in the midst of continuing debate about the legitimacy of a democratic nation using any force unless repelling an invasion. Not surprisingly, when war with Great Britain was joined in 1812, there was no strategy in place, none at hand, and no useful experience to fall back on. The results bore that out.

This strategic vacuum did not prevent the wish from becoming the father of action, however, and the opportunity to eliminate the infernal British presence to the North was seized upon. Unfortunately, insufficient numbers of troops were used in the wrong places, and little came of the offensive thrusts mounted. When Great Britain signed a peace treaty with France in 1814, it was free to apply the full weight of its armed forces against the United States. American defense finally won the day, although it was a near thing.

The generally poor performance of the military forces during the war and the fear aroused by the British landings on the U.S. shores prompted President James Madison to appoint a Board of Engineers to study methods of defending the country. In its report, issued in February 1821, the board recommended that the basic strategy for defending the country should be to counter the enemy at sea, a reprise of Secretary Stoddert's earlier suggestion. In addition, they concluded that a system of fortifications on the seacoast was needed to both support the navy and provide a point to concentrate troops, whose task would be to counter any enemy force that might make it to the shore. This maritime strategy suited the Navy very well, but it left the Army garrisoned in forts with little guidance on how to fight outside of them.

In any case, a time of relative peace settled in on both the American and European continents, and the will to execute programs to support and sustain the strategy slowly faded away. The size and capability of the Navy ebbed and flowed over the next years. That of the Army generally just ebbed while, at the same time, it was changing its character. Previously, it had been influenced largely by the pre–Napoleon European model where soldiers were disciplined and orderly, rights of civilians were observed, and attempts were made to control bloodshed.[14] When Dennis Hart Mahan joined the faculty of the United States Military Academy at West Point as professor of civil and military engineering in 1832, a new model was featured.[15] While studying in France before assuming his position, Mahan had become imbued with the all-out spirit of Jomini's Napoleon, and began teaching that style of warfare. Since nearly all leaders would be students at West Point, his influence was to pervade the doctrine of the army for many years.

The First Modern War: The Civil War

From a larger perspective, in the mid-nineteenth century military forces were diminishing in importance; economic power was emerging as the measure of national might. The Industrial Revolution was well underway and, fueled by consumer demand, was spreading; those countries participating were becoming more wealthy. The technology and production techniques emerging from industrialization were changing the entire landscape. The American Civil War, often called the first modern war, was to be the showcase of the improved implements of war now being produced.

Both the North and the South entered that war in 1861 with differing strategies in mind, both confident that theirs would be successful. Southern leaders calculated that creating a stalemate early in the conflict would cause the North to decide that maintaining the Union by force was not worth the price. In practical terms, this meant successfully defending the Confederacy against any attacks by Union forces. Supporting military strategy opted for an active rather than passive defense (that is, to defend by attacking) on the theory that, although their forces were superior in marksmanship and could move on interior lines of communication, the borders to be protected were too long and the manpower of the North too great to attempt to defend every spot Union forces might choose to attack. By taking the fight to the enemy, and by being able to concentrate forces, their attacks might be successful. They believed that success would help convince foreign governments to support their cause with arms and other goods, support badly needed since the Confederacy was largely an agrarian society. If this additional support could be garnered, wearing down the enemy might be possible.

The North, on the other hand, had the reunification of the Union as its objective and thus had no choice but to assume the offensive. At the outset, General Winfield Scott, the Army general-in-chief, proposed to seize Confederate land and force the capitulation of the Confederate capital at Richmond by isolating it. Unfortunately, this pre–Napoleonic strategy, which had worked well in the Mexican War some ten years earlier, was time-consuming, whatever its ultimate chance of success, and there was little patience for it in the North.[16] Instead, the choice was made to move in force to engage and defeat southern forces in battle, and to capture the Confederate capital at Richmond by force of arms, all good Jominian strategic principles.[17]

Although the North had a government in place, an industrial base for material support, and a large manpower pool, the Union Army seemed to lack the organization to sucessfully bring these advantages to bear early in the war. A succession of Union generals commanding the Army of the Potomac on the eastern seaboard botched every operation attempted, a situation so frustrating to President Lincoln that he began to study military writings and tried to direct the war himself for a short while.

By 1864, however, General Ulysses S. Grant had surfaced as the most competent northern commander and had been named to command all armies as general-in-chief. Grant, seizing the strategic initiative, decided to cut the Confederacy in two and roll up the Confederate forces in each half. This was to be accomplished through simultaneous and coordinated attacks by the Army of the Potomac and the Army of the West in the hopes of causing the Confederate Army to either divide their forces or open exploitable gaps. The strategy was successful, particularly in the west, where General William T. Sherman's army broke through, marched to the sea, then turned north to complete the encirclement of Lee's Army of Virginia. All southern forces were finally brought to heel, in part by direct military action, but every bit as much by attrition of its manpower and economic strength.

Casualties on both sides had been particularly high because of technological improvements and a general failure to plan for the expanded or new capabilities that resulted from them. Advances in ship construction (ironclads), transportation (railroads), command and control (telegraph), and weapons (land mines, torpedoes, rifled field artillery) were commonly known, but military strategy, tactics, and supply were slow to make the changes necessary to take full advantage of them.

Technological advances were important, but they were overshadowed by the altered character of warfare. This was not a case of two professional armies maneuvering in a confined area, but a conflict between citizen armies, backed by the total resources of the sponsor nations and fought over a broad landscape. The significance of large numbers of troops and plentiful material resources became manifest. It was "staying power," the ability of a nation's political, economic, social, and military forces to persevere despite heavy losses of men and equipment that ensured success. Classic strategy was thought to be dead. It was not, of course; it was merely in transition.

The German military historian Hans Delbrück, after studying Clausewitz, had concluded that there were only two types of military strategy: that of annihilation, which meant overwhelming or destroying the enemy's forces so that he could no longer fight; and that of attrition, where operations would be designed to wear down the enemy so that he chose not to continue fighting.[18] The Civil War had clearly demonstrated that industrialized nations were capable of supporting annihilation strategies. It did not bode well for those on the receiving end.

Strategic ideas kept coming. During the mid–1880s, while at the Naval War College, Captain Alfred Thayer Mahan began a study of the preceding two centuries of British military and naval history with the objective of identifying the effect that England's control of the sea had on military operations. He concluded that the use of sea power was the decisive factor in most of the battles. What Jomini had done to analyze land-based operations Mahan did with maritime strategy. Extrapolating his assessment of the British experience, he postulated that defeating the enemy's navy would ensure the protection of a maritime nation's lifeline, its seaborne commerce. Therefore, a navy with a global reach provided by forward bases for coaling and provisioning, one powerful enough to win battles, was required. Mahan gave little thought to a navy directly supporting land battles by means of amphibious attacks or bombarding forts. Nevertheless, his rationalization of a strong navy to support nascent maritime inclinations satisfied the economic and imperialistic notions of many.

Mahan also enlarged on Clausewitz's view of military force as a political weapon by linking strategy to national policy. He suggested that strategy (naval strategy, in his terms) needed to have sufficient breadth in order to be useful in peacetime as well as in war. This thinking fit neatly with an emerging theory that held that a country's armed forces should prepare for war during peacetime, matching potential enemies in strength and technical progress.[19] The traditional "passive" defense strategy was changing to an active one. The enemy fleet was to be engaged far from shore.

Mahan's ideas were a revelation to a U.S. Navy that for most of its hundred years had focused on coastal defense and commerce raiding. They impressed others as well. His writings have been credited with influencing significant early twentieth-century events, including Britain's decision to retain a navy capable of continuing her dominance of the seas, which gave impetus to Imperial Germany's naval development and affected naval thought in France, Italy, Russia, and Japan, among others.

Near the turn of the century, Sir Julian Corbett was also expounding on maritime strategy at the Royal Naval War College in Great Britain. Corbett maintained that a navy would be unable to gain total victory in a war on its own. Therefore, he recommended using naval forces to assist in establishing control on land.

Corbett notwithstanding, strategy at sea until World War I was all Mahanian—outnumber and destroy enemy ships of the line. Naval forces were to engage each other in combat in the hope that political and military events ashore would be affected by victory or defeat at sea.

Lessons Unlearned: World War I

By the turn of the twentieth century, the anachronistic empires of Europe were poised on the edge of a precipice. Social change, residue of the Industrial Revolution, and the incessant undercurrent of nationalism conspired to finally push them over, culminating in the turmoil of World War I. The precipitating incident was the assassination of the Austrian Archduke Francis Ferdinand and his morganatic wife, Sophie, by Gavrilo Princip, a Slav nationalist, in Sarajevo in June 1914. This act was seized upon by activist Austrians as a pretext for intervention to end unrest in Serbia and restore the prestige of the House of Hapsburg.

The affair threatened a rather tenuous balance of power maintained among the empires; therefore, promises of support and alliances, official and otherwise, were unshelved and presented for collection. Germany stood by her ally Austria-Hungary. Russia decided she could not let Austria-Hungary dominate the Balkans. France braced for a German onslaught while working to ensure British participation. As the ramparts of the Old World shook, the level of intercourse among nations became more strident, mobs cheered the coming war, and the military establishments begged their respective governments for permission to mobilize, a process of calling up and moving reserves that took some time. What was not appreciated, certainly not by the political and diplomatic elements of governments, was the irreversibility of events once the order to mobilize had been issued.[20]

As the armies mobilized and the few who tried to arrest the juggernaut found themselves brushed aside, the Old World began its death spiral. Only the British empire was to survive the war that followed in much the same condition as when it began. The Hapsburg (Austro-Hungarian), the Hohenzollern (German), the Ottoman (Turkish), and the Romanov (Russian) empires were all to collapse as a result of the war and the peace process which followed. One can reasonably argue that the world has yet to recover fully from the trauma.

When Europe stumbled into war in 1914, lessons from the American Civil War about time and resource consumption had been so obscured by several relatively quick and somewhat painless conflicts fought in the 1870s that as the fight began, all of the extant military strategies were based on outmoded thinking.

Entry into World War I during the fourth year of fighting provided a unique experience for the United States. Ever since the War for Independence, when it was allied with France, America had acted alone in any conflict. Now, with sides already chosen, if the enemy, the so-called Central Powers (the German and Austro-Hungarian empires), were to be defeated it made sense to at least cooperate with those already opposing her. Thus, the United States "joined" the Allies, not as a full-fledged member, but as a collaborator.

Nothing had transpired during the Spanish-American War in 1898 or in fracases with Mexico in 1910 and 1916 to shake the U.S. military's conventional strategic wisdom of forcing the enemy into a climactic battle. Here, as in Europe, lessons from the Civil War were long forgotten. The United States concurred in the Allied strategy of blockade and frontal assault. The mode of employment was to amass resources until able to attack in such numbers as to overwhelm the enemy and thus end the war, a design that, unfortunately, was guaranteed to take a long time to bring off.

Moreover, the enemy did not cooperate. The Germans launched attacks that compelled a still-training U.S. Army to fight alongside the other allies. The American production base was just getting geared up when the armistice was announced, so its full capability was not realized.

The United States had entered the war with a missionary spirit. Once committed, President Wilson saw participation as an opportunity to establish an "international liberal democratic order based on prosperity from trade" in the world.[21] Earlier, he had offered to mediate the dispute, seeking "peace without victory." Although rebuffed at that time, he personally led the U.S. delegation to the peace talks once an armistice had been achieved.

Faced with allies insisting on a vengeful peace and bent on continuing old ways, Wilson worked tirelessly to incorporate the concept of a world organization where peaceful means of solving problems might be employed, a League of Nations. He was successful with the Europeans, and provisions for the League were woven into the draft of the peace treaty; however, he had not tended to his domestic political fences. The isolationists in the Congress had had enough meddling in foreign affairs and did not support involvement in the League. They were joined by others with real concerns about automatic response provisions in the so-called Covenant for the League pledging action from the United States, conditions they felt violated strictures in the U.S. Constitution. Wilson, his back up, was not willing to compromise; consequently, the Senate rejected the treaty by refusing its consent. Although the League was formed, it was missing its most important member.

The machine gun, the tank, and the airplane all made their debut in numbers during World War I. From their first use as observation platforms early in the war, aircraft rapidly were used to counter enemy aircraft, support ground troops, and intercept enemy lines of communication. This new weapon system led some to imagine that, if properly employed, it might eliminate traditional warfare and make armies and navies obsolete. Bombardment from the air promised to be much cleaner and quicker; losses might be reduced. If aircraft could do all this, the cost of war should be much less both in currency and in lives, a particular concern in the wake of the war.

After World War I, an Italian, Guilio Douhet, collected and presented the prevailing views on the potential use of air power. His approach went well beyond any utility the airplane had actually demonstrated to that time. His notion was that the advantages of height and speed achieved by an aircraft were of such magnitude that it would be nearly invulnerable. It followed, then, that a nation should have an air force equipped with long-range bombing aircraft with crews trained and ready to release large quantities of bombs on enemy population centers, seats of government, and industrial concentrations at the very start of a conflict. This action, he contended, would destroy the opposition's will to fight and force the enemy government to stop hostilities.[22]

Others, particularly General Billy Mitchell of the U.S. Army, foresaw more applications for aircraft and pushed as hard as they could to bring reluctant or unwilling governments and armed services to "see the light." Military writers J. F. C. Fuller and Basil Liddell-Hart postulated using the combination of tanks supported by aircraft,[23] the U.S. Navy developed a real interest in airplanes, and the Royal Air Force replaced the army as an instrument of overseas policy for Great Britain.

At sea, Corbett's ideas resurfaced because, although naval operations certainly had made contributions to the final victory, the few naval engagements that had occurred were not decisive in themselves. What could be seen only dimly at that time was that dominance at sea in a total war between highly industrialized nations would be achieved only after a gradual accumulation of victories, amid heavy attrition of forces; there would no longer be a decisive "battle" at sea any more than there would be on land. Technological change as much as any deliberate action was responsible for this.

The appalling loss of life and property resulting from the all-out and widespread conflict of World War I shocked many. Even the United States, which had experienced relatively few casualties and no physical damage, recoiled. Diplomatic efforts at reducing the likelihood of more conflict continued for the next several years. Despite not being a member of the League of Nations or the World Court, the United States attempted to maintain a position of influence in the world for a time. Washington was the site of the first Five Power Naval Conference, which produced treaties limiting the size of major navies. The American secretary of state joined with the prime minister of France to promote a pact renouncing war, the Kellogg-Briand Pact, which was eventually signed by sixty-two nations.

This participation in the affairs of the world was short-lived, however, because, when the world economy tumbled into a depression in the 1930s the United States, for all practical purposes, retired from the stage. It could be argued that its failure to continue to accept responsibility in the larger world ensured that the second great war of the twentieth century would be fought. Isolationism ensured that U.S. strength could not be mustered and deployed rapidly.

The nation's experience in World War I had prompted thinking in new ways about the defense of the United States and the utility of some preparation.

The War and Navy departments began to develop war plans, which were to be kept on file. These plans were based on the conclusion that there was little threat from a war-torn and exhausted Europe. Japan, on the other hand, was seen as able to mount one. The Japanese had entered World War I on the side of the Allies as a debtor nation, but had emerged stronger, with major foreign reserves and a corner on the textile market in east Asia. Unfortunately, its economy was still not fully developed and was so sensitive to world conditions that when the world economy collapsed, Japan's did as well.

Under these conditions the Japanese army began to gain more influence, while despite the depression Japan's shadow still fell over all foreign interests in that part of the world. Given this, Plan Orange, a war plan outlining operations against the empire that was originally drafted in 1914, was dusted off.

Plan Orange projected that U.S. forces would progressively expand control of the sea area of the Pacific westward as fast as possible, solidifying lines of communication, and then conduct operations against naval forces and sea lanes to apply pressure, both military and economic, on Orange (Japan).

This plan survived, with periodic revision, for nearly 20 years before it was superseded.[24] War Plan Red, another contingency formulated earlier in the century for operations against Great Britain, was also updated, just in case.

The worldly viewpoint these activities represented suggested a need for more and better armed forces. After all, if experience to date were any guide, wars were now to be long, gritty, all-out affairs where a nation's strength would be measured not solely in numbers of military units, but, more important, in the depth and breadth of manpower, available economic capacity, and stability of its society. This shift in emphasis was ill-timed; the Great Depression ensured that no expansion would take place very soon.

Across the sea, war-scarred Europeans were confronted with a resurgent Germany under Adolf Hitler. As the war clouds gathered, the sentiment of a majority in the United States was again that the country should not become involved.[25]

In service of this fervor, Congress passed neutrality acts in the mid-1930s that embargoed loans and the shipment of arms to all belligerents, specified a "cash and carry" policy for goods bought in the United States, and declared the ships of belligerents off-limits to traveling American citizens.

Something Old, Something New:
World War II Strategy

As conditions continued to deteriorate, the need for military and diplomatic dialogue became apparent. A Standing Liaison Committee was formed in 1938 that brought together representatives of the State, War and Navy departments for purposes of coordinating the nation's efforts. Amazingly, it was the very first official linkage between the military and the makers of policy in the United States.

President Roosevelt himself took a more direct hand in foreign policy development and execution by proposing a series of measures to Congress that would help Great Britain and increase preparedness in this country as well. He also met with Winston Churchill, the British prime minister, to plot a joint course should the United States be dragged into the war. Despite these moves, when war neared, the generals and admirals began to take over in typical fashion from the diplomats.[26]

This was to be another coalition war, but this time the United States would, once engaged, participate fully. To ensure unanimity of effort, planning with Great Britain was begun before the United States was a belligerent. Joint talks (the ABC-1 meeting) were held in January 1940 to discuss a combined strategy in the event the United States should join the war. In the course of these meetings it was agreed that Germany was the only enemy with the potential for mustering the military and industrial prowess and the manpower necessary to defeat the Allies. As a consequence, Allied operations would be concentrated in Europe. The United States would stand on the defensive in the Pacific, deterring the Japanese with its fleet at Pearl Harbor.[27] Supplies would continue to be shipped to Great Britain and preparations made to send forces to Latin America, if needed.

After the declaration of war, the "Europe first" strategy was formalized. Execution, however, did not follow the script. The Combined Chiefs of Staff, an organization formed by melding the senior service officers from Great Britain and the United States for the purpose of recommending military operations, could not come to an agreement. The British, undoubtedly haunted by visions of the casualty lists of the earlier "Great War," wanted to fight the Axis at arm's length until overwhelming superiority of force could be attained. They proposed a strategy of long-range bombing of Germany, supporting subversive activities, assisting the Russians (who by this time had been betrayed by the Nazis, switched sides, and joined the Allies), and conducting other operations at the periphery of Nazi-held territory—no head-on clashes with the Wehrmacht. The U.S. Joint Chiefs agreed with the first three but took issue with the last. The American strategy envisioned confronting the German Army as soon as possible, utilizing a massive invasion of the continent across the English Channel.

Bringing off that kind of operation in the European theater early in the war would not be easy because the United States was still struggling to get on a wartime footing. If that option were selected, a long period of inactivity would follow while men and equipment were stockpiled in England in preparation. From a political standpoint, this delay would be damaging because the population of the United States, always impatient, would be demanding action. Furthermore, there was a shipping crisis similar to the one in the earlier war, the Germans were again winning the war of attrition at sea, and the number of merchant ships available to carry the men and equipment across the Atlantic, already in short supply, was being rapidly reduced. Resource allocation decisions were bound to interfere with an early invasion, so the British strategy was adopted initially and resulted in amphibious invasions of North Africa, Sicily, and Italy. When the forces were ready, the amphibious invasion of the continent so dear to U.S. strategists' hearts was executed.

Naval operations, in the meantime, were conducted as if there were two separate conflicts underway. On the Atlantic side, American and British navies maintained sea lines of communication, isolated Germany, and supported the armies on the continent – a maritime strategy. In the Pacific theater, the tasks of the overwhelmingly American fleets were to defeat Japanese naval forces and conduct a sea-air blockade, actions best characterized as part of a naval strategy.

Coalition warfare carried the day. During the war strategy was plotted in several meetings of the Allied heads of state, Roosevelt, Churchill, and Stalin, at Casablanca in 1943, Teheran in 1944, and Yalta in 1945. Although they often did not agree initially on what should be done, by meeting's end they always reached a consensus. The effort against Germany in particular was allied in thought, word, and deed – the Pacific war much less so.

In that area it was largely an American show, although there were relatively small numbers of British and Commonwealth forces involved from the beginning, and Russian forces that assisted at the end. The defensive strategy originally decided upon was quickly abandoned as a combination of Japanese aggression and U.S. success caused the latter to commit a large portion of its resources to the Asian theater of operation.[28] Although U.S. Army forces were present in significant numbers, they were used in a naval role, conducting amphibious landings supported by Air Corps bombing on one attack axis, while Marines supported by naval air were doing the same on the other.

The invasion of Japan, which was to be the logical culmination of the Pacific war (although casualties estimates for such an undertaking were set very high), was not required after all. A strategic bombing campaign, including nighttime delivery of incendiary bombs, was undertaken by the American Air Force, and was followed by the delivery of atomic bombs on the cities of Hiroshima and Nagasaki. Although in a narrow sense an atomic bomb was merely another explosive weapon, its thermal, radiation, and blast effects set it apart. A new strategic age had literally burst on the scene.

But there were lessons to be learned from the old. Three theories of strategy in warfare had been developed and "tested" by the Allies up to the end of World War II. All left something to be desired, although each made a contribution to the final victory.[29] The maritime strategy of using naval power to influence the outcome on land had been helpful in defeating Germany. The naval strategy of defeating the enemy's fleet and strangling his commerce was correct for Japan. Air Force strategic bombing had done considerable damage in both countries. But no one was sufficient in and of itself.

Despite commitment to a strategy of annihilation by the United States, achieving that objective using only conventional explosive weapons appeared open to debate as the war ground on. The mass of forces, the sophistication of weapons, and the dimensions of the battlefields in total warfare between alliances simply made a decisive battle on land or at sea impossible; it was necessary to wear the enemy down.

Then came *the* bomb. Instantly a strategy of annihilation on a scale previously only dreamed of seemed possible. It was obvious that old conceptions of warfare needed to be revised. This new age was to be formidable.

CHAPTER III

The Strategic Heritage of the United States from World War II to the Present

The end of the war found the United States fielding the greatest military machine in history; America had become *the* world power. This colossus had been built by stimulating the productive power of industry and by arousing and maintaining the will to win in the ordinary citizen.[1]

Ultimate success in World War II had been the result of several factors but principally was brought about by the strength of the coalition. Achieving the victory had required patience, understanding, and above all compromise, because each member had brought something different to the alliance in terms of objectives, methods, and means. The Allies had argued about but finally agreed on an overall strategy of taking their enemies serially and defeating them utterly, and then had executed it.

Although they had shared this trial by fire, the Allies were not affected equally. The United States stood astride the postwar world with a mighty military and a fully productive industrial base. Hulking in its shadow was the Soviet Union, which after suffering more than 13 million casualties and much damage in the fighting was, nevertheless, already gaining strength and rebuilding. The European powers were worn out. England was merely a shell, appearing much the same on the outside but drained financially. France was worse. None of the physical and little of the social devastation suffered by those countries who had "hosted" the actual fighting had touched the United States. While there certainly was mourning for those of its sons and daughters who would not return, there was also widespread optimism about a world now free to ". . . emulate American ideals of self-help, entrepreneurship, free trade and democracy."[2]

It was thought in some quarters that war might well be obsolete as a policy alternative because the United States, as sole possessor of the atomic bomb, had the means to deter, or even to punish, those who might want to try it again. The United Nations, a rebirth of the idea of an organization of nations committed to solving problems peacefully, was established in 1946 and had begun functioning. In other words, the sun of peace was shining; however, on the horizon storm clouds were gathering.

As was its wont, the United States began returning its forces from overseas and discharging most of them. The Soviets did not do the same. Indeed, their refusal to withdraw forces from the countries they had occupied on the way to Berlin or to honor the agreements of the Yalta and Potsdam conferences regarding self-determination for those same countries rekindled the fundamental fear of communism that had developed after the Bolshevik Revolution but was shelved during the war. Soviet-backed communist governments appeared in Hungary, Rumania, Bulgaria, and Poland, and Soviet activism in Greece and Turkey made the situation worse. Postwar Europe seemed powerless against Soviet force; only the United States was strong enough to counterbalance it.

Preparing for a Leadership Role

Recognition of that fact stimulated the Truman administration to action. The wisdom and experience of such men as George Kennan, W. Averill Harriman, Charles Bohlen and others, all of whom had served in diplomatic posts in Russia, were tapped in an effort to understand Soviet intentions in the postwar world. They concluded that the United States would have to assume a leadership role in peacetime if the fabric of society in Europe, a fabric woven over centuries, was not to unravel completely. Should such a dissolution occur, it was thought that the resulting Soviet-dominated Europe would directly threaten the United States.

Accepting leadership means action. The strategy chosen was one of simply "containing" Soviet expansionism. If this were accomplished, the thinking went, the Soviets would eventually forsake their aggressive ways and change. Containment of the Soviet Union became the bedrock of U.S. foreign policy. Initial efforts were aimed at preventing the Soviets from taking over, or dominating, governments in countries made weak by the war. While most overtures were to be diplomatic, military force, including the use of the few atomic weapons in the arsenal, remained an option. In enunciating this policy, President Harry S. Truman pledged to "...help free peoples to maintain ... national integrity against aggressive movements that seek to enforce upon them totalitarian regimes."[3] If this commitment were to be fulfilled, the structure for making and executing national security policy decisions, including those of the military, needed to be modernized.

From the earliest years of the republic, an uneasy truce had existed between the civilian controllers of the army (the secretaries of War) and the generals. At bottom was the question of who would command the forces. An official opinion issued by the Attorney General in 1855 stated that the presumption existed that the Secretary of War commanded, since he was executing the President's instructions. This did not convince the uniformed officers, who continued to argue the issue. It was not finally resolved until 1903, when a legislative act specified that the Secretary of War exercised command through delegation from the President.[4]

There had also been a good deal of friction and little coodination between the War (Army) and Navy departments, which throughout their existence had occupied completely separate and very powerful political worlds. An attempt at forcing cooperation had been made in 1903 when the Joint Army-Navy Board was formed to address all matters requiring coordination, but it had not been a roaring success.

Shortly after the conclusion of World War I, it became obvious that having to process the often competing priorities of the Army and Navy separately was a waste of substantial time, money, and energy. Since no suitable answer was at hand, the question of how one might combine them in some useful way became the subject of more than 12 studies between 1921 and 1945. Some fifty bills and resolutions on the subject were submitted to the Congress; few of the bills ever got out of committee and none were enacted.

The post–World War II environment provided an opportunity to address the subject once again. President Truman, arguing that integrated planning, unified programs and budgets, and economies of scale in procurement would result, urged Congress to combine the Army and Navy into a single Department of Defense. The services were fighting each other over the same subject. Plans for unification proposed by the Army both during and just after the war were opposed by the Navy; it countered with its own plans, which the Army promptly rejected.

Since there was little agreement in 1946 on what the role of the military would be during peacetime, adversarial positions were natural. The services were in a self-protective mode. Whatever else happened, the Army wanted to ensure equality with the Navy, the Navy worried about maintaining its autonomy in the face of a perceived threat from the Air Corps, and the Air Corps, desperately wanting separate service status, feared that it would not be achieved if any sort of consolidation occurred. Thus the debate raged on over large issues (roles and missions) and smaller ones (funds and promotion systems). In late 1946 and early 1947 agreements were finally forged and a National Security Act was drafted, passed, and took effect on

September 17, 1947, when the first Secretary of Defense, James V. Forrestal, was sworn in.

Although the unification of the armed forces was not legislated, the Act accomplished much of what was required to support the country's expanded role in the world.[5] Most important, it created a framework within which military and foreign policy could be blended into one agenda addressing national security. Three new agencies and a national military establishment were to be its resources.

Arguably, the most important new agency was the National Security Council (NSC), established to advise the President on the integration of domestic, foreign, and military policies relating to the security of the nation. Another, the Central Intelligence Agency (CIA), was formed to gather and collate all intelligence; the third, the National Security Resources Board (NSRB), was to advise the President on the coordination of military, industrial, and civil mobilization whenever that might be required. In theory, the three were to work together; the NSC, comprised of the highest officials responsible for diplomatic, military and industrial planning, would be informed by the CIA and the Resources Board and would generate policy recommendations in all matters affecting the security of the nation.

The same Act created a National Military Establishment headed by a Secretary of Defense, who would coordinate the activities of, set general policy for, and exercise direction, authority, and control over the individual service departments (the Army and Navy retained their autonomy and the Air Force joined them as a separate service), thus ensuring strong civilian control of the military establishment. The Secretary would be the President's principal assistant for national security.

Congress did not want to merge the armed forces but did desire the benefits of unified force commands, which had been employed with some success in World War II; it authorized the establishment of a permanent unified command mechanism. The resulting structure had two chains of command, one encompassing the actual fighting troops, the other the support forces.

The National Security Act also gave statutory legitimacy to the Joint Chiefs of Staff (JCS), which had been formed in 1940 to carry out joint planning with a similar British organization. The Joint Chiefs were named as the principal military advisers to the President, the Secretary of Defense, and the National Security Council. They were specifically charged with preparing strategic plans and actually establishing the unified commands. Under the Act, the unified commands were to be directed through an executive agent arrangement by a designated service chief; for example, the Chief of Staff of the Army might be designated the executive agent for the European Unified Command.

In the everyday world, meanwhile, communism seemed to be

inexorably on the move. The seizure of power in Czechoslovakia together with the breakdown of talks on settling the fate of Germany and the subsequent blockade of Berlin in 1948, heightened the apprehension of the western European nations and the United States. This anxiety led directly to collaboration and a collective defense treaty that France, the United Kingdom, Belgium, the Netherlands, and Luxembourg signed in Brussels. It also led to the development of the North Atlantic Treaty (when the United States joined in) with its "attack against one is an attack against all" provision, and the organization formed under it (NATO), which grew from a consultive political forum into a military command structure. Enlisting in such an effort was a truly radical step for the United States, where "entangling alliances" had been considered akin to the plague for a century and a half. Once bitten, America embraced the concept of coalition defense through alliances with a vengeance, signing some six multi- and bilateral treaties over the next ten years.

The formation of NATO caused the Soviets to create a similar arrangement. They gathered their satellite nations into an alliance that convened in Poland and was duly dubbed the Warsaw Pact. The world was now divided into two camps, each led by a nation whose leaders

> ...tended to see [the] rivalry as a clash of principles, with their own national features tied to the success of such concepts as capitalism and socialism, individual liberty and state security, religious freedom and scientific materialism...[6]

Conflict seemed inevitable, and the specter of a nuclear holocaust cast a longer shadow each year.

Defense Planning in the Nuclear Age

When evidence that the Soviet Union had detonated an atomic warhead came to hand in September 1949, the foundation of American national security was shaken. It was clear that the whole concept required updating. Previously, threats to the nation took time to develop; an enemy had to mobilize, transport, and position forces before much damage could be inflicted, a process that would take weeks, if not months. Now, with the advent of high-flying and long-range aircraft, very destructive weapons might be brought to bear only hours after the decision to attack was made. Senator Arthur Vandenburg captured the essence of the problem when he said, "Our oceans have ceased to be moats which automatically protect our ramparts."[7]

This situation called for continuous efforts on a broad economic, political, and military front directed toward maintaining the peace (as opposed to simply planning for war). Constant vigilance would be required. Large standing military forces were needed because there might be no time to mobilize in the traditional sense. Bernard Brodie, sometimes called the first writer on strategy of this new era, declared that whereas the principal objective heretofore was to win a war, it now was to avert one.

By 1950 the Soviet menace seemed to be looming particularly large. In January of that year the secretaries of State and Defense were asked by the President to review U.S. objectives and the strategy for achieving them in peace and war. The combined State and Defense study group concluded that the Soviet Union's ideology, the power of their conventional forces, and their nuclear potential posed a major threat to the nation. Their report, which was later adopted in the National Security Council as NSC-68, was more a political than an analytical document. It concentrated entirely on estimating the likely capabilities of Soviet forces and assumed a specific intent on the part of the Soviet government with respect to using them.

> The assault on free institutions is worldwide now, and in the context of the present polarization of world power, a defeat of free institutions anywhere is a defeat everywhere.[8]

The report's thesis that the Soviets were bent on expanding throughout the globe was designed to frighten policy makers into supporting the significantly increased military strength recommended to counter such action. Although not disagreeing with the conclusions, President Truman decided that the time was not propitious for the budget increase necessary to achieve the required force levels. He soon changed his mind when the North Koreans attacked South Korea a couple of months later.

Historically, Korea had been a pawn in a continual struggle between Japan and China, with the Japanese in control from 1904 through World War II. As that war came to an end, the Russians were assigned to take the surrender of Japanese forces north of the arbitrarily chosen 38th Parallel; the United States would do the same to the south.[9] The United Nations had attempted on several occasions to organize countrywide elections, but had failed. However, elections were held in the south in 1948 and Syngman Rhee was elected president. The United States government did not trust Rhee (he was suspected of harboring ideas of unifying the peninsula by force) and chose not to provide him with military equipment capable of being used for an offensive. Perhaps the North Koreans (and, as many people believed, the Soviets) interpreted this, along with the fact that Secretary of State Dean Acheson's "forward defense line" was drawn so as to exclude Korea, as an indication of lack of interest. If so, they miscalculated.

Despite concern among many officials that the Soviet Union had orchestrated the Korean adventure as a prelude to moves elsewhere, President Truman viewed the situation as a test of the United Nations' ability to counter aggressive acts between or among states; he ordered the case placed before the Security Council of that body. As luck would have it, the Soviets were in the process of boycotting the Council and thus were absent from an historic meeting during which, had they been present, a resolution calling on the North Koreans to stop the incursion and return behind the border would almost certainly have been vetoed, perhaps forestalling any action. As it was the resolution passed, and, after two days, when North Korea ignored the order to desist, the Security Council requested member nations to furnish assistance to South Korea.[10]

The Korean War, which raged intermittently between 1950 and 1953, puzzled, angered, and frustrated many, both in uniform or out. The North Koreans had no navy to speak of, and did not rely much on supply from the sea; thus there was no naval challenge. The much vaunted U.S. air power moved in rapidly, but was unable to interdict the major supply routes on land. In essence, naval superiority and the most massive air force in existence were all but meaningless, and the possibility of atomic weapon employment by the United States apparently did not deter the North Koreans at all.

This "police action," as it was sometimes called, did have wide-ranging effects. Perhaps the most important was that it highlighted the fact that, as Bevin Alexander puts it, "Simple verities about total victory and the conflict between good and evil that had guided American policy for many years were inadequate in the dismaying world that arose from World War II."[11] It also established a precedent of armed intervention by U.S. forces in an area outside the western hemisphere, and the necessity to expand U.S. armed forces for operations in Korea provided an opportunity to increase numbers elsewhere according to the recommendations of NSC-68. The defense budget increased from $11.5 billion in 1950 to $45 billion by 1952. Forces were deployed to fixed sites or areas forward in Europe, that is, close to the Soviet Union, so that any engagements would take place there and not on the U.S. mainland, and a NATO military structure was erected. Finally, the strategic environment had dictated a completely new way of fighting a war. It had been the first conflict in which an ". . . administration entered, fought and ended the . . . war for political objectives which took precedence over, in its mind, the conduct of battle."[12]

President Dwight D. Eisenhower, who was elected on his promise to end the war, was convinced that his threat of the use of nuclear weapons had finally brought about the cease-fire and subsequent peace talks on the Korean peninsula. He was also convinced, along with his Secretary of State, John Foster Dulles, that the conflict would not have occurred at all if the United States had relied on American air power and its capability to deliver atomic weapons. While accepting containment of Soviet expansionism as an objective, the two decided to alter the way the United States reacted to what were seen as "tests" of democracy by adopting an explicit strategy of deterring wars instead of fighting them.

Eisenhower was also determined to reduce the defense budget. Since nuclear forces in general went "farther" than conventional ones (that is, fewer were necessary to achieve equivalent firepower) and were therefore cheaper to buy and maintain at the ready, the decision was made to anchor future deterrence of war with the threat to use nuclear weapons not only in answer to any local aggression, but against the source or instigator of the aggression as well. This response style became known as massive retaliation.

It soon became clear, however, that reliance on only these weapons would not suffice; in situations other than a direct confrontation between superpowers, their use simply was not credible. The unwillingness to employ nuclear weapons to stave off a French defeat by a communist revolutionary force in Indochina was an excellent example.[13] What is more, as the Soviet Union built more of their own weapons, any massive retaliation by the United States for aggression in a third country might well bring down a counterstrike. Massive retaliation was a hollow strategy.

Military strategists were strangely silent during the ensuing debates about nuclear weapons and strategy. Civilians in research institutions and universities emerged as the creative thinkers in these areas.[14] Although generally trained in history or social sciences, these civilians were capable of bringing game, psychological, and economic theory to bear on national security problems. From them came the central concepts of the nuclear era, the theories of mutual deterrence and arms control, the science of crisis management, and the doctrine of the limited war.

When President John F. Kennedy took office in 1961, his administration, led by Secretary of Defense Robert S. MacNamara, subjected the inherited strategy and accompanying force structure to rigorous analysis. As a result the policy of deterring war, whether general or limited, conventional or nuclear, was reaffirmed. In the Kennedy formulation, however, emphasis was to be placed on the settlement of disputes by diplomatic rather than military means, although the capability to enforce settlements using the military would remain. In order to back up this strategy, the number and capabilties of long-range nuclear systems had to be adequate to deter a deliberate nuclear attack on the United States and her allies, while, at the same time, strong conventional forces were needed to do the same for nonnuclear conflicts. Thus did the doctrine of "flexible response" replace massive retaliation. Flexible response sought to meet force with like force; that is, an attack made solely with conventional weapons would be resisted with conventional weapons.

The principal virtue of flexible response was that it seemed less likely to provoke any unwarranted escalation to nuclear weapons. This desirable effect notwithstanding, the strategy was perceived in some quarters as a dilution of the deterrent effect of the "nukes." The NATO allies in particular, who had been reasonably comfortable behind the U.S. nuclear umbrella for years, were not happy.

They preferred the notion that the United States would rapidly escalate the nuclear ladder in the hope that that would force an end to hostilities before much damage was wrought.[15]

It was during these years that the Defense Department came to dominate foreign affairs. By the early 1960s budgetary considerations were assuming more and more weight in strategic calculations. A Planning, Programming, Budgeting System (PPBS) had been installed in the Department of Defense to better rationalize requirements and control expenditures, and the mathematics of systems analysis were applied to the requirements calculus.

A new theory for calibrating deterrence emerged from all of these ruminations. Nuclear-force capabilities were to be maintained at a level that would ensure that the number remaining after withstanding a Soviet nuclear attack would be adequate to launch a retaliatory strike of such magnitude that the level of destruction in the Soviet Union would be enough to deter them from attacking in the first place. This formation became known as "assured destruction." Conventional forces were also required, they were expanded numerically, and their capabilities broadened when some troops were trained for guerrilla fighting.[16]

Formalized planning scenarios were now used as part of the PPBS force planning and sizing process. In the Kennedy-Johnson years, forces were to be sized for two and a half wars; that is, for simultaneous wars with the Soviets in Europe, with China in Asia, and with some lesser power somewhere else. The Nixon-Ford years produced a contraction of both strategy and goals not because the world was a safer place, but for budgetary reasons. Asian countries were now to defend themselves unless the Soviets were clearly involved; one and one-half wars (China had been coopted and was no longer an enemy) was the planning guideline. In the late seventies President Carter, in the wake of the Shah of Iran's ouster, declared the Persian Gulf to be an area of vital interest to the United States, and a new force was developed to react to general contingencies in that area.[17]

By the early 1980s, most of the scenario distinctions had disappeared as, under President Reagan, the military was charged with maintaining the force structure and capability to fight the Soviets on three fronts simultaneously, a war-fighting strategy sometimes called horizontal escalation.[18]

The Planning Legacy of the 1990s

In the early 1990s, planning is in general disarray. While not powerless, the enemy of the last 45 years has lost much of its bite, at least for the time being, and has not been replaced. Predicting the next crisis area in the Third World is extremely difficult. Flexibility must perforce become the byword in all things concerning national security.

Since World War II, containment of Soviet expansionism and deterrence of nuclear war have remained U.S. policy. In both cases, a military strategy of choice has been to maintain sufficient military power and organization to cause the Soviets to calculate that more would be lost than won if they initiated military action. Forming and maintaining coalitions (thereby increasing resources), forward basing of U.S. forces (to signal commitment, and to keep battle from the shores of the homeland) and the maintenance of a military force structure capable of responding to either a conventional or nuclear attack were the methods chosen to execute the strategy. If the Soviets were not deterred and did initiate conflict, the Armed Forces' task was "to secure all U.S. and allied interests, and deny the aggressor any of his war aims," while limiting conflict to only the scope and intensity required to end it on terms favorable to the United States.[19]

Changes to this fundamental strategy have been, for the most part, made only at the margin. For example, increases in weapon system capabilities have typically altered only target lists. In the early 1970s, nuclear strike plans against small target sets were drawn to provide measured responses and to eliminate the necessity for all-out retaliation. An antiballistic missile (ABM) treaty with the Soviet Union, requiring that both sides remain vulnerable by virtue of not building and deploying antiballistic missile defensive systems, was signed, as have others concerning the numbers of nuclear weapons. This anti–Soviet strategy has been very successful; there has been no armed conflict between the two superpowers.

Lesser confrontations have occurred, however, including, in 1962, the first genuine scare of the nuclear age. The Soviets had been discovered stationing offensive missiles in Cuba; President Kennedy decided something must be done. Although many of his advisers were calling for armed attacks on the missile sites, the choice was made to offer Soviet Premier Khrushchev an avenue out of the situation short of a clash of arms. A naval blockade of Cuba was announced, U.S. forces were placed on alert, and the Soviets were advised to remove the missiles and warned not to bring in more. As tension mounted, the Soviets "blinked" and a potential catastrophe was averted. But there always seemed to be another waiting in the wings.

The next crisis appeared in Southeast Asia. In the aftermath of World War II, France, despite the desires of the United States, had rushed back in to control her former colony of Vietnam. However, its presence was no longer welcome. Opposition to French rule had spread, particularly in the north, and the dissidents now had a military organization, left over from battling the Japanese. Fighting broke out almost immediately. France requested and the United States delivered both economic aid and military equipment. At a conference in Geneva in April 1954, Vietnam was partitioned into North and South at the 17th Parallel, with France assigned as "guarantor" of South Vietnam. The Viet Cong, a revolutionary movement of communist guerrillas in the south who were allied with, if not taking orders from, the government in the north, became more active. The United States read this as a communist takeover attempt, and, bypassing a France beset by difficulties elsewhere, offered aid directly to the government in the south. The end came suddenly when, unable to fend off the revolutionary forces, the French suffered a stunning defeat at Dien Bien Phu in May 1954. They finally withdrew in 1956 and the Republic of South Vietnam, with support from the United States, was born. Fighting between government forces and the Viet Cong continued.

The rapidly deteriorating situation was seen by the leadership in the United States as a test of the nation's ability to help others trying to combat communist "wars of liberation." Military "advisers" were sent to help train the Army of the Republic of Vietnam (ARVN). Eventually, the North Vietnamese actively joined in, sending troops as well as supplies south. When the ARVN proved less than effective against the increased threat, U.S. soldiers and airmen were ordered into battle. By 1964, U.S. government policy was to continue to add forces as necessary; it was thought that if Vietnam were "lost" the remaining states in Southeast Asia would inevitably fall as well (the domino theory).

There was little agreement in the higher reaches of government as to how the conflict might be brought to a conclusion. The U.S. military wanted to inflict a level of damage sufficient to get the North Vietnamese to quit, that is, to defeat them in traditional terms. The civilians in charge, on the other hand, concerned about the Chinese or Soviet reaction, simply wanted to apply enough pressure to force the North Vietnamese to the bargaining table. The enemy yielded to neither, and the tension between the civilian authority and the military leaders intensified as the gulf between the objectives of the two camps widened. Bad things began to happen as the war dragged on for nearly 10 years.

It was a difficult war to fight at best. At one time and place it was a classic confrontation between guerrillas and a professional army where the latter's hightech weaponry seemed to make little difference; at other times and places it was organized army unit against organized army unit. Various inducements (bombing halts were the primary ones) were employed to lure the North Vietnamese to the bargaining table. However, even when negotiations commenced, little was accomplished. As years passed without a "decision," segments of an American public that had never fully embraced U.S. involvement became more vociferous in their opposition; American society reeled from the strident protests sounding throughout the country, the military complained because it was not free to prosecute its kind of war, and the civilians in charge became more and more frustrated because nothing seemed to work. There was much finger pointing. Finally, in 1973, some 20 years after the initial involvement, a bargain of sorts was struck and all American troops were withdrawn.[20]

Shadows of the Vietnam War linger yet. It was a war unlike any other in the American experience. Perhaps the most glaring difference, one shared with the Korean War, was that, no matter what face you put on it, U.S. forces had not defeated the enemy. In this case, the American public saw that "up close and personal" as the pervasive eye of the television brought it into homes on a daily basis. The army of journalists on the scene documented atrocities by soldiers on both sides, identified various attempts by the government to distort unpleasant information, reported on corruption and profiteering (a good old American wartime custom), and exposed the burgeoning use of drugs by American servicemen. When the war was finally over, there were no homecoming parades, only recriminations and a determination in many to ensure that there would be no more such adventures.

There have been no more protracted military efforts since that time, although U.S. military forces have been in combat in various locations around the world. The strategic posture of the United States remained as before, designed to counter a heavily armed Soviet bloc as government and industry strove to add capability. Maximum weapon ranges increased to thousands of miles, while technologies contributing to weapons going higher, faster, and farther, invisible to defensive eyes, were pursued with vigor. Other efforts worked to enhance accuracy and control. Technical terms, including the bits and bytes of "computerese," have become part of our everyday vocabulary.

Quite suddenly, as the last decade of the twentieth century neared, the strategic picture abruptly changed, relations with the Soviet Union mellowed, the Warsaw Pact was abandoned, and the defense establishment was forced to consider a world without worthy opponents. Planning went into hibernation while appropriate enemies were sought. While no menacing ones could be found, irritating situations were plentiful, so forces were employed as peacekeepers in Lebanon (unsuccessfully), and as liberators in Grenada and Panama (successfully).

In 1990, Iraq invaded Kuwait, its small neighbor to the south, charging Kuwait with flooding the oil market to drive prices down and with "stealing" Iraqi oil along the disputed border.[21] This naked aggression was condemned by the United States and others, and, later, by the United Nations in the form of a resolution calling for immediate withdrawal. Iraq ignored all calls for a return to the status quo. This first prompted U.S.- and U.N.-sponsored economic sanctions, then military operations to evict Iraqi troops by force.

As the likelihood of combat increased over a period of several months, there were both anguish and belligerence in the United States. Since on paper Iraq had the fourth largest army in the world, one supposedly battled-hardened in an eight-year war with Iran, the possibility of a drawn-out and bloody conflict, reminiscent of Vietnam, haunted many. At the same time, despite the fact that Iraq posed no direct, but only an abstract and indirect threat to the United States, there was a rallying 'round the flag that prompted a remarkable patriotic surge (one which was capitalized on by many an entrepreneur). In the actual conflict, allied forces easily and quickly defeated a poorly led and clearly dispirited Iraqi army,[22] first from the air, then on the ground. The war lasted 44 days. Most Americans exulted in the victory, more from a sense of relief than anything else. Few stopped to consider that it was really not much of a contest. The forces of Iraq are out of Kuwait, but nearly all of the problems that seem endemic to the Middle East remain.

Through these years of near and actual conflict, the world has, to an extent, learned to accept the potential larger terrors of this age while continuing to work to reduce, if not eradicate, them. Significant efforts to control the proliferation of nuclear weapons have been undertaken, as have preliminary moves to limit, in some way, the size of nuclear arsenals and the plenty of conventional weapon systems as well, at least among the strongest powers. The evolving political, social, and technical forces of societies interacting with others who harbor opposing interests and aims have brought the world to its present place. Throughout most of history, war was generally considered to be a principal means by which one group could force its wishes on another. As societies evolved, however, war seemed to have ". . . [lost] its one virtue, its power of decision."[23]

For nearly 45 years since the end of World War II, the Soviet Union was the bully against which all needs were measured; other threats paled beside the capability with which it was credited. Bearing the standard against this threat for all these years has altered American society.

CHAPTER IV

The Contemporary Strategic Environment

The United States clearly came of age as a world power when it began to assume global responsibilities in the post–World War II years. Admittedly, it did so only grudgingly when indications were clear that the Soviet Union was not going to leave other countries alone. The Cold War that soon developed between the western alliance, led by the United States, and the eastern one, led by the Soviets, strengthened the resolve of American leadership to halt any Soviet expansion, but it also focused the political and military power of the country very narrowly. The competition that formed the "conflict" in this war permeated all facets of life, from economics to amateur sports.

During the 1950s there was a whiff of paranoia in the air. It seemed to many that the United States was under continual siege by Soviet, or, more generally, communist agents. Indeed, for much of the time, it was assumed that any activity inimical to U.S. interests almost anywhere in the world must be communist, or, more specifically, Soviet inspired. Accepting this characterization not only served to make what often were very complex issues appear simple, but also inhibited the type of objective analysis that might have helped explain the variety of forces at work in the world.

Debate Over the Role of the Military

As the period of tension with the Soviet Union lengthened from years into decades, the consequences of this single-mindedness and the commitments it engendered began to chafe. First and foremost, in the absence of a shooting war, the cost of equipping and maintaining a larger-than-normal military establishment came to overshadow all other considerations, including the specific reasons for establishing it in the first place. Few

questions were asked about what was to be done, many about who and
what were to be used in doing it. Further, the general unanimity of opinion
about the proper course of action that had developed in the immediate
post–World War II years dissolved as attitudes toward Soviet actions took
on a distinctive political coloration. Individuals were classified as hard-
liners (hawks) or "soft" on defense (doves), depending on the level of their
support for establishing military force levels and procuring of weapon
systems, and how they would define the conditions under which forces
might be put in play.

Since in terms of financing military forces and equipment the executive
branch proposes and the legislative disposes, some shared view of what is
required to maintain national security would seem useful, if not necessary.
The Packard Commission, a blue-ribbon, presidentially appointed panel
that examined management in the Defense Department, concluded that,
unfortunately, "...there is no rational system whereby the Executive
Branch and the Congress reach coherent and enduring agreement on national military strategy, the forces to carry it out and the funding that
should be provided."[1]

In the light of the single enemy focus, some would argue that the point
is moot because the fundamental changes that seem to be occurring in the
relationship between the Soviet Union and the West obviate much of the
need for formal military strategies and the maintenance of a strong defense.
That opinion is not shared by all. Many believe that the nation's military
strength should remain the same as it has been, a position based on a fundamental distrust of Soviet intentions or on a doubt about the ability of
Mikhail Gorbachev to pull off the massive restructuring of the Soviet
economy and political system he has recently undertaken. Others of the
same mind simply cite the fragility of human institutions and the seeming
inevitability of conflict among men.

Whatever the long-term effects, the disintegration of communist rule
throughout the Soviet bloc and consequent lessening of tension are likely
to, in the near term, usher in a particularly unstable and potentially
dangerous time for the United States:

> [F]or almost half a century the vague, shifting and unremitting struggle
> with the Soviet Union has been the organizing principle of our national
> life. We have used the Soviet Union as the great simplifier around which
> we have defined virtually every foreign policy issue that we consider
> important.[2]

Depriving the national security apparatus of this focus may well set it
adrift, vulnerable to all sorts of predatory budget-cutters and neoisola-
tionists who mistakenly assume that, should the Soviets "come around,"

the world will necessarily be a safe place. This is dangerous thinking on two fronts. First, the collapse of communism will eradicate the need for neither a national security policy nor the forces to execute it. After all, the Soviet Union is likely to remain a military superpower with respect to the *capabilities* of her armed forces, whatever her intentions to use them.[3] Although force sizes, structures, and equipment lists may have to be changed to match current conditions, and probably should be, achieving agreement on exactly what those conditions mean for the United States must precede any adjustments. Second, and, perhaps more important, the stability of the world now does not depend solely on the nature of the relationship between the United States and the Soviet Union, nor will it in the future. A quick tour of the world's contentious spots like the Middle East and Southeast and Southwest Asia will show that the actors in these areas are not always as responsive to the lead of the superpowers as one might wish. A peek at the array of sophisticated weapons in their armories will also be enlightening.

Given the forecast emergence of new power centers and the very real likelihood of more nuclear actors as technological capability becomes more widespread, the world may, in fact, turn out to be less stable than it was when the two alliances more or less balanced each other. It gives one pause, for instance, to contemplate the unquestioned economic and potential military power of an Asian combine of some sort with China, Japan, and Korea as principal members.

Unfortunately, the United States appears to be both temperamentally and organizationally ill prepared for the type of multipolar world that may be emerging. Strategy to date has been confined to preventing a superpower war and little else, thereby ensuring that defense planning would be one dimensional.[4] A very recent example of this focus can be found in the Middle East. There were no thought-through strategies for reacting to Iraqi adventurism despite a fundamental distrust of its leader, Saddam Hussein; strategies had to be developed on the fly. Other planning that has taken place has not been particularly forward looking; it has generally been based on the assumption that the future would simply be an extension of the past.[5]

The result of this myopic view has been that American activity in the international arena during the last several decades has been almost completely reactive. Unable to refer to a framework or master plan, the leadership of the United States formulates actions only when forced to. What is more, when alternatives have been identified, decision makers have had great difficulty in choosing a course of action when faced with the necessity to do so. Crises, whether real or imagined, have often resulted in little meaningful action but plenty of posturing, usually for domestic political purposes.

Even when action has been taken, it seldom correlates with the relative importance of areas or interests; in other words, responses to crisis do not seem consistent with a larger design. It seems to be a fact that many individuals serving in both the executive and the legislative branches of government are as insular in thought as many of their nineteenth- and earlier twentieth-century predecessors were. They all appear more concerned with their individual and collective short-term fates than they are with the long-term welfare of the country. This preoccupation with the domestic political scene ignores the fact that in economic, environmental, health, and even political terms, compartmentalization of issues into domestic as opposed to international categories has not really been possible for years; distinctions will be even harder to make in the future. Put another way, domestic actions almost always have some international impact, and vice versa.

Ignoring the implications of this point has historically resulted in a chronic emotional and psychological unpreparedness for conflict, when it has occurred, in most of the U.S. population.[6] This seeming aversion to military preparedness ensures that the armed forces will be caught in varying states of undress when called upon for action. It is neither a desire to "fight," often born of frustration when others do not behave as they "should," nor the physical readiness measured in trained troops and available equipment, that is of importance here. It is the understanding and acceptance of the need for action, a rationale based not only on the specific reason prompting activity, but on its place in the larger scheme of things. Tensions or interactions between and among nations should be recognized not as discrete events, but as part of a flow that must be considered in its entirety when evaluating situations. In short, an historical perspective is needed to make preparedness meaningful — not necessarily because history repeats itself, but because it provides clues to motivations and the consequent behavior.

Americans typically do not take the long view, and certainly not when it comes to the evolution of the world society and the role the United States should play in that process; such a view is also not encouraged by the leadership. In fact, the shorter the memory the better, in particular concerning election campaign rhetoric and promises. This tendency to focus only on the "now" has sometimes prompted visionary leaders to be devious in maneuvering the public to position the country for action. A study of this phenomenon would surely include the pre–World War II years when President Franklin D. Roosevelt quickly grasped the implications of a Hitler-dominated Europe and then guided a generally isolationist American public into some preparation for participation in war.

An opposite motivation for deceiving the public is also part of the historical record. Leaders or the government have on occasion deliberately misled the public to mask activity or, more often, failed actions in the hope that the electorate will not turn them out. Actions during much of the Vietnam War, where both the government and the military deceived the public with respect to their intentions, their actions, and the outcomes, illustrate this behavior.[7]

There seem to be reasons other than this near-term focus problem that act to inhibit preparation for conflict. The traditional fear of a standing military force, which has been a part of the American psyche, to a greater or lesser degree, since before the War for Independence (despite the fact that many Americans cannot remember when there was not a good-sized standing army) continues to be cited. It is likely that this concern is reflective of a more general feeling that "in liberal democracies, war is viewed as fundamentally unnatural or illegitimate inasmuch as it threatens the constitutional principles of such societies—above all, the right to life or the principle of self-preservation of classical liberal theory."[8]

A more pragmatic explanation is that the American public has traditionally been unwilling to "pay" for an intangible like security in the absence of a clear and present danger. What is more, administrations have often been loath to point out the necessity to do so for fear of "rocking the boat" and being summarily discharged at election time. These attitudes and actions have ensured that, once one war ended, manning levels achieved by the armed forces during the conflict would be cut back so far that the bulk of a new force had to be both raised and organized prior to being capable of engaging in the next.[9] This environment has also meant that little meaningful planning was accomplished between conflicts, a situation characteristic of most of the years of the nation's life until well into the twentieth century.

The most notable exception to this modus operandi has been the planning of the weapon exchange as the opening act of general nuclear war. Here, there are few options to planning ahead. Should a large-scale nuclear attack against the United States occur, the time available for response to an incoming attack will be measured in minutes—clearly insufficient time to begin planning a retaliatory strike. Since the threatening party (at least the current one) has been known, detailed planning can and has taken place in advance. The result is a national plan for the employment of strategic nuclear forces under various conditions, called the Single Integrated Operational Plan (SIOP). This plan, which "marries" individual strategic force elements (and their warheads) to specific targets, was formulated and is updated by the Joint Strategic Target Planning Staff (JSTPS). The SIOP contains a very specific retaliatory plan should the U.S. be attacked by nuclear missiles.

The plans for general war with the Soviet Union where only conventional (nonnuclear) weapons are used are much less specific. Strategies contained therein closely resemble those used in World War II. There also are plans prepared for just a few other eventualities, although the treatments are very general in nature. Given that the United States has commitments arising from four multilateral and three bilateral treaties, the planning is limited.[10] Beyond the several obligations of these treaties, there are informal ones with other countries, most importantly with some so-called nondeveloped nations. There are no plans in a true sense for operations in these areas, yet it is here where the highest likelihood of involvement, and thus a certain level of danger, lies. Since many Third World countries are amassing weapons with capabilities that may well make the cost of intervening in their affairs high, it seems prudent to identify the most likely location for contingencies affecting the interests of the United States and to formulate strategies in advance of their need so as to be prepared.

Defining National Interests

National interests are "...the country's perceived needs and aspirations in relation to other sovereign states constituting its external environment."[11] They are a product of "...American political, economic, and psychological interrelationships with other countries of the world."[12] They are not, however, engraved in stone, nor are they of equal value. Interests may best be differentiated by assessing the potential danger that denying them might occasion. There can be, for instance, survival interests (those whose denial would jeopardize the continuance of the state), vital interests (those whose denial would most likely result in serious harm to the state), major interests (those whose denial might harm the state), and peripheral interests (those whose denial would mean little, if anything).

Unfortunately, identifying national interests is not a well-developed skill (at least not in the United States); in any case, it tends to be deferred until some threat appears, often a military one, at which time whatever is threatened is immediately declared vital. However, lists are not kept, and reviews of any sort are seldom made. Few if any Americans, in government or outside of it, could, in a short period of time, produce a list of national interests that a majority would agree on. Since the national security organization was formed to protect them, it is little wonder that the existence of a national strategy—and a national military strategy, except in the broadest terms—is suspect. Unfortunately, as William V. Kennedy puts it, "...the U.S. has no means to assess its international interests free of White House ideological obsessions and the entrenched bureaucratic interests of the two departments, State and Defense, that dominate the development of U.S. foreign policy."[13] Correcting this deficiency would be extremely difficult, since the political and economic implications of national defense have become at least as important as the level of security provided.

Beginning with the charge that the post–World War II Truman administration had "lost" China to the communists, and continuing through the attack on the Eisenhower administration's management of defense matters (the substance of which was based on a nonexistent missile gap "discovered" by the Kennedy team), to bomber "gaps" and the Reagan buildup, much of the ebb and flow of defense planning and spending has been a result of politically rather than reality-based perceptions of threat and need.

In the two-party political system, one major sport consists of the party not in power charging the one that is with being derelict in keeping America strong.[14] If successful in gaining power, the newly seated group sets about "correcting" the problem. Samuel Huntington has described a five-step cycle that captures the emergence, ascendance, reshaping, and final form of strategic policy changes.[15]

1. New strategic concepts based on a recalibration of the threat are put forth by some group (either the "ins" or the "outs") that has detected or uncovered the need for new definitions (Huntington calls these "upside strategies").

2. Public support for an increase in capabilities for defense forces is whipped up.

3. A buildup in defense occurs in areas designed to counter the new strategic threats.

4. The recognition that the buildup is at the expense of social and other programs sets in and support for it decreases.

5. A strategy that fits the level of defense capability actually achieved through steps 2 and 3 is formulated ("downside strategies").

The recent Reagan administration years fit this pattern exactly. Reagan was elected on a platform that, among other things, decried the condition of the nation's defense (which had been managed by the opposing Democratic party for the previous four years) and called for a buildup in national security forces. The first years of his administration were characterized by large defense budgets, but during the last few, defense received fewer dollars as priorities were reassessed.[16] At the present time there is even more downward pressure on defense spending, as enemies seem to be melting away and social and budgetary pressures increase.

This politicalization of national security is particularly significant because beliefs about the degree of danger posed by the enemy's nature and capability dictate strategy selection and the amount and direction of military spending. In the past when prospective enemy capabilities and intentions were overstated or deliberately misconstrued,

the atmosphere of contrived alarm made the public vulnerable to demagogic appeals, disarmed responsible criticism of military expenditures, and narrowed the spectrum of politically permissible debate in Congress and in the media on alternative foreign policy and national security strategies.[17]

At the best of times, it is difficult to achieve any sort of consensus on direction and resource allocation in the United States because there are so many more or less independent power centers clamoring to be heard. Each has its own assessment of the threat, which is, more often than not, slanted to provide a basis for its own broader agenda. Where political considerations alone dominate assessments and actions, the nation is not well served. For, in America as elsewhere, influence is power, and the "organization" that carries the day adds to its ability to influence tomorrow's decision.

The economic aspects of defense are closer to the bone. The number of dollars in the defense budget to support the size of force prescribed has given rise to an entire industry whose primary customer is the U.S. government, with the Department of Defense as its agent. The economic attraction of the defense "business" may be estimated by noting the number of companies, both large and small, that have found it a lucrative full-time business since the end of World War II; before that time this was only true during wartime. Because the rewards in this area are high both for government and industry, budgetary considerations have come to dominate all others.[18]

Defense is not only important, it is big business. While defense accounts for roughly one-fourth of the federal budget, it comprises about two-thirds of so-called discretionary spending, which may be spent without a change in law. These dollars represent an opportunity for the Congress to create public works projects within the defense budget. They can, for example, conduct some "economic engineering" by delivering or sponsoring a program that can provide jobs or income in a representative's district or a senator's state. While the outputs of some of these programs have military utility, others have none. These pork-barrel projects, which the military does not need or want, consume about ten billion dollars a year.[19] In truth, however, you will not hear the military complain much. If a branch of the armed forces has a pet program, that branch will spend time and effort lobbying sympathetic (and powerful) congressmen on behalf of what is desired. Industry does the same, often managing to continue supplying products to the military when the service is maintaining that they are no longer needed, to get a new system approved and forced on a service, or to keep one alive after its rejection.[20]

All too often strategic dialogues between or among the military services are "resource distribution fights" as each battles for a bigger share of the pie. Most of them occur because the individual armed services retain the status of separate fiefdoms. Each proposes to buy what is required to fit its strategic and tactical view rather than what may be important from a national perspective. The Chairman of the Senate Armed Services Committee, commenting on the hearing on the 1988 Department of Defense budget, observed, "You don't have anybody's [overall] strategy. You have a Navy strategy, an Army strategy, an Air Force strategy, a Marine strategy."[21] The requests are all "justified," of course, usually by analysis produced within or through the organization itself (sometimes a service goes to the extent of "creating" its own strategy within which requirements can fit).[22] The results are nearly always arbitrary (Why a 600-ship Navy, not 590 or 610? Why 40 tactical fighter wings, not 39 or 41?), but they become mantras within each service. This is not to suggest that any one service is selfish or single-minded when in action against an enemy; rather, it is to say that they all are at budget time, when the other services are the enemy. Each seems convinced that it should receive the bulk of resources because of its much greater contribution to national security.[23]

Identification of what is needed to defend the country, of course, varies with both perspective and loyalty. Many Air Force devotees, both in and out of uniform, are convinced that more penetrating bombers will provide the edge. Navy supporters denounce this and proclaim that salvation lies with yet another aircraft carrier, and so on. There is in each, and in the Army as well, an institutional bias to keep things as they are.

In this current environment, all of the services are under siege by budget cutters as the enemy against which the forces were arrayed has begun fading into the background. Expensive systems currently ready for production, like the B-2 bomber, or still in development, like the AX Navy attack aircraft, become prime targets for budget cutters. Since most of these systems were designed (and rationalized) for employment in set-piece scenarios in which the Soviets (and the Warsaw Pact in Europe) were the enemy, their utility against other opposition or in other mission areas needs to be proved. Because there is no opponent that matches up in size or capability to the big Red, some stretching is often required to arrive at a justification for continuing the programs.

The same is true with respect to the personnel and equipment already in operation. For example, the Navy has maintained that even in the face of at least a changing, if not a declining threat, its size and makeup should remain essentially the same as it has been. The arguments presented in support of this proposition are based on some unvoiced assumptions that may or may not stand up to the light of day. Most notable is the implication that the same number of aircraft carriers are required to be deployed as have been for the past several decades. All the services have the same problem. After years of describing the Soviets as ten feet tall, their audience has trouble believing, no matter the explanation, that the threat to the United States is the same now that the giants have been reduced to normal size.

When an opportunity for defining an enemy or a set of circumstances against which one can measure, or validate, a requirement presents itself, all rush in. The UN-Iraq War filled this bill. Having painted the Iraqis at least six feet tall, the proponents of stealth, the multipurpose bomber, and other technology programs now point with pride to what was — or could have been — accomplished with their particular "widget" during this particular fracas. It is, of course, not clear that another Iraq is anywhere in the future.

What seems to be missing in all this is the national perspective — an answer to the question, what will best serve the nation's objectives across the widest spectrum of contingencies? Developing this perspective should be the Secretary of Defense's purview, but his ability to do so is questionable. First of all, his is a political appointment. The Secretary is appointed to his position by and holds it at the pleasure of the President. His personal inclination as well as his professional loyalties will, in all likelihood, cause him to view the world and its threats in a particular way. Because he will pick his own people to serve in the appointive slots in the department, it is unlikely that another strategic perspective will be represented on the executive side.[24] That view will have to come from Congress through its budgetary machinations, if from anywhere.

When it comes to the defense budget, however, it is every man for himself. If the services agree with the Secretary of Defense, all is well. If not, they are permitted to — and will — go to Congress separately, where they will meet with elected representatives, many of whom have their own fish to fry relative to major programs. The intentions of Congress in this regard have been ambivalent.

When the position of Secretary of Defense was created, it was fairly weak. However, nearly all of the amendments to the National Security Act over the intervening 44 years have attempted to strengthen its authority at the expense of the military departments (strictures have been kept in place to ensure that the military services could not be merged while Congress was not looking, however), but service secretaries have been guaranteed access to Congress on any matter after simply informing the Secretary of Defense of the pending contact.

Thus, if the Secretary chooses not to support the individual service requests, the services are perfectly free to, and regularly do, lobby individual members of Congress to obtain what they want.[25] It is not clear why Congress continues to insist on allowing this direct access, although the likely explanation lies in the fear of domination of the system by a particular administration. What in fact exists is a tyranny of the armed services, who can and do interpret the military threats arrayed against them in any way they choose and then take whatever path is necessary to obtain what they believe is best for their service.[26]

Balancing Military Capabilities

If the nation is to retain a balanced military capability, however, there is a need to improve coordination among the services. President Eisenhower began the process of streamlining the Defense Department in 1958, which continued through the Goldwater-Nichols Department of Defense Reorganization Act of 1986. This, the most recent amending act, continues Congress's efforts to strengthen civilian control, improve the quality of military advice, and enlarge the role of the joint commanders. These changes were enacted because the Congress believed that the military departments had too much power, that getting usable "joint" advice from a "corporate" jcs was impossible, and that strategic planning was poor, particularly in the light of declining budgets.

Goldwater-Nichols, among other things, names the chairman of the Joint Chiefs of Staff as the principal military adviser to the President, the National Security Council, and the Secretary of Defense, and requires him to consult with the joint commanders when acting in that capacity. The Joint Chiefs are removed from the chain of command; the Chairman is only "in the channel" if authorized. If he is so anointed, then orders are passed through him; otherwise, they need not be. Figure 2 represents the current organizational arrangement.

The President and Secretary of Defense constitute the National Command Authority (NCA). They are members of, and are advised by, the National Security Council.[27] Military advice is provided by the chairman of the Joint Chiefs of Staff and possibly by the other chiefs, who also head the individual services. The operational chain of command runs from the National Command Authority to the unified and specified commanders, who organize and employ forces in peacetime and will fight them in war.[28]

The unified commands, currently organized on the basis of geographic or mission areas, are permanent entities with fixed responsibilities and the forces of at least two military departments available to them. For example, in peacetime a unified commander such as the Commander-in-Chief, Pacific Command, will ensure that the forces assigned him remain ready for action, oversee bilateral military training exercises with the military forces of other nations, arrange for senior officer and U.S. Navy ship visits to these countries, conduct civic action programs in selected locations, and provide humanitarian and medical assistance throughout his area. During crises or wartime, of course, the unified commander will command and control the forces assigned him and fight the war in his theater, or area of responsibility. The importance of these commands has prompted the Congress to provide them with an ever-increasing voice in planning and procurement activities.

There are currently nine Unified Commands:

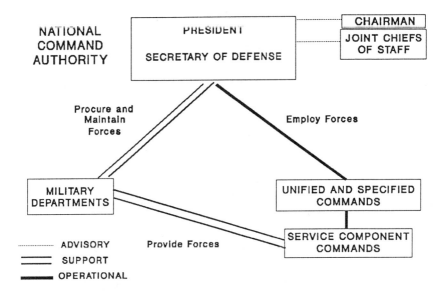

Figure 2. Department of Defense Organization with Chains of Command

United States Atlantic Command (USLANTCOM)
United States Central Command (USCENTCOM)
United States European Command (USEURCOM)
United States Pacific Command (USPACOM)
United States Readiness Command (USREDCOM)
United States Southern Command (USSOCOM)
United States Space Command (USSPACOM)
United States Special Operations Command (USSOC)
United States Transportation Command (USTRANSCOM)

The Specified Commands, on the other hand, are organizations that perform single functions and utilize the forces of only one military service. There are currently two Specified Commands:

Military Airlift Command (MAC)
Strategic Air Command (SAC)

Unified commanders have arrayed under them individual military service groups called component commands. Occasionally, for special operations or in specific areas of the unified commander's area of responsibility, another command will be organized from the various services (e.g., a joint task force). There are other units and entities that appear here and there, and alliances such as NATO have separate chains of command that interact with the national system described above.[29]

It is possible, perhaps even likely, that the Unified and Specified command structure just described will be changed. A radical restructuring, which will require Congressional review and approval, has been proposed to provide a framework for reducing U.S. military force posture while maintaining adequate national security. Under the proposal the eleven commands just enumerated would be reduced to four: Strategic Command, Atlantic Command, Pacific Command and Contingency Command.

The other chain of command depicted in the figure provides administrative support. It contains the individual military departments charged with procuring and maintaining combat-ready forces and equipment to be assigned for use by the service component commander in satisfying the needs of the unified commander.[29]

These chains of command ensure that rational and coherent defense planning is carried out, which otherwise might be hampered as the services train and buy equipment based on roles and missions defined for each. The basic assignments go back to a broad agreement forged in Key West, Florida, in March 1948. Service maneuvering at that time caused the first Secretary of Defense, James V. Forrestal, to corral the chiefs (as heads of services) in Key West to hammer out which service would do what, hoping to reduce, if not eliminate, duplication. This effort was only partially successful. Periodic flare-ups over roles have occurred over the intervening years. The contemporary environment is considerably different from the time when the initial decisions were made, yet the duties assigned have not changed much despite occasional evidence that a particular mission may be given short shrift by a service, particularly where the mission supports another branch of the armed forces. The most obvious current example of this phenomenon is the close air support (CAS) mission of the Air Force in direct support of the Army.

The aircraft the Air Force now uses for fulfilling that mission (the A-10) is old and considered vulnerable to contemporary enemy (read Soviet) defensive weapon systems. The Air Force, after being forced to address the problem by the Secretary of Defense, has continued to recommend an aircraft with dubious credentials for that particular mission, but with other obvious (to the Air Force) benefits. For instance, buying aircraft for this mission would likely reduce the unit cost on each fighter variant of that same aircraft already being procured in numbers, and having additional aircraft would also provide a system useful for other Air Force missions that have nothing to do with CAS. Both of these are excellent reasons for selecting an aircraft, provided it does the job needed by the Army. Many feel it does not.

All of these differences might be easily resolved if the protagonists were able to work together. The rivalry among the services is legendary and not likely to improve much, despite rhetoric to the contrary. At the next level, relations between the Department of Defense and the Congress are at best poor, and getting worse. Each accuses the other of a variety of misdemeanors. The most telling (and most often repeated) charge made of the Congress is that it overregulates the Defense Department. In the middle years of this century, just a few major committees and their chairmen constituted the power centers in the Congress. Since that time, that power has become diffused — but not diluted — among many committees and individuals. This is particularly true with respect to the budget process, where six separate committees have the opportunity to analyze the Defense budget. Increases in staffs that support the committees allow for very detailed examination of the budget requests each year.[30]

A bill of particulars prepared by the Defense Department in 1990 alleged that actions by Congress make operations nearly impossible. For example, the tremendous increase in the number of reports is cited as requiring a significant amount of time in the drafting of them, time that could be better spent on activities directly related to defense tasks. Another problem detailed is that of congressional "meddling" with department programs through techniques such as mandating that funds be used only for certain items, setting minimum employment levels, and requiring that specific technologies be used. All of these, Defense claims, result in turbulence in programs, in additional costs, and in an inability to truly budget or plan.[31] From the other perspective, an unbiased observer would argue that the Department brings this sort of treatment on itself by ". . . routinely finessing, evading, and sometimes openly defying reasonable congressional committee attempts to find out what is going on."[32] After all, the Congress is accountable to the American public for the actions of "the agencies it funds."[33]

Whether these two powerful and strong-willed organizations will be able to reach an accommodation is yet to be seen. Clearly, one is needed. The level of micro management by Congress is all out of proportion to its effectiveness. Although there is a six-year defense plan (which used to be five), it is misnamed. In practice it is six one-year plans that include procurements stretching over as many as ten years. Because each program ends up being reviewed annually, each is vulnerable to "adjustments" — the effects of which ripple throughout the entire establishment, invariably raising costs and always altering plans. This is not to say that program adjustments should not be made. Clearly, they should when called for. The task of deciding which are needed is made infinitely harder because there is no reasonably explicit strategy to use as a measuring stick. In addition, the fundamental question of who should select from among alternatives remains unanswered.

Most of these behaviors related to economics or politics have become ingrained over the decades in a single-enemy, largely bipolar world. As tensions lessen and the forecast multipolar world emerges, the utility of doing business as before comes under serious question. Defense experts remain cautious (and rightly so) in the midst of general celebrations over the end of the Cold War. The national security establishment is diligently trying to formulate some credible threat against which U.S. troops may need to be arrayed, and the services are stockpiling arguments that favor or support their cherished hardware programs. Congress, at the same time, must legitimately be concerned about reducing the federal deficit, the viability of the industrial base supporting the defense industry, the economic effects of severe reductions in that industry, and the constitutional charge to provide for the common defense. It clearly is time for a cooperative effort.

The director of the Soviet Institute for the Study of the U.S.A. and Canada, Georgi Arkbatov, was right indeed when he told some Western visitors, "We are going to do a terrible thing to you — we are going to deprive you of an enemy."[34] Arkbatov seems to recognize American ambivalence concerning the standing of a military establishment in a democratic society and the conditions under which it should be employed. These beliefs regarding the use of force constitute the strategic culture of the United States, a culture that will play an important role in determining the approach the United States takes in interacting with the rest of the world through the nineties and beyond.

CHAPTER V

Elements of the Strategic Culture: Geography and Politics

Strategic and even tactical military considerations almost never shape military programs in the United States.[1] Rather, their dimensions are the result of the relative strength of political and other pressures. The nation's strategic culture, defined as an amalgamation of attitudes and convictions about the role of a military establishment in a society and the circumstances under which it should be used, is one of those shaping forces. It directly influences the amount of financial, political, and social effort the nation is willing to commit in establishing and maintaining military forces. The strategic culture will have been shaped by the country's geographic location, its political philosophy, its form of government, and its military experiences and traditions.

Geographical location leads the list because it determines the need to actively defend borders and establishes, to a great extent, a country's capacity for independent action. It determines if threats to a nation's existence are likely to be continuous or only intermittent. Where a nation has a contiguous neighbor, significant forces, both diplomatic and military, might well be needed to ensure the physical security of the state if the other were particularly strong, or belligerent. A nation in the middle of several others has even more needs. While natural barriers such as rivers, lakes, and mountain ranges provide some protection, the mere presence of other states on borders necessitates a certain level of interaction, whatever one's inclination might be. Island nations, on the other hand, enjoy a degree of immunity from threat and more freedom of choice regarding their involvement with others.

The United States in this respect benefited greatly from its location, particularly in its formative years. The country emerged from its War for

Independence more than a little disorganized, insolvent, and unable (and unwilling) to afford to keep any sort of defensive force in being. Despite the presence of foreign troops in adjacent territories to the north and south, there was time for nation building free of the fear of spillover from the seemingly endless conflicts among the older European states, because the Atlantic Ocean presented a formidable barrier to their supply and reenforcement.

Nevertheless, early federal governments remained uneasy about the security of the new nation because of the mere presence of the British troops to the north, Spanish to the south, and Indians, British, and French to the west; they took steps to remedy the situation. First efforts centered on New Orleans, which, as the gateway to the great Mississippi River, controlled access to the interior of the country. While negotiations with the French were underway for acquisition of the city by the United States, the Napoleonic War intensified in Europe. President Thomas Jefferson seized the moment and threatened Napoleon with a United States allied with Great Britain if a settlement were not forthcoming. Needing money to finance his campaigns and already faced with a formidable alliance of states, Napoleon finally responded by offering to sell not just New Orleans, but the entire Louisiana Territory. The deal was completed in 1803.

Early in the next decade, the United States and Great Britain began to quarrel over freedom of the seas and the rights of neutral nations. Some segments of the U.S. population were all for taking advantage of the situation to conquer Canada and annex it. Efforts in this direction were set in motion, but military actions initiated bent on conquest were unsuccessful. This War of 1812 was ended by treaty in 1814, with no new territory gained.

In the south, General Andrew Jackson, the hero of America's victory at the battle of New Orleans, took it upon himself to preempt any designs the Spanish might have on territory. After Seminole Indians retaliated for the burning of a border village by U.S. troops, Jackson led a punitive expedition into Florida that attacked Indians, Spanish, and British alike. The Spanish, weak and unable to protect their possession or its inhabitants, ceded Florida to the United States in 1819.

Ever fearful of European adventurism, the United States became alarmed by British overtures to other major European states who were making noises about intervening to quell unrest in the wake of revolutionary movements in Venezuela, Mexico, Argentina, and other Latin American states. The government was concerned enough to create what might well have been its first formal foreign policy. The Monroe Doctrine, announced in 1823, declared that the entire American continent was no longer available for colonization by outside powers.[2]

In the interior, settlers were moving the western frontier of America to the edge of the great plains and beyond, to the waters of the Pacific

Ocean. Near mid-century, this migration gave rise to a rapidly spreading notion that the United States was *meant* to occupy the entire land from sea to sea; that was its "manifest destiny." If this were so, more work was needed because there were still areas controlled by foreign powers in the western territories. In a period of less than ten years, the map was filled out. Texas, after first declaring itself an independent state, was annexed in 1845, New Mexico and California territories were purchased as part of the settlement of the war with Mexico (which had resulted from the Texas annexation) and the rival claims of Great Britain and the United States over the lush and fertile Willamette Valley in Oregon Territory were settled. Although a British presence in Canada to the north, and Mexico to the south continued to be somewhat vexing, oceans at the east-west extremities provided assurance that there would be no threat emanating from those directions. This "free" security was capitalized upon to continue growth and development without much fear of outside interference.

After 1870, settlers followed miners into the plains area of the West. Products of the Industrial Revolution, like barbed wire for fences, windmills and irrigation, and the railroads made farming and ranching feasible from an economic standpoint. The railroads became the biggest of businesses during the latter decades of the nineteenth century and into the twentieth. Their presence enabled the population to spread throughout the country and provided support to individual enterprises, wherever they arose.

Favorable geographic location also permitted the military strategy for the nation's security to be based at sea; defenses against an attack from overseas would be posted far from the country's shores, and preparations on land would be confined to the fortification of important ports. This strategy required relatively few military forces, allowing the government to maintain its armed forces at a minimum level of manpower, equipment, and funding until a threat directly presented itself.

Another dimension of geographic location is the availability of natural resources. In the United States they were plentiful, the land fertile, the weather favorable, and the settlers energetic. The economic potential of the New World was tapped soon after settlers arrived. A trade based on the export of agricultural products and raw materials and the importation of finished goods quickly arose. Great Britain, for example, became dependent on American tobacco and cotton. The abundance of natural resources also served to support a growing manufacturing sector which, spurred by the Industrial Revolution, began overtaking agriculture as the engine of the economy. The opportunities, under these conditions, along with a fairly liberal immigration policy, ensured an increasing population and a large and semiskilled work force available to the economic sector because little manpower had to be devoted to defense.[3] The interactions of the growing productivity, trade, investment, and other elements of the economy soon propelled the United States into the ranks of world powers. By the early twentieth century, using almost any measure other than the size of its military forces, the United States was a great power, with the potential of becoming a superpower, and was beginning to eclipse the major European states. This phenomenal growth had been made possible not only by favorable geographical position, but also by the form of government established by the inhabitants once they had cast off the English yoke.

While many of the early settlers of America were pleased and grateful to have found relief from the oppression they had faced in Europe, they soon found that ties to the old world still meant some, although, perhaps different, problems with governmental bodies. In the British colonies, inhabitants felt that the economic power they had developed entitled them to better treatment than they were receiving. Appeals to the British Parliament brought no relief and so they revolted — originally to draw the king's attention to their plight, ultimately to gain independence. Choosing to fight rather than capitulate to the British Army, they found themselves without an effective military force.

The population at that time was comprised largely of settlers from Great Britain whose experience with the dictatorship of the military that followed the English civil war (1642–1651) left them with a fundamental distrust of standing professional armies. They had, as a consequence, entrusted local defense to townspeople; these militia served as the initial fighting forces when the War for Independence began. The need for a more traditional organization was recognized, however, and the formation of a Continental Army was quickly authorized and volunteers enlisted. The Continental Congress maintained control over the Army (and Navy) by authorizing strengths and providing provisions and material.[4]

After the successful uprising, the colonists turned to building their individual lives under an alliance of the states, but trying times soon returned. The Articles of Confederation, which were the governing statutes for the six years from 1781 to 1787, did not prove satisfactory because they vested all the power in a Congress that was ineffectual. Both the government and the people were laboring under a massive debt; crushing taxes were the norm. Many were unable to pay them and had everything they owned seized. The money that had been issued during the Revolutionary War was worthless. Another revolution seemed at hand. The deteriorating situation forced the realization that institutions were needed to guarantee the liberty so valued and so dearly won. An important consideration was that these institutions would need to counterbalance each other so that no single one could arrogate all power to itself.

Representatives from the states gathered in Philadelphia in 1787 to create a national government that would embody those institutions necessary to maintain order and protect liberty. In the most general sense, they wanted to abandon the ways of the old world they had left, while capturing as many of the ideals and ideas about liberty and freedom then known — and upon which they could agree. However, the preceding several years had taught them that in order to ensure some amount of liberty for all, everyone would have to give up a little. The governmental form adopted provided for a separation of powers, assigning specific activities to the federal government with its three branches, the executive, the legislative and the judicial, and other activities to the states. A system of checks and balances among all the powers centers was included.[5]

With respect to the security of the nation, three cardinal issues were addressed: the conduct of intercourse with other nations, the control of the security forces, and the power to commit the nation to war. Probably influenced by the acknowledged thinkers Locke, Montesquieu, and Blackstone, the drafters of the Constitution assigned the control of foreign affairs and war specifically to the chief executive.[6] The President was expressly named as the Commander-in-Chief of the army, the navy, and the state militia when they were called into federal service; departments of War and State were established in the executive branch to assist the President.[7] As a check on the executive branch, the power to declare war was allocated to Congress.

When it came time to establish the structure of the military forces, there was some recent history to draw upon. Success in the War for Independence seemed to have validated certain precepts useful to a nation devoted to individual liberty. First, it appeared that enemies could be successfully confronted by a nation in arms, rather than a professional army. Thus, a "dual" army system was specified consisting of a small standing army of soldiers (enlistments were limited to two years) and a body of state-formed militia units available to be called to federal service. Second, civilian control over the military could be maintained.[8]

Unfortunately, the drafters of the Constitution were unable to resolve a fundamental point of political philosophy: should the federal government be strong and dominate the states, or should the states rule? The Constitution struck a compromise between these positions; the reality was that the individual states were dominant during the next fifty-some years.

Because this was so, the federal government still had few specific responsibilities as late as the middle of the nineteenth century. The conduct of foreign affairs, the collection of customs duties, the survey and sale of lands in the West, and the distribution of mail comprised the list. There was, of course, the more general responsibility of providing for the common defense, but there was not much of a call for any because of the natural barriers that protected the United States. Many elected representatives resigned for want of something to do.

However, as the nineteenth century unfolded, the redrawing of the nation's maps made necessary by the Louisiana Purchase and the addition of the Oregon Territory, Texas, and the Southwest was creating a need for a stronger central government. This idea met stiff resistance from some of the states. One very contentious point was the question of slavery. Many Southerners, committed to slavery not only as an economic but a social necessity, felt that it must expand or it would die away. Consequently, the formation of each new state was viewed as an opportunity by both the pro- and antislavery forces to add to their number. The issue came to a head in 1860.

Earlier crises over the practice had been defused by various stratagems like the Missouri Compromise (1820), under which Missouri was admitted to the Union as a "slave" state and Maine as a "free" one. As more new territories grew toward statehood, the issue kept surfacing. Politicians took sides, often without regard for party affiliation, resulting in fractured political camps as the presidential election of 1860 approached. The Democratic party put forth two candidates, as did the Whigs, clinching the victory for the candidate of the newly formed Republican party, one Abraham Lincoln who was thought to oppose slavery.

South Carolina was convinced that he did and, asserting what it considered to be its right, seceded from the Union in December 1860. Other southern states followed, and in early 1861, they formed a government to serve what they called the Confederate States of America. President Lincoln, inaugurated in March 1861, determined that the Union should survive, was prepared to save it by force of arms. The Confederacy declared war on May 6, 1861. The Civil War answered, but did not settle, the question of precedence. Although federal institutions and power have proliferated since then, the issue of state's rights still exists in the minds of many. Happily, differences of opinion on this subject are now settled in the courts.

The country continued to grow in power, if not prestige. For the most part, the advantages conferred by its geographical location continued to be enjoyed until technological achievements in modes of transportation, like the steamship and the airplane, and in communications, like the telegraph and telephone, began to shorten the at least apparent distance between continents and, in that sense, to lessen the nation's security. It gradually became necessary to shift more responsibility to the armed forces, which had remained relatively small in number through the years.

Even with only modest numbers on the force lists, reliance on a small regular force augmented in times of emergency by state militia and volunteers had its problems. First of all, there was absolutely no stability in the size of, or equipment for, the regular forces. If a threat (real or imagined) loomed or a conflict started, the services would be rapidly built up, only to be immediately scaled back once the threat disappeared or the conflict was over. For example, after the Civil War the Navy was reduced in size from 971 ships to 29. This was particularly unfortunate because the Navy had just begun the transition to using steam as a propulsion system. The Army suffered equivalent reductions. In the absence of any visible threat, the deterrent value of forces in being was forsaken. Interestingly, the friction leading to the secession of states and eventually to war in one way underscored the soundness of this arrangement. Had a large permanent force been under arms, they would, most typically, have been used by one side to suppress the other. The practice of immediately reducing both forces and budget following a war gradually became an art form, one that, unfortunately, did not change with the times; the United States would be slow out of the blocks in nearly every conflict she jumped or was drawn into. Such a posture may, in fact, have contributed in some ways to the origin of World War II and, perhaps, Korea, but, in any case, resulted in unnecessary casualties and expense.

Second, the viability of fielding a citizen army of any size relied not only on the militia being made available (they belonged to each state), but on other citizens volunteering for duty. The militia system did not last. It was replaced, toward the end of the nineteenth century, by a National Guard that was in principle somewhat the same, but because its training and equipment were purchased with federal funds, the national government had much more say in its employment. A reserve component of each armed force was added later.

From the standpoint of volunteers, no significant problems in filling regiments were experienced while the economy was primarily agricultural. This volunteer form of national security force was practical at that time because threats to the country could only develop very slowly, particularly because of the natural barriers created by the two oceans bordering the United States. Furthermore, in the late eighteenth and early nineteenth centuries, most wars were still small affairs fought for specific and limited objectives. A government could maintain its armed forces at a survival level of manpower, equipment, and funding until a threat directly presented itself. After the economic upturn coincident with the Industrial Revolution, however, volunteers were not so plentiful. By the Civil War, with its massive armies and large numbers of casualties, both sides had to resort to conscription to fill out regiments. It was also needed for most of the wars of the twentieth century.

Third, there was no military policy and no effective military organization when there was no war. There were occasional organizational reforms in the small professional services, but not much lasting change. Diplomacy provided the security for the country. Secretaries of State and diplomats in early administrations were extremely competent. They were operating, however, in a world where their contemporaries were often spies with a reputation for unscrupulousness, lying was accepted, and secret treaties were the norm. In the abstract, this behavior was abhorrent to the principled leaders of this fledgling country. It was precisely this shadowy maneuvering and improper use of power that persuaded them that it was wise to limit intercourse with foreign powers.

The fear that a large standing army might be used to enforce internal governmental edicts rather than as a tool for strengthening the country persisted throughout the nineteenth century. This largely philosophical objection was joined with the more practical one of being disinclined to pay the cost of having a sizable armed force. For many years, the federal government had little in the way of funds and fewer ways to garner them. Although the Constitution authorized the government to levy taxes, the power was interpreted fairly narrowly for much of the country's history. The size of the regular Army and Navy gradually increased but remained relatively small until after World War II. Instead of depending on a professional and well-trained military, the country relied on "ad hoc forces and amateurs of every kind."[9]

There was, nevertheless, a practical value to having these employees of the federal government around, particularly in the growing-up years. In the early, relatively powerless days of the national government, the Army provided a much-needed ability to engineer and complete public projects the states refused to undertake, some of which were important to the military, such as roads, but most of which served the populace as well. In the same vein, Army engineers, graduates of West Point, provided much-needed professional expertise to supervise the construction of railroads and canals. The Army was also involved in most of the exploration of the country, mapping and charting the wilderness territories as well as providing protection for the western movement of settlers. Indeed, to many in the West, the Army was the only governmental representative they would ever see. Navy ships plied the seas seeking commercial opportunities. The captain of each ship was essentially an ambassador without portfolio, authorized to negotiate and sign treaties.

In more recent times, the military has also been used for "social engineering." Not too many years ago, youths in trouble with the law were given a choice between jail and the service. The armed forces, desegregated by President Truman's Executive Order in 1948, helped lead the country toward equal opportunity, a journey which, it might be noted, is still in progress. Finally, with so many men serving in the armed forces during the Second World War, the powerless, women, racial minorities, and the handicapped were given opportunities to work.

The economy has always benefited from association with the military, particularly when it was engaged in war. As early as the pre-Civil War days, government contracts for weapons and supplies often subsidized the development of consumer products, from the safety razors and wrist-watches of World War I to the space-age electronics and materials of today. The conflicts of the twentieth century have stimulated the basic economy through increased arms production and a healthy investment in research and development of products. It was the purchase of arms by our allies in World War II that revitalized factories and financed the escape from the Great Depression of the late twenties and early thirties. More recently, military interest in space exploration has contributed greatly to national successes there, and to commercial applications of products developed to support the effort.

Today, the tradition of using the armed forces because they are there and already on the payroll continues. The Department of Defense has been given significant responsibilities, along with some more money, in the battle against drugs. While such activities have only a tenuous connection with the tasks of the armed forces, the government reaps the benefit of engaging extra bodies and sophisticated equipment (which may or may not be what is required) in the struggle without, in a very real sense, having to pay for them. There are, of course, opportunity costs in the form of lost training time and lowered morale, to mention the most significant, but, in a country whose focus is always in the near term, these are not likely even to be considered, let alone counted. Clearly, a country that has traditionally held its military forces in low esteem has certainly not eschewed some of the advantages of having one. Those forces have come in handy on other occasions as well.

CHAPTER VI

Elements of the Strategic Culture: The American Military Experience

American military forces have performed admirably, if not always with distinction, in combat. The first pages of the nation's military history were written shortly after the Europeans began settling in the New World, when the native Indians resisted being moved off what had been their lands and retaliated. The initial recorders of that history were the members of the militia of the colonies, those citizens who had volunteered to be called to arms in times of need.

Protecting Our Interests: From the Revolution to 1914[1]

Militiamen, in general, were untutored in the way of "formal" military matters and had no opportunity to learn until the Colonial Wars (1689–1773), when many joined British Army regulars in operations against the French and their Indian supporters. This marriage of styles turned out to be an uneasy one at best. The typical militiaman, used to freewheeling showdowns with Indians, was more interested in finding a tree to shield him as he fired than he was in the lock-step, close-order drill maneuvers that were an important part of European "set piece" battles. These "combined" operations, however, did present an opportunity for the colonists to accumulate some formal military knowledge. As a result of these experiences, they tended to favor a mix of the Old World's close-order maneuvering and the hit-and-run, personal marksmanship, and individual activity practiced by the Indians.[2] Militia were the first in action against the British in what became the American War of Independence.

After skirmishes at Lexington and Concord, British troops fell back in some disarray to their quarters in Boston. Militia performance — including that of the minutemen, the group relied upon to respond rapidly — had been uneven, with patriot tactics rapidly deteriorating into an every-man-for-himself mode. The British were unimpressed and thought the colonists cowardly because of their preference for firing from concealment rather than "playing the game" and meeting the redcoat formations in the open.

Once the decision was taken by the Second Continental Congress to fight for independence, all colonies were requested to provide militia. A call for volunteers to fill out a Continental Army was also made and, caught up in the spirit of the moment, many individuals signed up for enlistment periods as short as six months.[3]

The war itself proceeded unevenly. After a tactical defeat at the battle of Breed's (Bunker) Hill and a victory at Fort Ticonderoga where some precious cannon were captured, the Continental Army undertook an ill-fated two-pronged attack on British forces in Canada, which had been approved by both the Continental Congress and General Washington. After a lengthy trek through the Maine wilderness by one wing of the force, during which that group suffered almost unimaginable hardships, the storming of the walled settlement of Quebec that followed resulted in a defeat. This outcome was almost preordained; the number of attackers was severely reduced because expiring enlistments depleted the ranks just prior to the assault.[4]

In general, the Continental Army performed poorly through the first years of its existence. Plagued by poor supply and little training, it was no match for the British regulars arrayed against it. In the few face-to-face battles of the first years of the war, the Americans generally did not show well. Support of the army was atrocious. There was little money, and profiteering was rampant among suppliers; consequently, the Army had little to sustain it except desire. It was also largely untrained. General Washington, however, was determined to have a European-style fighting force even though, with the exception of a few officers, he did not have many who knew how to make it behave like one. Gradually the supply system improved, and serious training was conducted under Baron von Steuben in 1778 and 1779.

At sea the Atlantic Ocean belonged to the British. A Continental Navy had been formed in 1775, when several frigates were authorized and laid down, but trained seamen for this fledgling outfit were scarce because Congress had also commissioned privateering (which amounted to piracy with a license), an activity more remunerative than serving in an organized navy.

With the privateers operating off the coast of England, where they were moderately successful, the Royal Navy was able to maintain the blockade of the colonial seaports it had established early on.

Ultimate victory, however, was assured when in 1778 France declared war on Great Britain. The principal effect of this action was that North America became a relatively minor theater in a larger war. However, it also meant that more support was forthcoming, including French troops and, most important, units of the French Navy. The Continental Army, which by now had matured into a decent fighting force, swung to the offensive and, with the French fleet holding off the Royal Navy during siege operations, forced the surrender of a British Army force at Yorktown.[5] This was, essentially, the last action of the war in North America. The Continental Congress disbanded the Army and Navy immediately after the war for both fiscal and ideological reasons: the government was broke and standing armies were distrusted. However, problems with Indians on the frontier necessitated the reversal of this policy and a small army (about 4000 men) was raised.

The new United States Constitution charged the Congress with raising and supporting armies and providing and maintaining a navy. It also required them to set up militia and prescribe their use. The Uniform Militia Act of 1792 followed making each able, free, white male citizen between the ages of 18 and 45 a member of his state's organization (sometimes called the common militia).

The United States Navy gained some dimension as a force shortly thereafter when French truculence at sea prompted the laying down of six frigates.[6] This near war with France resulted from some bad faith on the part of the U.S. government. France was at war with England and wanted the United States to fulfill some mutual assistance obligations incurred in the 1778 treaty which had ensured the colonial victory, by helping out in West Indies operations against the Royal Navy. The U.S. Congress, concerned about commercial trade, reneged on its obligations. The French began seizing U.S. hulls. The few ships then comprising the Navy went to work and prospered, capturing French vessels which were then refitted, rearmed, crewed, and sent back to sea under the U.S. flag. This flurry of military activity was ended by treaty in September of 1800, when France recognized U.S. neutrality and agreed to stop seizing American merchant ships, at least those not carrying contraband. Once this threat was over, there was a rush to cut back military forces. The Army, which had been strengthened only slightly, was again reduced, and the Navy allowed to maintain only six of the 13 frigates then in commission. There would be time enough, it was felt, to build up if necessary.[7]

For several years, the Muslim states (Morocco, Algiers, Tunis, Tripoli and Berber) located in an area along the southern edge of the Mediterranean

Sea known as the Barbary Coast had provided a haven for pirates. These rogues terrorized shipping throughout the Mediterranean and occasionally sailed out to attack vessels plying trade routes in the Atlantic. After the War for Independence, when United States merchant ships were no longer physically protected by the Royal Navy, "tribute" was paid to protect shipping. Still, the piracy continued, and by 1801 the situation had become so intolerable that a four-ship naval squadron was dispatched from the United States to the Mediterranean. For the next 15 years a single squadron, augmented at times, conducted operations in that area with varying degrees of success. Tripoli was blockaded; the other Barbary Coast states were neutralized by threat, treaty, or payoff; and finally the U.S. Marine Corps was employed, gaining another line for their hymn in the bargain.

Before that scenario was played out, however, another conflict on U.S. soil was to be fought. The British, embroiled yet again with Napoleon, began stopping U.S. ships on the high seas searching for "contraband," often "impressing" American seamen into involuntary service, and occasionally seizing the ships. Even more maddening to the new nation were their activities on the North American continent, where British agents provided arms and gunpowder to Indians, inciting them to attack settlers in conflicts over westward expansion and the fur trade. American protests about this behavior were ignored and tensions increased. Although both sides were generally reluctant to see the situation worsen and result in war, there were some in the United States who saw this period, when Britain was occupied on the Continent, as an opportunity to conquer and annex Canada. The regular military, however, was not prepared for any sort of a conflict, let alone what would be required to control the vast reaches of the land to the north.[8] Nevertheless, war was declared in 1812.

Since it was not a struggle for national survival, this was not to be a popular war. The New England area, for example, which had a substantial trade with England and essentially fed that portion of the British army in Canada, refused to send militia. In any case, volunteer units were gathered, armies were formed, and expeditions planned. The only British targets within reach were those in Canada, so the national sights were fixed on the keys to seizing that country, the defended settlements at Montreal and Quebec and the anchorage at Halifax. The first invasion effort, mounted with volunteer militia and some regulars, was launched from Detroit and aimed at Montreal, but it quickly came to naught. For one thing, militiamen refused to cross the border because, they stated, their task was to turn away invasions, not participate in them. Two other equally inept attempts were made, with both thrusts suffering defeats at the hands of combined British and Indian forces. What began as an offensive war quickly became defensive, and desperate naval battles on the Great Lakes were required to prevent reciprocal British incursions into U.S. territory.[9]

In the Atlantic, the small ocean-going Navy harassed British shipping and conducted some memorable battles with enemy ships of the line. The only land action reflecting well on the Americans was the Battle of New Orleans, where General Andrew Jackson led his troops in a daring night raid that so befuddled the British landing force that he defeated it shortly thereafter. Interestingly, the Treaty of Ghent, which actually ended the war in December 1814, had been signed before its last battle.

Faith in the militia was fading. Its performance during this war had left much to be desired. The troops guarding Washington had broken and run in the face of the British raid, although, as counterpoint, it was militia steadfastness at Baltimore which caused the British forces to retire. In any case, the authorized size of the army was increased slightly, and public support for keeping the armed forces prepared lasted until an economic downturn in the 1830s.

During the peace that followed this war, the military was kept busy. The army engaged in exploration and the engineering of roads and railroads. It also built forts, which turned into economic and social centers of activity on the advancing frontier. As that imaginary line pushed westward, clashes with Indians increased in frequency. One such conflict, where soldiers were chasing mounted Indians on foot, resulted in establishment of mounted infantry in 1833. The navy, meanwhile, was busy opening commercial ventures overseas and conducting scientific explorations in South America, the Middle East, and China and Japan in the Pacific.

This period of relative peace was finally broken when the government of Mexico, reacting to the United States annexation of Texas in 1845, broke diplomatic relations. President Polk and the Congress responded with a declaration of war. No militia were needed this time; volunteers rushed to augment the small regular army. The combined forces attacked and seized the Mexican provinces bordering Texas while the navy blockaded her eastern coast, all with little effect. The esteemed Winfield Scott, General-in-Chief of the Army, then conjured up an amphibious attack aimed at capturing the city of Veracruz, followed by a march on the capital, Mexico City. It was a masterful operation using pre–Napoleonic techniques of maneuver, bombardment, and siege. After successful execution, a negotiated settlement ended the war. This action had been one much like those fought everywhere to that time; the next was to break the historical mold.

The War Between the States has been called the first "modern" war, one in which an entire nation's manpower and industrial strength were engaged.[10] Although volunteer regiments rushed to the War departments of North and South, conscription became the law in both lands after it became obvious that the quick decision hoped for was not to be. The Confederacy enacted such legislation in 1862 in order to increase the size of the army; the Union did the same in 1863, although the stated purpose was to "motivate" men to volunteer. The war was, quite unexpectedly, a titanic struggle.

It began with the Confederate shelling of Fort Sumter in the Charleston, South Carolina, harbor. President Lincoln, with Congress in recess, seized the initiative, ordering a blockage of southern ports and an increase in the size of the Navy, and accepting nearly a quarter of a million volunteers for the Army. The forces of the warring parties massed and first touched at Bull Run on July 21, 1861. The next several years were characterized by movement and maneuver by Confederate troops and rather more stolid, plodding positioning and pursuit by Union forces. Interestingly, most of the officers commanding on both sides were West Point men who had been instructed in the Napoleonic style of war popular at that time.[11]

Unfortunately, the warfare environment had changed considerably since Napoleon's day. The breech-loading and repeating rifles and improved artillery had raised firepower potential of even a single unit considerably, the railroad had made rapid initial and later deployment of troops a reality, the telegraph allowed for rapid communication, and command of forces and observation balloons enhanced the collection of battlefield intelligence. The armies were, in short, more efficient killing machines than those that had gone before. Great battles were fought and appalling numbers of soldiers fell on both sides. While the North, in a sense, could "afford" the high casualty rates, the South, already beset by inflation and shortages across the board, could not. For example, railroads had become indispensable as a means of both supplying and relocating troops, but shortages of rails and the scarcity of repair crews resulted in reduced rather than enhanced mobility for the South's dwindling forces.

Offshore, the North was exploiting yet another of its beginning advantages. The Union Navy maintained a blockade of southern ports throughout the war and also provided gunfire support and transport, particularly in the West. The Confederacy, which had no fleet at the start of the war, gradually built one, but employed it largely in commerce raiding. An epic clash of two ships of these opposing navies forecast a new era when the ironclads *U.S.S. Monitor* and *C.S.S. Virginia* dueled off the Virginia Capes.

The Civil War saw no truly "decisive" battles in the Napoleonic sense. Rather, it was a wearing down of one side by the other. Only that side able to produce a nearly unending supply of manpower, materials, and firepower could eventually force the issue to a climax, and it did. From this perspective, the Civil War foreshadowed the large struggles to come in the twentieth century; few went to school on it and no planning resulted from it.

With the surrender of Confederate forces west of the Mississippi on May 26, 1865, hostilities between the North and South were finally over. Some Europeans had anticipated massive assaults on Canada and Mexico by a vengeful United States bent on getting even with Great Britain for supporting the Confederacy and France for its machinations in Mexico. They need not have worried. For one thing, Americans had had it with war. With no threat visible, both the Army and the Navy were quickly cut back to a size just slightly larger than they had been before the war. Maintenance of a modest force was deemed to be all that was required.

The period immediately following this war saw the Army in a new role, administering local governments. Consecutive Reconstruction acts provided the authority for the Army to maintain discipline, supervise elections, and act as judge and jury in cases of wrongdoing. As much as a third of the Army garrisoned the lands of the vanquished Confederacy until 1877; the remainder expanded the fight against the Indians as large segments of the population moved westward with the laying of track for the railroads. Eventually, Indian uprisings were eliminated, and in 1887 the survivors were made "wards of the government." Since this principal occupation of the regular army was no longer necessary, it was further reduced in size. There were no military policy and no effective military organization. But signs of change were visible.

First, performance when called up during labor unrest in 1877 essentially put paid to the common militia with its once-a-year muster and three-month service period. It was replaced by a "National Guard," a volunteer militia with two- to three-year enlistments, which was better organized and more responsive to federal direction. Second, the Navy, after moving toward steam as a propulsion system, had been forced to revert to sail on wooden ships, which were falling apart. Modern ships of steel powered by steam were appearing in European navies, while argument raged in America about their utility. Without coaling stations a steam-powered ship had a much shorter cruising range than did one under sail, prompting those opposed to modernization to claim that a foreign navy composed of steam ships was even less of a threat than an all-sail fleet. The "modernizers" countered by stating that if an enemy should decide to attack, the Navy would be unable to stop them. A sort of compromise was reached in the Naval Appropriation Act of 1883 when three steel cruisers were authorized with the proviso that they be unarmored and carry a full sail rig. The Navy's stock continued to rise when Captain Mahan's writings prompted the Secretary of the Navy, Benjamin F. Tracy, to recommend a significant expansion of the country's seagoing force.

Near the end of the nineteenth century, an explosion of revolutionary fervor focused attention on the island of Cuba off the Florida coast, where the inhabitants were seeking to rid themselves of Spanish rule. The so-called yellow press in the United States, led by William Randolph Hearst's *New York Journal* and Joseph Pulitzer's *World*, portrayed the Cubans' plight in such stark terms that it stirred both a sympathetic and imperialistic reaction in readers.[12] On February 15, 1898, the battleship *U.S.S. Maine*, dispatched by President McKinley to Havana harbor to stand by during riots in that city, sank after being rocked by an explosion. The Spanish, of course, were blamed.[13] Spain denied any knowledge or culpability but apologized anyway, clearly anxious to avoid any difficulties with the United States. The disclaimer was ignored. The Congress exacerbated the situation by demanding that Cuba be given its independence, and called on Spain to withdraw its forces. The Spanish government, feeling the U.S. action to be unwarranted, severed diplomatic relations two days later, causing the Congress of the United States to declare war.

This had to be an overseas fight, the first of its kind for the United States, since Spanish forces were located in the Philippines, Puerto Rico, and, of course, Cuba. Although most of an expanding U.S. Navy was in the planning stage and thus still on paper, it was, nevertheless, considerably larger and more fit than that of Spain. Army participation included regulars, National Guardsmen, and volunteers, including the First U.S. Volunteer Cavalry, also known as the Rough Riders, whose second in command would soon be the President.

In the Far East, Admiral Dewey, after obtaining coaling ships from the British and a base in Hong Kong, sailed his U.S. Asiatic Fleet to Manila Bay and quickly defeated the Spanish fleet there. Closer to home, the U.S. Atlantic Fleet set up a blockade of Cuba and was able to bottle up that portion of the Spanish fleet in the waters of Santiago harbor, where they had gone to take on coal. It soon became clear that unless there was pressure on the Spanish forces around the port, their fleet was not about to venture forth.

After a farcical movement to, and embarkation on, ships at Tampa, Florida, the Army was put ashore in Cuba and moved on Santiago.[14] In less than a month U.S. Army forces pressured the Spaniards so much that the fleet chose to sail in order not to be included in the surrender. The Spanish ships were forced to exit the harbor singly at roughly ten-minute intervals because of a narrow and partially blocked navigation channel. It was like shooting fish in a barrel; every ship was either sunk or damaged so heavily that it required beaching. The Spanish surrendered in Cuba on July 17, 1898. All that remained was Manila.

Troubles there developed after Dewey's naval victory and resulted in a battle with the Philippine people. Emilio Aguinaldo, a Philippine rebel who had been exiled by the Spanish, had returned, organized Filipino followers into an army, declared an independent Philippine Republic, and lay siege to the city of Manila still held by Spanish forces awaiting an

American take-over. When U.S. troops arrived, fighting broke out against Aguinaldo's army. It deteriorated into guerrilla warfare as the Filipino troops disappeared into the jungle. There was brutality, including torture, on both sides. The fighting stopped for a time after Aguinaldo's capture by ruse in 1901, but continued to break out sporadically until a pacification campaign on all the Philippine islands was undertaken some years later.

The dimensions of the United States were to change significantly as a result of this war. Hawaii, Samoa, and Wake Island were annexed, and "title" to Guam, Puerto Rico, and the Philippine Islands was received, in consideration of which $20 million was paid to Spain under the Treaty of Paris, ratified in February 1899, that ended the war. These new possessions required a larger army for "pacification" purposes and Elihu Root, the Secretary of War, in his annual report presented in December 1899 pointed out the need for augmentation of regulars and other reforms intent on making the Army more responsive and professional. One important organizational issue contained in the report was the identification of a need for a staff organization to study problems and make war plans.

Theodore Roosevelt's election as president meant relatively good times for the military, since a flurry of legislation benefited the services. In 1903, the Dick Act reorganized the National Guard as a reserve to be equipped by the federal govenment and trained by regular army personnel. The General Staff Act in 1903 replaced the Commanding General of the Army with a Chief of Staff and authorized a staff to support him. Decidedly imperialistic military activities cropped up, as well. On the Navy side, Roosevelt had the battleships of the fleet painted white and sent them cruising around the world in an unprecedented (for America) show of strength. However, the next problems showed up closer to home.

Nicaragua, which for a time had attracted and welcomed economic investment by U.S. citizens, was beset by a revolutionary movement. When several Americans were killed, a contingent of U.S. Marines was landed to protect American interests.[15] They stayed until 1913, among other things training a constabulary. The Marines were to return again in 1927 on a pacification mission. In Mexico, social revolution erupted in 1910. While U.S. Army troops patrolled the border, Navy ships steamed outside ports in the Gulf of Mexico, showing the flag. Eventually, after an "insult" to the U.S. flag and the discovery that Germany was delivering ammunition to the Mexicans, Veracruz was stormed once again, this time by the Marines. After mediation by Argentina, Brazil, and Chile, the troops were withdrawn. In 1915, Haiti was rocked by insurrection, whereupon the busy Marines were introduced to take over the police force; they stayed for 19 years. One year later, there was revolution in the Dominican Republic. More Marines were landed to protect U.S. citizens. When a constitutional government was installed in July 1924, the Marines departed.

Engagements Abroad: World War I

Across the Atlantic, the decrepit monarchical power structure of Europe had been slipping inexorably toward war since the turn of the century. The United States officially maintained its distance by proclaiming itself to be neutral. Questionable British behavior in respecting a neutral's rights on the high seas after the war began in 1914 had Americans and the State Department seething, but most of the country wanted to remain aloof. Although not loath to participate economically — after all there were huge profits to be made in time of war — the isolationist streak still ran deep. Finally, Germany's use of unrestricted submarine warfare in the face of American warnings, and the discovery of an overture hinting at alliance made by the Germans to the Mexican government, prompted the United States to join the allies as an "associate," that is, willing to coordinate operations, but not to integrate them. This nicety aside, the armed forces were not really prepared for much of commitment.

A punitive expedition in 1916 against Mexico, in retaliation for raids in the United States, had given officers some experience in combat, but the troops were poorly trained and sites for training the influx of recruits required to fill out a combat army did not exist. Earlier that year, a National Defense Act had expanded the regular army, tied the National Guard more closely to the federal government, and authorized a volunteer army during war and a navy "second to none." In response to the Mexican "incursion" its provisions were employed to initiate a mobilization activating the National Guard and calling for volunteers. This operation uncovered some serious problems in both equipment and personnel. For one thing, there had not been a sufficient number of volunteers; therefore plans for peacetime conscription were prepared, a precaution that came in handy very soon. For another, the Army had few modern weapons (four machine guns per regiment), few aircraft, and the country's industry was on a peacetime footing.[16]

The Navy was building, but was still relatively small and ill suited for the initial jobs assigned it when in 1917 the United States joined the European war that, by that time, had been dragging on inconclusively for some three years. Despite its battleship orientation, the Navy was ordered to start convoy and antisubmarine operations almost at once. The naval building program was switched to construct destroyers and the naval air arm was strengthened to conduct antisubmarine warfare (ASW).

The war had rather quickly settled into a stalemate on the western front after some poorly executed "knockout" punches thrown by each side had failed to connect. There were no "edges" to the battlefield, just two entrenchment lines, over 500 miles long, facing each other. All the attacks launched were frontal assaults resulting in frightening losses on both sides for years. On the eastern front, the Russians, although ill prepared and poorly equipped, had fulfilled their promise to the French and attacked shortly after the war began. The specter of Russians running loose in the Prussian countryside had caused the German High Comand to shift combat units from the western to the eastern front, units which might have made a difference in France, but did, in fact, soundly defeat the Russians. Fighting continued while the regime of Czar Nicholas II crumbled internally, with the victorious Bolsheviks eventually seizing power and negotiating a separate peace.

The Allies, their troop strength depleted,[17] wanted to use arriving American troops to fill out their formations. General Pershing, who had been dispatched to Europe to assess the situation and to command the American Expeditionary Force (AEF) when it arrived and was given the freedom to decide when and how the AEF was to be employed, refused. He planned to use it in an offensive mode; the AEF could assume the defensive only when preparing for an offensive. As for command arrangements, his instructions from Secretary of War Newton D. Baker had been:

> Cooperate with the forces of the other [allied] countries . . . but . . . the underlying idea must be . . . that the forces of the United States are a separate and distinct component of the combined forces, the identity of which must be preserved.[18]

Pershing had estimated the force needed to win the war at three million men. The logistics problems accompanying the provisioning and supply of that size force were immense. Since the only large-scale war fought by U.S. forces had been on its own soil some 50 years before, there was no infrastructure or experience to fall back on when considering supplying large numbers of men across an ocean. Further, the merchant marine had been neglected for years. Since no preparations had been made, U.S. forces had to use British and French equipment.

While the AEF trained, the Germans launched a last-ditch attack that broke through Allied lines in the vicinity of the Argonne Forest. Pershing quickly offered units to help stem the tide; U.S. Marine and Army brigades fought at Belleau Wood, and an Army division did the same at Château-Thierry. After blunting the German attack, the Allies launched one of their own all along the front, with AEF units operating in concert with others. The push, abetted by shortages of food and near-revolution in Germany, resulted in an armistice on November 11, 1918.

A sideshow of this Great War had been initiated in the vast spaces of Russia. The Russian revolution had ended when the Bolsheviks seized power and reached a separate peace accommodation with the Central Powers

(Germany and Austria-Hungary) through the Treaty of Brest-Litovsk in March of 1918. The Allied Supreme War Council, which directed the war for the allies, determined that troops should be sent to Russia to prevent munitions shipped and still in place there from falling into German hands, to prevent Murmansk from becoming a German submarine base, to help restore the crown to the Romanovs (or failing that, to assist in establishing a pro–Allied government), and to ensure that Czech troops fighting there on the side of the White (royalist) Russians would be able to get home.

President Wilson acquiesced in these rather outlandish terms of reference and allowed U.S. troop participation, although his orders to the Americans reflected much different thinking. American troops were to help the Russians in governing or in defense, as the Russians requested, and to preserve the munitions there for Russian use. This new "invasion" of Russia was opposed by a resuscitated Russian Army now in the west. In some truly awful weather, the home team inflicted reverses on the generally green troops of the Allies. In Siberia to the east where the White Russian forces were fairly strong, troops of Japan, France, Great Britain, and Italy were all situated around Vladivostok when the contingent from the U.S. Army arrived, insisting their presence was for occupation and general guard duty only. With the Japanese bent on possessing eastern Siberia and coopting the White Russian leaders, the situation culminated in White Russian troops attacking the Americans because they would not "play the game." The U.S. unit maintained strict neutrality until withdrawn on April 1, 1920, some six months after U.S. troops on the other side of Russia had departed.

The next two decades were filled with both peace and tension. While the reminders of devastation and body counts of the war were still fresh, there was a willingness among nations to cooperate in attempting to limit the potential for war. There was a concomitant interest in containing the growth of likely enemies. To this end, the major powers met in Washington, D.C., in 1922 and concluded the Five Power Naval Treaty, which put limits on both the size and numbers of naval forces. The treaty limited the displacement of battleships to 35,000 tons and the total tonnage of battleships and battlecruisers for each of the three large naval powers, the United States, Great Britain, and Japan, in a ratio of 5:5:3.[19]

The Japanese sought and were granted a stipulation that signatories were not permitted to add either bases or facilities in the West Pacific. The treaty also permitted the U.S. Navy, which was beginning to appreciate the potential of air power, to convert the hulls of two cruisers under construction to aircraft carriers. Finally, it was agreed that a ten-year shipbuilding "holiday" would be observed. The participants of that conference met again in London in 1930 to create limits on cruisers and to extend the building holiday to 1937. The cooperation manifested by these treaties would, unfortunately, soon disintegrate as the world economy collapsed.

Budget cutting was the dominant principle in the United States; the bills from the war just past had to be paid. The Army was pared to its usual postwar skeletal force. The Navy fared a little better because of the naval treaty, but neither force was very potent. To further exacerbate the situation, the worldwide economic depression that began in the late twenties so limited spending that choices had to be made between men and modern equipment. For the most part, men were chosen at least in part because picking out *the* enemy (from among several possibilities) was difficult. Since the nature of equipment required would be greatly influenced by this enemy's identity, compiling a list of what to buy in the face of this uncertainty was too difficult.

Preparing for World War II

A small rearmament, principally for deterring the Japanese (and probably viewed as an economic spur as well), began in 1933 as the National Industrial Recovery Act granted President Franklin Delano Roosevelt the power to use public works funds to build ships. By executive order, 32 ships were to be built over a three-year period. Congress stopped it. The following year the Vinson-Tramall Act authorized another 102 ships, but only a few were funded and shipbuilding was extremely slow. It would be the end of the 1930s before many ships would be ready.

The harsh terms the armistice had imposed on Germany and the worldwide economic depression ensured acrimonious relationships in Europe, and strains of martial music were once again being heard. Hitler had come to power in Germany in 1933 and was rebuilding his armed forces in violation of the Treaty of Versailles. When Spain exploded in civil war in July 1936, Germany and Italy came to the support of the antigovernment fascist forces with both equipment and men. On the other side of the world, the Japanese first subdued Manchuria and then attacked China in 1937 in an effort to expand their Greater Asian Co-prosperity Sphere, a Japanese concept developed largely for the purpose of keeping themselves supplied with raw materials.

As Europe again went to war, President Roosevelt, under an authorization granted by the Congress, moved to establish an Air Corps within the Army, create the post of Chief of Staff to the President, and form the Joint Chiefs of Staff. Several field commands that brought the forces of the different services under one commander were also created. The Joint Chiefs quickly assumed the planning and coordination functions of the Joint Army-Navy Board and acquired a supporting staff to assist.

Orders for arms and equipment began pouring into American businesses from England and France. Factories that had long been idle

while caught in the grip of the Depression came to life as the President announced that America would be the "Arsenal of Democracy." Eventually,
the impoverished state of U.S. forces was noticed. The "Two-Ocean Navy"
acts authorized the increase of Navy tonnage by 100 percent, and the Selec-
tive Service and Training Act established the first peacetime draft.[20] By
December 1941, the Army had over a million men in training. Because there
were only 29 new construction and 19 conversion and repair shipyards in
1940, the Navy was not likely to get much bigger in a hurry no matter the
legislation.[21] The United States was better prepared than usual when the
Japanese bombed Pearl Harbor on December 7, 1941.

Although the agreed-upon Allied strategy called for a holding action
in the Pacific while the Axis powers in Europe, primarily Germany, were
finished off, Japanese activities dictated some changes. After a string of victories in early 1942, Japanese planners decided to challenge the U.S. Navy
again, this time in hopes of completely destroying it. The battle they sought
was joined near the Pacific island of Midway, where U.S. carrier air power
won a decisive victory.

This encounter proved to be the turning point for both countries.
Japanese forces, having lost most of their mobile striking power, could no
longer challenge the U.S. Navy directly and reverted to the defensive. The
United States, on the other hand, recognized that staying on the defensive
played into the enemy's hands, so the Joint Chiefs of Staff authorized offensive thrusts in both the central (Guadalcanal and Tulagi islands under Admiral Chester Nimitz) and southern (Port Moresby under General Douglas
MacArthur) Pacific areas. They were the opening moves in a two-pronged
offensive drive which would move inexorably toward Japan.

The case in Europe was much less clear, in part because the German
army was so strong. The British did not want to challenge it directly until
the Allied strength had been built up; the United States wanted to attack
as soon as possible. When the military men could not agree, President
Roosevelt intervened (as he and Churchill were wont to do occasionally)
and supported the British position because he thought that it was necessary
to have some action quickly both to keep the coalition together and to
satisfy the demands of the American public, who would soon be clamoring
to know what was being done to "get it over over there."[22]

A joint invasion of North Africa (Operation *Torch*) was planned and
executed in the fall of 1942. Other operations on the periphery followed,
in Sicily and Italy in 1943; the momentum had passed to the Allies. The
buildup for the cross-channel invasion continued but was diluted by the
demands for these and operations in the Pacific. Eventually, production
caught up with demand, and Allied troops landed at Normandy on June
6, 1944. It was the beginning of the end in Europe.

Much had preceded this ambitious amphibious effort. The industrial might of the United States, reaching peak productivity by early 1943, had turned out unprecedented numbers of aircraft, tanks, ammunition, ships, and, most important, amphibious landing craft for both the European and Pacific theaters. The antisubmarine war in the Atlantic had been won by the men manning the escorting ships and aircraft, aided by technological development efforts that produced radar and sonar. The day and night strikes from long-range bombers attacking Germany had nearly ruined the Luftwaffe and forced some 30 percent of the Nazi war effort to be devoted to air defense. Finally, the coalition of Russia, Great Britain, and the United States, along with other, smaller powers, ensured that Germany would have to fight on multiple fronts by April of 1945. The combination of factors proved overwhelming.

While the first post–European war meeting of the Allies was taking place at Potsdam, President Harry S. Truman, who had assumed office upon the death of Roosevelt in 1944, was flashed the news that the detonation of a nuclear device had been successfully accomplished at the Los Alamos research site in New Mexico. Weapons employing the device were constructed and B-29 bombers were ordered by the President to drop the special bombs on two cities in Japan. The Japanese, already on the verge of suing for peace, capitulated.

At the end, the American military machine was a colossus. Some 16 million men had been under arms; more than 1200 major ships and more than 3000 heavy bombers were being operated. The country, divided by class tensions and still mired in the Depression when rearmament began, was now united, powerful, and bursting at the seams with potential. However, since there seemed to be no call for all of that might, the United States rushed to begin withdrawing forces from overseas and reduce the total number of servicemen on duty. But this was not to be a typical postwar period; conditions had changed. Soviet activism and Allied fears combined to create a climate of ideological polarization and increasingly high levels of tension as the United States and the Soviet Union, the superpowers of the world, settled into a war of words, ideas, and political maneuvering—a "cold war."

The military services, their identities preserved in the reorganization of the military establishment under the National Security Act, hardly noticed; they were preoccupied with other matters. The Navy in particular was distracted, because the awesome power of the atomic bomb had convinced many that security lay in being able to deliver such weapons from aircraft with sufficient range to reach nearly anywhere. This meant developing and buying new aircraft for the now independent Air Force, an activity bound to come at the expense of the other services in a time of shrinking defense budgets.

When the "supercarrier" being built for the Navy was cancelled by Secretary of Defense Louis Johnson so that more Air Force groups could be procured, the Navy leaders reacted. This "revolt of the Admirals," as it is often called, provoked a hearing before the House Armed Services Committee to look into charges of "favoritism" (among other things) made by senior naval officers. Finally, the turbulent waters were calmed.[23] While one eye followed the internecine service battles and the other warily watched the Soviets, on the other side of the world the North Koreans moved against the South. Most of the world, the U.S. included, was caught off guard.

Containing Communism in Korea

After the decision was made to go to the aid of South Korea, it was necessary to hastily reconstruct a viable military capability.[24] The closest troops, the Eighth Army on occupation duty in Japan, were readied and began arriving in South Korea within days, determined to halt the North Korean advance. Unfortunately, this was largely an administrative army, with few weapons and little training for combat. Although game, they were no match for the North Korean forces.

At home, efforts began to supply troops both for Korea and Europe, where many felt the next blow would soon fall. The number of draftees was increased, reservists were called back to active duty, and the National Guard was federalized. An American Army was established in Germany, construction began on bomber bases throughout England and elsewhere, and General Dwight D. Eisenhower, who had been the commander of all forces in the European theater when the war ended, was recalled and asked to command all the Allied forces forming up under the NATO umbrella.

At the front, the Eighth Army had been pushed back onto the tip of the Korean peninsula. General Douglas MacArthur, who had been the military governor of Japan and named to command United Nations forces, hatched a plan for an amphibious insertion of troops at the port of Inchon on the western coast of South Korea. This landing had the potential, if successful and rapidly exploited, for trapping most of the North Korean Army. After grudging approval by a reluctant Joint Chiefs of Staff who had little faith in the plan, the operation was executed under extremely difficult landing conditions. Troops poured ashore and headed for Seoul, the capital. The North Koreans, although not enveloped as hoped, were forced to retreat across the border. A fateful decision now presented itself. The original objective of United States and United Nations actions had been to restore the border and stop the fighting. Now, the success of Inchon dangled the possibility of reunification of Korea before hopeful eyes. The temptation was too great. The objective was changed, and the forces were given the go-ahead to eliminate the North Korean Army.[25]

Thus authorized, pursuit continued north of the border, but North Korean troops continued to elude a decisive confrontation. Within months, UN forces had moved up the peninsula and were approaching the Yalu River, which marked the border with the People's Republic of China (PRC). The PRC, apprehensive about the juggernaut they saw rolling toward them — one they considered might not stop — began signalling their discomfort. These warnings were ignored or discounted, and in December 1951, with the UN troops nearing the Yalu, elements of the PRC Army, which had been infiltrating through UN lines for days, attacked. After a week's worth of fighting, the Chinese withdrew. Unfortunately, this was read as a lack of commitment on the part of the PRC, rather than as the final warning it was meant to be. United Nations troops continued north until some were actually at the Yalu when the Chinese struck again. This time, the American and ROK troops were overwhelmed and retreated, amid calls for, among other things, nuclear strikes on the PRC side of the border. This retrogression continued down the peninsula past Seoul, where order was finally restored and UN troops were able to establish a defensive position around the 38th Parallel. A military stalemate ensued. Discussions between North Korea and the United Nations aimed at ending the war were begun in 1952 and rather quickly resulted in a cease-fire and the establishment of a demilitarized zone around the post–World War II demarcation line.[26]

The armed forces emerged from this war somewhat shaken; although performance was generally good, there were disturbing signs in some areas. First, despite having not just control, but command, of the air and sea for most of the conflict, the Air Force and Navy had been unable to effectively interdict the supply routes sustaining the North Korean and Chinese armies. Second, elements of the Army had not reacted well when confronted with the unorthodox tactics of the Chinese army; headlong retreat had resulted causing untold additional casualties. Finally, the callous, if not brutal, treatment of prisoners of war by the North Koreans had produced strange results. Some American POWs actually died in captivity because they lost the will to live. In a phrase, they gave up. Others collaborated with the enemy. These behaviors were not typical of performance in other wars.

After this conflict, the Eisenhower administration shifted the emphasis in military capability. Its doctrine of massive retaliation (discussed earlier) required forces configured for delivery of nuclear weapons occasioning rapid expansion in the Strategic Air Command (SAC), an organization devoted solely to that mission.[27] Service responsibilities were divided neatly, if not equally. The Air Force, in particular SAC, would strike the Soviet Union. The Navy's mission was to protect the sea lines of communication to Europe, while the Army's was to stop a Soviet attack there.

By the mid-1950s, land-based missiles powered by rockets and carrying nuclear warheads had been added to the arsenal and created yet another turf battle between the Air Force and the Army. Submarines were both nuclear powered and launchers of nuclear-tipped missiles.[28] Technological advances had also permitted the development and manufacture of smaller nuclear weapons so that even a mortar-sized round was possible. A Joint Strategic Target Planning Staff (JSTPS) was formed to produce a coordinated nuclear strike plan from the increasingly complicated but separate ones of the Air Force and Navy. However, it was not operations against forces of the Soviet Union, the basis for all U.S. planning of the time, which demanded attention in the early 1960s; it was another divided country in Asia.

Vietnam and After

Involvement in Vietnam started simply enough; a Military Assistance Advisory Group was established in 1950 to manage American supplies provided to the French, who were busy battling communist insurgents. As French influence in Saigon waned, that of America waxed. By the late 1950s, the United States was underwriting some 98 percent of the cost of maintaining the army of the Republic of Vietnam, and 80 percent of the cost of running its government. With Moscow seemingly embarked on a policy of supporting so-called wars of liberation, it did not seem prudent to ignore the threat to Vietnam. Instead the ante was raised.

President Kennedy sent personal envoys General Maxwell Taylor and Dr. Walter Rostow to South Vietnam to assess the situation in 1962. Their report stated that a military contingent was required to underscore our commitment and shore up morale. Without American presence, they warned, the Viet Cong would be successful in dominating the country. Military estimates of what was needed varied widely, from a high of a million troops to ensure victory, to a low of 8,000, a number that would, it was said, be enough to "stabilize" the situation.

True commitment in Vietnam began when 16,000 soldiers were dispatched as advisers. Military equipment also flowed in but nothing seemed to make much of a difference, including changes in the Vietnamese government. The pace was stepped up when the United States conducted air strikes against North Vietnamese targets in retaliation for reported torpedo-boat attacks aimed at two U.S. destroyers, but little progress in bringing about a solution was made. The war, which had begun with guerrilla-type operations in the South, seemed to be becoming more of a conventional conflict as North Vietnamese regular troops were infiltrated. More U.S. troops were dispatched. Various tactics were tried: search and destroy, defended hamlets, and pacification, among others; each was somewhat successful, but none decisive. Nor was the air war being conducted against North Vietnam successful. The hope was that this would bring them to the bargaining table, but the escalating aerial bombardment brought limited political response and little disruption in the flow of supplies, despite rather extravagant and misleading claims to the contrary.

The election of Richard Nixon as president in 1968 brought renewed enthusiasm for pursuing the war to a climax. The level of bombings was increased, and terror tactics against communist sympathizers were inaugurated. The results were marginal at best. Finally, in January of 1973, an agreement was consummated that called for both the United States and North Vietnam to remove all troops and support from the South. American troops were withdrawn, and air and naval forces ceased operations against the North. Two years later, South Vietnam, where some 47,000 Americans had been killed in combat during the longest war in U.S. history, was overrun by forces from the North.

The military establishment was in near disarray at the war's end. Protest had not only racked the homeland, but was present at the front as well. Race riots occurred everywhere, "fragging" (throwing a fragmentation grenade into someone's, usually an officer's, tent or room) became fairly common, aircraft were sabotaged. As the war dragged on men refused to carry out orders, pilots refused to fly missions, sailors picketed their commanding officers on ships. There were few celebrations when the war was finally over.

Specific reasons for this phenomenon are difficult to isolate, but several general observations seem pertinent. The services had a different look in this war, particularly the Army and its draftees. The average inductee "was much less educated, less ambitious, came from a poorer family and was in worse physical condition than the typical American of the 1960s."[29] The average G.I. was single, around 19 years old, smoked pot, and had little faith in his leaders. The type of war also helped rend the fabric. Jungle fighting in areas littered with booby traps and a fanatic enemy who was sometimes indistinguishable from civilians all promoted a "bunker" or siege mentality in U.S. troops. Finally, at a time when it was desperately needed, there was little effort by senior governmental officials to sustain the rationale for U.S. participation.

Since Vietnam, only a few military operations have been carried out; most have been undistinguished. A secret attempt to rescue American hostages seized during the turmoil in Iran was aborted when several of the mission's aircraft were lost in a collision while they refueled in the desert short of their target. Several hundred Marines, ashore as part of a peacekeeping force in Lebanon, were killed when their barrack was blown up by terrorists, and an American cruiser in the Persian Gulf to protect shipping, shot down an Iranian civil airliner. On a more positive note, invasions of the Caribbean island of Grenada to expel the 800 or so Cuban workers there, and of Panama to install a democratic government in that nation were, despite their questionable legality under international law and the U.N. charter, successful military actions. Air attacks by Navy and Air Force aircraft in Lebanon and Libya met with qualified success. In the early days of 1991, U.S. air, land, and sea forces poised in the Saudi Arabian desert and on the waters of the Persian Gulf and Arabian Sea moved with other U.N. forces to evict Iraqi troops occupying the nation of Kuwait.

Iraq's invasion of Kuwait in August 1990 set in motion the formation of a coalition of 28 countries allied in opposition to further Iraqi adventurism. Their buildup of military forces totaled more than three-quarters of a million air, ground, and sea forces (more than half a million of which were from the United States); finally, in January 1991 military operations began with the goal of ensuring permanent withdrawal of Iraqi troops.

United States forces employed most of the high-technology weaponry acquired over the past decade, including stealth aircraft and land-attack missiles, as part of a vast air armada which was to inflict considerable damage. After pounding various strategic and tactical targets in Iraq and Kuwait for 38 days, action on the ground was initiated. The coalition forces quickly moved to the attack and, through a combination of deception and maneuver, rolled over and outflanked the Iraqi forces. Mercifully for all, it was soon over. Overwhelming superiority in weapons, supply, organization, and leadership had resulted in achieving the objective of ridding Kuwait of unwanted foreign troops.

Although the military had pretty much recovered from the agonizing post–Vietnam years even before the satisfying victory over Iraq,[30] it is probable that the speed with which it was accomplished and the very low number of casualties suffered by U.S. forces will be a major step in restoring the public's faith in its military. Whether that renewed confidence will manifest itself in a proclivity for rushing forces to trouble spots immediately or in a new sense of strength in negotiations for peace is not clear.

The sum of the military's experience accumulated since the end of World War II, all in limited war and low-intensity conflicts, has not always been pleasant, but it has been instructive. Some important lessons, dearly learned, need to be remembered. First, fighting a nonindustrialized nation is different from combat with an industrialized one in both kind and degree. It follows, then, that tactics and forces useful in one type of conflict are not optimal for the other. Second, careful planning and inspired leadership are more important than ever. Third, the armed forces need to remember to do what *needs* to be done, and not simply what *can* be done.

CHAPTER VII

Elements of the Strategic Culture: Values

Although the geographical position and the political and military heritage of the United States discussed in the preceding chapters provide the raw materials of the nation's strategic culture, its actual shape can be described only after those elements are interpreted through the mores, folkways, and values of the larger national culture.[1] In a nation where the population is homogenous, shares common beliefs, and agrees on a precise description of acceptable behavior, that culture is likely to be well defined. The wider the range of values, perspectives, and behaviors tolerated, the less distinct it will appear. The national culture that has developed in the United States in large measure fits the latter category, because nearly all the population were immigrants.

Individualism and the National Interest

The original British settlers were joined over time by immigrants from nearly every country of the world. Because freedom of expression was guaranteed to all, newcomers were not required to abandon their native culture. On the contrary, when there were unifying elements already present among the new arrivals, such as race, religion, or nationality, they tended to cluster together in communities. Membership in these communities was in some ways more important to individuals than it was in the larger national one they shared with all other Americans. Given this, it was not unusual for the American culture to absorb features of the subcultures in varying degrees.

Another reason for the blurred edges of American culture is the unwavering belief in the individual; it is the individual who is typically credited with molding and maintaining the strength of the United States. Fulfilling this passion for freedom required control of the surrounding environment by the individual. The early days of trying to survive on the largely

virgin American shores required a massive team effort. Once the foothold
was solidified, however, manifestations of this individualism appeared,
particularly in the pioneers who continued to move west, in advance of
government and other human beings, in order to maintain freedom of action. As the frontier collapsed in the water at the edge of the Pacific Ocean,
individuals had little choice but to matriculate into surrounding communities. As the numbers of individuals swelled, governments, both national
and local, that had been formed to serve the groups, grew in size and influence. As the infrastructure became more complex, individuals became
members of several communities (work, church, and leisure) some of which
overlapped, and others which did not, each serving to restrict individualism
and thus, to a degree, freedom and the control which went with it. Nevertheless, the myth of individualism remains a vital part of the cultural
heritage despite these strictures.

For these and other reasons, gaining a national consensus on almost
anything is very difficult; engaging the attention of everyone is nearly impossible. For example, a large percentage of Americans do not actively participate in the political process. Nearly half, in fact, do not vote for their
national leaders; even fewer participate on non-election days.[2] As a result,
a relatively small but active minority of citizens defines and manages the
affairs of the nation. Leery of stirring the large, apparently uninterested but
potentially powerful total electorate, these power brokers and wielders ex-
pend little effort in identifying or defining issues except when absolutely
necessary or when a public outcry will be useful in achieving their political
ends. Ceding all power to this group has several undesirable side effects.
Principal among them is a tendency for members to concentrate at least as
much on maintaining their own position as on advancing the interests of
the country.[3] Involving citizens in the business of the republic is not
routine. In fact, "the machinery of electoral politics does not encourage the
participation of citizens in confronting the most fundamental choices facing the nation."[4]

Former Secretary of Defense Casper Weinberger observed that democratic countries cannot develop and carry out "grand strategies" as can
totalitarian states because of the fluctuation of public opinion. Speaking of
the Reagan administration, he said, "[although the administration's] ends
and goals are clear . . . our employment of means is obviously limited by
the give and take of free politics."[5]

While this sort of statement is made every day by various administrations, members also busy themselves removing as many of the limits as
possible by hiding their objectives. For example, it would be nearly impossible to quibble with the objectives of the announced current national
security strategy because of the very general way in which it is articulated.
Arguments invariably arise when generalities need to be transformed into

specific actions at a time and place. The virtue of generalization, in strategic terms as in others, is that nearly any activity can be (and has been at one time or another) justified on the basis of national security.[6]

National interests, for example, which should be the basis of any national strategy, tend to be defined in public by the leadership in such a way as to be nearly valueless, if not unintelligible. Developing a long-term national security strategy that can be articulated forthrightly and endorsed by the population as a basis for continuing military and foreign policies under these conditions may be impossible.

Nevertheless, attempts must still be made because, as Kenneth Keniston has stated, ". . . all men have and need conscious and unconscious premises that shape their experiences, their interpretations of life and their behavior; and in every individual or society those premises are organized into a more or less coherent . . . whole."[7]

Creating a whole that is consistent, systematic, and acknowledged is difficult because many of the premises or beliefs are not only subsociety specific, they are probably hierarchically arranged in a heterogeneous nation. That is, it seems likely that there is a set of beliefs, probably a small one, upon which every American would agree. Then, there are larger sets shared by smaller groups of people who populate either a geographic region or an economic or social class. It is unlikely, for example, that un- or undereducated members of the working poor from the South or West would have exactly the same total belief system as an academic in a Northeastern university or an oil tycoon from the Southwest.

Issues of national security and military strategy tend to be widely aired only when raised by the candidates during national elections, when the Executive and Legislative houses of the government are locking horns, or when some catastrophe – real or contrived – occurs. What passes for "public debate" at other times is, in reality, a few professionals or politicians presenting their arguments in the pages of academic, specialized, or technical publications. Normally, citizens

> . . . remain plunged in ignorance of the simplest military facts and their leaders, seeking their votes, do not dare undeceive them . . . no one in authority has the wit, ascendancy or detachment from public folly to declare fundamental brutal facts to the electorate.[8]

Leaders, it seems, believe that military issues are so complex that the average citizen will be unable to comprehend them; therefore, their resolution is better left to the experts. This assertion is not only unproven, it is self-serving. After all, the burden of explaining an issue adequately should be on those who define it, not on those expected to aid in the solution.

One result of keeping the public at arm's length regarding the appropriateness of policy and national commitment is to further distort the nation's experiential filter, already suspect. All societies tend to view the world from their own perspective, weigh the actions of others on their own cultural scales, and judge them by local standards. As with any other country, the United States has a unique history that has been captured in literature, folklore, rituals, and symbols and promulgated through educational systems, both formal and informal. Interpretation of this accumulated experience shapes the manner in which Americans view the larger world and therefore influences national behavior and the formation of the strategic culture. However, the accuracy of the reported experience that forms the basis for behavior and judgments is open to question. In recent years the difficulty of determining the reality of history has become all too evident. Books written in the past 10 to 20 years describe historical events in ways remarkably different from descriptions in books written earlier. For example, early accounts describe the founding fathers of the United States as nearly perfect as humans can be. More contemporary biographies have illuminated their all-too-human foibles. In other cases, historical events have been interpreted in several ways at the time of occurrence, and quite differently the further removed the account is from the actual event. As the interpretations multiply, the salient features of the original happening begin to blur. Tolstoy is credited with having said that history would be an excellent story, if only it were true.

Determining reality has not, as one might suppose, become easier in the midst of the communications explosion of recent years. If anything, it has become more difficult. The leaking of "information" (which may or may not be factual) as a trial balloon, as part of a disinformation campaign, or as a public-relations gimmick has become a cottage industry. Although responsible investigative reporting by the communications media has uncovered wrongdoing in high places by some holding the public trust (Watergate is the best example), routine pursuit of the truth does not seem to be high on anyone's priority list.

Clearly, the capability to present and analyze all the strategic issues exists. Indeed, the total amount of information that can be made available to any one individual has increased by orders of magnitude in the last 50 years as new technologies in the print, broadcast, computer, and communications fields have been introduced. Because of the ability to "cover" events almost anywhere, however, less is covered in depth. The pressure is to condense in order to cover more in a given period of time, with the result that the sensational but isolated event all too often becomes the only window on very complex situations. This focus on the "happening" has become even more pervasive as available technology has allowed for our immediate "presence" at the scene of nearly any action. Unfortunately, we get to see only what a director (correspondent, editor, etc.) somewhere decides we

should see, not necessarily what may be important. Since we have no independent way of knowing the truth, we must assume that events occurred
in the way they were reported. Thus what has been provided as the description of an event, true or not, becomes part of experience that will shape
thought and behavior.

American Perceptions and Reality

The impact of these "environmental" factors is exacerbated by the
many facets of the American character, for "man ... not only tends to be
prisoner of his perceptions, his perceptions also are slaves to his predisposi-
tions."[9] These elements or characteristics tend to be like coins, two-sided;
one side portrays a view of Americans as they themselves wish to be perceived, while the flip side shows reality. The two are not often the same.
Whether the head or the tail is up will depend on the circumstances.

Forced to choose the one characteristic they would most like to have
considered representative of their country, most Americans would probably select being moral; they would like the United States to be seen as
always able to first recognize and then choose to do the "right" thing. In
government, for example, there is a "tradition of regarding moral aspiration and moral indignation as instruments of foreign policy."[10] Homage to
this predilection can most easily be seen when a moral justification is invariably developed at the national level (sometimes painfully) and then offered
to the public, often after the decision or action has been taken. Americans
like to be on the "right" side of every question. If the location of that side
is not clear, it is often assumed to be synonymous with the position of the
United States; Americans tend to see the country's goals as noble and
just.[11]

Although the "right" side of any question is seldom absolutely clear,
that almost never keeps a judgment from being made because many
Americans believe in their country unconditionally. They end up applying
a curious double standard when weighing national behavior. That is, they
tend to excuse their own government from responsibility for disastrous outcomes of actions taken because the *motives* are assumed to be pure,
whereas the activities of other countries are judged solely on outcomes.
Members of this group would assert the right of the United States to interfere or intervene in the governmental processes of other nations on the
theory that any intervention is bound to be for the purpose of protecting
the "rights" of all people, but would raise a hue and cry should another
country attempt to influence an outcome here.[12] Other Americans would
look at such behavior and view it in exactly the opposite manner. Their
credo is to believe that the United States's motivations should be discounted

entirely, while those of others should always be considered. Under this premise, America is usually wrong in whatever it does, whereas other's behavior is always acceptable. That these two groups can, for the most part, exist side by side is a tribute to the tolerance emblematic of the American culture. Certainly, one important ingredient of being moral is "playing fair," playing according to the rules. Unfortunately, these ethical Marquis of Queensbury rules often are "understood" rather than written, but their presence is, nevertheless, important. An American is most comfortable where rules are codified in some fashion so that conduct (performance) may be judged and, if transgressions are discovered, the guilty party identified and punished.

In this quest for the moral high ground it is useful to have enemies who act in particularly shady and nefarious ways. If they do not, crediting them with doing so seems to work just as well. Americans have always been able to conjure up a bogeyman. From the late 1700s through the first decade of the twentieth century, Englishmen were imagined on the opposite side of every border, scheming to inhibit the United States in some way.[13] Some time after the Bolshevik revolution in Russia, communists and Soviets supplanted the British.[14] Rhetoric helps reinforce moral positions. Characterizing the enemy as truly evil and putting the worst possible interpretations on his actions serves to buttress the distinction between good and evil and strengthens the we-they formulation favored by so many. This is possible because, as Strobe Talbott puts it,

> Americans live in a celebrity culture. At home they are in a constant search for heroes, while abroad they are on the lookout for supervillains . . . whose indisputable nastiness makes it easier to comprehend why so much of the outside world often seems an unfriendly if not dangerous place.[15]

Emphasizing the "badness" of enemies helps gain public support for contemplated action. That support is absolutely crucial in national security matters where sacrifices may well be needed at all levels of society in order to effectively carry out a strategy.[16]

Reinforced by the economic and military superpower status America has achieved, the belief that the United States is a moral nation often manifests itself in a penchant for always being sure about what is best for others. This attitude has had a remarkably long run in the United States. By the end of the nineteenth century, this feeling of moral superiority swept across the United States, fostering the conviction that America would serve as a shining example of freedom and economic vitality for the rest of the world. Contemporarily, this attitude often results in well-meaning but heavy-handed interference in the affairs of the governments of other sovereign states. Supervising elections, putting pressure—economic or otherwise — on governments to "dump" certain officials, and the supporting of guerrillas are all examples.[17] Needless to say, Americans are more comfortable looking outward when making judgments. Instances of racial, social, religious, and economic intolerance, as well as bigotry and persecution, are not only part of American past history, but are still with us in the present. When objections are raised to these actions, they are typically dismissed with the nostrum that transgressions of other societies are so much worse.

Another aspect of the "moral" theme is the inclination to believe in the innate goodness of man, to believe that humans will, in the final analysis, do the right or honorable thing. Popular entertainments focus on exactly this theme, often portraying evil-acting people as finally having hearts of gold, sometimes showing an individual giving up his or her own life to save that of another. While such events do happen, it does not seem that they occur with great frequency (if they did, they would not make headlines). We are faced with much more evidence of the self-centered actions of man than of his sacrificing nature. When morality and self-interest are in conflict, there seems to be a tendency to substitute an examination of regulations for the moral responsibility of making a judgment about right and wrong; when translated into action, this generally means that if it is legal, it is considered ethical.

Yet another characteristic of the Americans is their belief in competition. Valuing here is based on the idea that the individual with the best idea or the one who can run the fastest, hit a ball the farthest, or build something the cheapest will "win," that is, be successful. Competition is an important element of American life that typically begins at home but is part of the educational experience in schools, continues in business, and has been extrapolated into international relations. Americans believe that, given a "fair" chance, America will "win" whatever the contest — economic, political, or ideological.[18] This attitude fuels efforts to reduce trade barriers to American goods, is behind proselytizing efforts like the Voice of America broadcasts, and tends to create a certain arrogance in relationships with other countries.

The truth about competing in the world does not quite follow the script. For the most part, American industrial might established a foothold behind protective tariffs and then blossomed during World War II when the country's geographical position ensured that its factories would be safe from the devastation of war being visited on much of the industrially developed world. From this running start the United States went on to establish a preeminent economic position in the postwar world as well. More recently, American business has been finding it harder to compete in the international marketplace.

On the broader "competitive" front, stories of manipulation, mismanagement, and outright cheating to gain an "edge" in business, financial, and even government activities fill the papers, and there are serious abridgments of individual freedoms every day. The federal government continues to add to an already horrendous budget deficit and seems unwilling to make the hard choices necessary to get it under control. While citizens of other countries might grant the availability of creature comforts in America, few would agree that its citizens are the chosen people.

An extension of this "America is best" theme is the contention that the U.S. military is a match for any and all. The evidence substantiating this conceit is spotty. From an historical perspective, U.S. military history has been neither particularly long nor particularly noteworthy. For the most part, when U.S. forces have clearly "won" in a conflict, it was against inferior opponents or was accomplished with the assistance of allies whose contributions are often quickly forgotten.[19] This is not to say that the individual American military man (or groups of them) is not as brave as, or as competent as, any other. Rather, it is to say that they are not nor have they ever been supermen. Unfortunately, the American public *expects* its military to be able to dominate all others. This expectation, abetted by an appearance of invincibility during the world wars, was frustrated first in the Korean War and again in Vietnam.

Americans have little patience with simply engaging the enemy, less for conducting drawn out operations, and none for "playing for a tie."[20] The military's reputation suffers when such events occur, for the most part unjustly so. The one-sided Grenada and Panama operations were satisfying precisely because they were short and, at least on the surface, successful, despite now-forgotten questions of legality and propriety. Once action has taken place, success or failure becomes the sole metric, not the legitimacy of the constitutional, policy, moral, or legal grounds that served as a basis for it. Because of the success achieved in the recent U.N.-Iraq War where U.S. forces played the major role, belief in the capability of the armed forces will be restored to a degree. Many citizens, particularly those who are not prone to examine issues in any depth, will be inclined to again raise their hand, index finger pointed to the sky, and chant, "We're number one!"

This demand for efficiency of force is particularly significant because the United States tends to draw quickly. That is, there is an inclination toward early application, or threat of application, of military force when seeking solutions to difficult international problems. The fact that no battle has been fought within the borders of the 50 states within the memory of anyone alive, a condition which has spared the vast majority of the populace the actual horror of combat, may be behind this "quick gun" attitude. Alternately, it may be an outgrowth of the American desire for settling differences quickly so that resources may be devoted to producing and consuming. Achieving "victory" in some way will provide that. The attitude here is no nonsense, look-you-straight-in-the-eye, and just-do-what-it-takes to solve the problem. This approach in the international arena creates a political environment in which "being tough" is viewed as a defining attribute of American leadership, especially in its presidents. It almost seems as though each one cannot wait for an opportunity to demonstrate his toughness.[21] One can only speculate what the effect might be if wisdom were the esteemed attribute.

Another important dimension of the American character is the belief in technological achievement. The rapid movement into industrialization and the scientific and engineering advances that have propelled this country into the forefront of technological competence in the world have made popular the notion that many, if not all, problems may be solved by the application of technology. Americans sometimes seem to be machine "junkies," and the pressure of economic competition works to drive the production of ever "better" machines: those which will go faster, have more range, are smarter and more accurate. Labor-saving devices dominate our markets, including the military one. This has built up a reliance on "engineering" solutions where, for example, the focus is on continually improving the product rather than the process. Answers can be readily provided; almost no one takes the time to figure out what the question might be.

Although Americans tend to favor fighting with technology rather than with manpower because of the high value placed on human life, it does not hurt that the search for technological solutions has spawned a robust defense community, now an indispensable sector of the society. That community, which consists of the uniformed military services, the civil service, and industries that supply military forces, was formed and grew large in the midst of the Cold War competition with the Soviet Union following World War II. The manufacture, sale, care and feeding of weapons and weapons systems is a billion-dollar business reaching, in one way or another, into nearly every corner of the country. The impact of defense dollars on both local and national economies sometimes leads to decisions being made on political rather than national security grounds.

The allure of substantial profits on the industrial side and the hope on the government's side that someone will produce the one system that will do it all (the panacea syndrome) exert powerful impulses on both. So long as the product developed and acquired fulfills a legitimate need, the system is functioning as it should. When intense lobbying of politicians is necessary to ensure the original acquisition or the continued production of an item no longer desired by the services, then the cause of national security is no longer being served.

The last facet of the American character that helps to shape the strategic culture to be considered here is the prevailing belief concerning the role of government in citizens' lives. The attitude that the least amount

of government is best remains the cornerstone of the American political
character, although exactly what "least" means varies widely. In the
agricultural, sparsely populated first years of the nation, least was truly
very little. However, as intercourse among people and among nations increased, more government was not only desirable but necessary to preserve
order, to protect the innocent from the predatory practices of a few, and
to defend the country's right to exist. While many, if not most, Americans
would like it best if the government intervened in their life not at all, this
same group is likely to expect it to regulate the behavior of others. This is
a country where many citizens do not want to be taxed more (or at all) by
the government, but do want that same body to decree that prayers must
be said in school and that abortions for any reason are illegal.

Fundamentally, the nation's preoccupation is with economic productivity and the enhancement of the individual's, not the group's, well being.
Since there is a suspicion that all levels of government serve special interests
rather than those of the individual, any regulatory actions that may affect
an individual's accumulation of wealth or power are highly resented. For
example, the taxation issue has progressed from the beginning revolt
against taxation without representation to a position where, despite
representation, candidates for an office who propose the raising of taxes,
whatever the merits of the proposal, are almost sure to be defeated. On the
other hand, those candidates who fashion platform planks based on reducing government often draw a large following. Given these feelings, the relationship citizens maintain with those who govern is a tenuous one. Form
often counts more than substance, and looking and feeling good seem
much more important than doing and being.

There are, of course, other dimensions of the American character that
reflect values of varied origins with unquantifiable numbers of adherents.
The litany just completed was not meant to be exhaustive, but merely suggests the composition of the lens through which Americans will experience
their environment and ultimately formulate their concepts of utility with
respect to the military. The myths and realities of the American character
are so intermixed that attempting to separate them would be futile. In
truth, they probably cannot be divided in any meaningful way because
Americans reject some of their reality as myth and accept some of their
myths as reality. The point is that out of this potpourri of attitudes, beliefs,
and behaviors comes action in the military arena.

United States participation in the U.N.-Iraq War is a wonderful study
in this regard. The day following Iraq's invasion of Kuwait, the United
States declared that such naked aggression was intolerable behavior, embargoed trade with Iraq, froze its assets in this country, and began prod-
ding the United Nations. In the next several days, the U.N. Security

Council first condemned Iraq's action and then established economic sanctions. President Bush ordered U.S. troops to the Saudi Arabia–Kuwait border to counter any further Iraqi threat to world oil supplies. In the next several months the military alternative, always lurking in the background, began to receive more press and attention. More U.S. troops were sent, and U.S. officials began forming up an alliance of concerned nations to share the load by contributing either forces or money. Reports of Iraqi atrocities in Kuwait increased, as did negative character studies of Iraq's leader, Saddam Hussein.

By mid-December an antiwar movement had also begun and was gaining a little momentum when the administration, which had been waffling about the vital interest to the country being threatened (loss of jobs was mentioned once), now began saying that economic sanctions would not be sufficient to force Iraq's hand. While the United States orchestrated activities, the United Nations finally authorized the use of force on January 15, 1991, if Iraq would not withdraw.

As the likelihood of military action loomed larger, the debate about the American president's power to commit forces to combat grew louder. The Congress, whose power was about to be usurped (if viewed from that perspective), wanted no part of that hot potato and so avoided the subject as if it were the plague until the last possible moment. By the time the official debate began, the outcome was predetermined. Having acquiesced in the force and rhetoric buildup, to undercut the President by refusing to support his action would make the U.S. "look bad," something considered by many to be a fate worse than death. In the event, the war began immediately after the United Nations deadline and was over quickly.

This adventure captured many of the elements of the American character. It was quickly transformed into a moral crusade against agression; the Iraqi leader, who had previously been at least tolerated by U.S. leadership despite some atrocious behavior during and after the earlier Iran–Iraq war, was personally vilified. The military option was quickly selected, Congress played almost no role, and the United States made sure it maintained control.

American Diversity and the Strategic Culture

The larger American culture is schizophrenic in many ways. Pacifists live side by side with interventionists. The combative Ku Klux Klan exists in the same culture as the gentle Amish; the skinheads and street gangs coexist with philanthropists and the millions of other average citizens who contribute billions of dollars to charitable causes each year. Most Americans like to believe that their lives reflect the value they place on morality, competition, technological achievement, practicality, and minimum government.

These cultural folkways and the self-perceptions that reinforce them, along with the country's geographical location and its political and military heritage, all coalesce to form a peculiarly American sense of how military power should be used. These somewhat diverse and occasionally conflicting attitudes and beliefs produce the following cornerstones of the American strategic culture.

1. *Fundamental decisions about national security and military policy in general are the result of a competition of ideas.* In reality, this proposition is only partially true. It implies that all points of view will be considered, the best idea(s) will emerge from the mix, and that each decision is arrived at in some structured way. What more typically occurs is that an element is taken from each proposition put forward and force-fit into a compromise upon which everyone will eventually agree, essentially a lowest-common-denominator approach. The fallacy in this "methodology" is that the objective has changed. Initially, the interest would have been in the accomplishment of a given job; when compromise is the name of the game, satisfying all the power centers in the tug of war becomes the primary objective.

An example of this sort of outcome is seen in the inclusion of multiple services in isolated military actions despite their continued difficulties in coordinating operations. The raid on Libya carried out in 1986 was executed by Navy aircraft launched from aircraft carriers a few hundred miles from the targets to be struck, and Air Force aircraft launched from England who had to travel hundreds of miles and engage in multiple aerial refuelings before arrival.[22] There is no question that the Navy could have done it all. Yet another example is the allocation of the defense budget. Each service receives approximately the same share of the budget, irrespective of its relative need. Complicating this matter further is the fact that every constituency belongs to a larger one. That is, despite the fact that each military service might fight the other internally, they will present a solid front when it is the Defense Department against State or some other executive branch organization. All of the executive join forces when battling the legislative, and so on.

Finally, the likelihood that the outcome will be the result of deliberate decision making is problematic. Descriptions of the decision-making sessions connected with various crises do not often inspire confidence. Although day-to-day operations may well include careful analysis and objective evaluation, there is not sufficient information to make a judgment. The public needs to recognize that decision making in crises may in fact depend on ad hoc procedures, be based on faulty or incomplete information, be afflicted with poor communications, misunderstandings, inappropriate use of authority, or even panic or human and mechanical error.[23]

2. *War is not the continuation of policy, but the failure of it.* Americans as a rule choose not to consider "time as a stream," but prefer to see events as discrete.[24] That is, most would not see war or the actual application of force as just another implement in the tool kit of international relations. Rather, foreign policy as conducted by diplomats and statesmen would be considered at an end once the threat to use force (implied or explicit) did not produce the desired result, a condition which would probably lead to military action. This attitude satisfies the traditional tenet that war is justified only as a moral crusade. While the position is sometimes difficult to maintain, weakening here would undermine the very foundation of the American conception of liberty for all and achievement on the basis of hard work (as opposed to conquest). The disruption to economic and social life resulting from a shifting of emphasis from a consumer-based market to a government one in time of war, a change no one would make willingly, further defines war as an aberration in the normal scheme of things rather than an outcome of a natural process. Guns-or-butter choices are not popular.

3. *Generally, force should not be used, but, once the decision is made to employ it, what is done should be free of political influence and any conflict should be rapidly fought to a victory.* This belief is allied to the one above. The population contains those who would advocate the use of military force only as a last resort, if at all, and those who are inclined to flex military muscles early in any dispute. The former would be unlikely to sanction preemptive action on the part of U.S. forces, and the latter would probably recommend it.[25]

Institutionally, the United States tends to favor talk and negotiation as methods of solving disagreements—as long as the other party does as well. However, it does not take much to prompt American saber-rattling. In fact, what was once called "gunboat diplomacy," where U.S. forces were visibly present while talks were conducted or notes exchanged, remains a popular technique. There are pluses and minuses to this sort of response. On the positive side, the forces provide tangible evidence of American interest in the problem at hand and serve as a reminder of the awesome power the country can bring to bear, if needed. From a negative standpoint, nations, as well as individuals, tend to resent intimidation and being shown up. If nothing else, they stand to lose "face," often thought to be a special province of Asian cultures but in reality very much a human reaction. Humiliating countries (or individuals), irrespective of their precipitating actions, is not the way to positively influence behavior over the long haul.

Having decided to use force, the American way is to start at the lowest level of military activity thought to be coercive, increasing the pressure only when the lesser effort did not achieve what was desired. Not much time is allotted for enemy decision making in response to U.S. actions, however.

4. *Economic power and superior technology rather than "military art" will ultimately carry the day in conflict.*[26] This attitude is one typical of a nation with plentiful resources and a belief in the superiority of engineering answers. It rests on this country's demonstrated productive capacity, its technological inventiveness, and "a political imperative to minimize casualties."[27] In truth, when you rely on a citizen army you have few choices in this regard, particularly when contemplating a medium- to large-scale conventional conflict. The bulk of officers and men will have had little training of any sort, let alone at the level that makes for a true fighting force. Thus, providing them with numbers of sophisticated weapons smart enough to be somewhat autonomous and with ranges such that they can be fired at the enemy far from the forward edge of the battle area (FEBA), is likely to improve combat survivability.

This has important economic and political implications. Men (or women, for that matter) have better (meaning more productive) contributions to make in a capitalist economy than to be soldiering. Coupling this practical dictum with the reverence for life (at least American ones) that is part of the country's religious heritage makes reductions in direct human confrontations, however achieved, desirable. This provides the rationale for preferring to fight with sea and air rather than land forces. Units operating in these media are more likely to be able to maintain distance from the enemy and a measure of mobility, factors that translate into survival rates. There also is a capability in these forces to do area damage through bombing or shelling or both. A weight of ordnance can be delivered quickly from long distances generally without fear of large losses to the attacking force.

Reliance on technological superiority feeds the hope of discovering the ultimate weapon, one that will truly make war obsolete. Many thought that the nuclear weapon might indeed be it, but genuine limitations on use have illuminated its weaknesses. Nevertheless, the search goes on within the Strategic Defense Initiative and other such programs.

Military art, essentially the planning for and maneuver of forces to produce victory, runs a poor third behind productivity and technology in terms of what might contribute to winning a war. There is a persistent belief that the beauty and symmetry of plans and their execution are wasted in modern conflict; time and dollars are much better spent in producing vast quantities of the implements of war, and, by making weapons "smart," providing a difficult problem for the enemy, a situation where he must defend each vital target everywhere, all the time. The U.N.-Iraq War may go a long way toward "rehabilitating" maneuver as a military art form. A small cadre of officers in the Army and Marines had been advocating more reliance and training in this area. The deception and flanking movements planned by

Central Command and executed in the desert by the allied forces worked wonderfully, particularly in conjunction with the pounding from the air the Iraqis had absorbed.

As one might expect, there are good and bad outcomes from having articulated a strategic culture. On the positive side, group cohesion and even good morale can result from a shared view of military utility. However, it can also breed inflexibility, overconfidence, and even intolerance of other cultures, all of which have an impact on the quality, direction, and thoroughness of strategic planning.

Expecting strategic planners to remove their cultural spectacles altogether is probably unrealistic. Yet, in some way they must recognize the "spin" that it causes them to put on interpretations of the environment and on the future they will try to fashion. Other factors are also at work.

CHAPTER VIII

Developing Military Strategy

The concept of strategy has expanded in concert with heightened economic and political intercourse among nations.[1] Beginning with Von Bülow's notion of strategy as the science of military movement to Liddell-Hart's concept of strategy as "the art of distributing and applying military means to fulfill the ends of policy,"[2] the field has developed into a broadly based discipline which encompasses several levels of application, from charting the general direction of a nation's course to much more detailed schemes for directly employing various resources to achieve specific objectives. Working in the field requires a substantial knowledge of geopolitics, military art, and psychology.

In today's world, all strategy is typically described as both an art and a science; it is an art because creativity and originality in conception and execution seem to be keys to success and thus are important in the development process. Strategy is at the same time a science, because a body of knowledge, assembled through observation, study, and experience, exists to support efforts at determining principles and precepts of warfare. In the United States, because of the assignment of responsibilities within the structure of the national security establishment, it is formulated in several levels of detail.

The highest level of strategy is that which guides the nation's conduct in the world arena. It should be broad-gauged and enduring, and applicable to all points of the nation's tangency with others. It has been variously called grand strategy, total strategy and, in this country, national strategy, and has been defined as "the art and science of developing and using the political, economic and psychological powers of a nation, together with its armed forces, during peace and war, to secure national objectives."[3]

National strategies should be based on national interests, aimed at the achievement of specific objectives, and supported with sufficient resources. The process should work something like this. Developing national strategy begins with an examination of those conditions the United States is interested in maintaining or bringing about in the world, including those in the economic, political, and cultural spheres. Current interests of the United States have been identified as:

1. The survival of the United States as a free and independent nation, with its fundamental values and institutions intact.
2. A healthy and growing U.S. economy to ensure opportunity for individual prosperity and a resource base for national endeavors at home and abroad.
3. A stable and secure world, fostering political freedom, human rights, and democratic institutions.
4. Healthy, cooperative and politically vigorous relations with allies and friendly nations.[4]

Objectives, which are statements of what must be accomplished in order to promote, protect, and preserve the identified interests, should then be developed. Some of the objectives derived from the above interests include maintaining the physical security of the nation and that of selected allies, becoming an integral part of the developing global economy, promoting the growth of "free democratic political institutions, as the surest guarantee of both human rights and economic and social progress," and building and maintaining productive relationships with other countries.[5]

Having identified the objectives, strategy is then developed to guide the employment of all the elements of power to be used in their pursuit. Once strategies have been developed, the required resources may be identified and procurement begun. While this process is described (and shown) as flowing smoothly from interests to objectives to strategies to resources, in practice there are feedback loops in continuous operation which will often lead to adjustments in each. Figure 3 depicts the flow just described.

Again, the national strategy is at the apex of a hierarchy. Immediately below it are organizational strategies. At this level, functional entities (departments of the executive branch, Defense, State, Commerce) are charged with both formulating and carrying out strategies derived from national ones that will assist in achieving their objectives. These economic strategies, political strategies, military strategies, and others are often enunciated as "policies" and are quite general.

At the next level are operational strategies. Here the subordinate units within a department (or other functional entity) develop strategies for employing resources at their level. It is generally here that resource requirements are generated and the strategies employing actual forces are created. These must support the strategies at the national and departmental levels.

The last tier is that of execution strategies. Here strategies which result

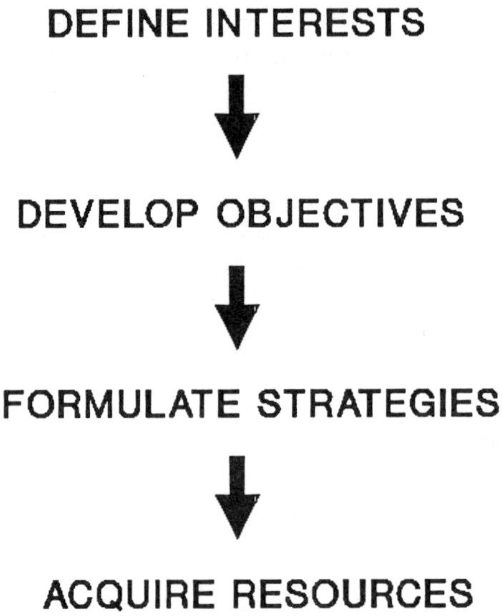

DEFINE INTERESTS

DEVELOP OBJECTIVES

FORMULATE STRATEGIES

ACQUIRE RESOURCES

Figure 3. Developmental Flow

in specific tactical activities are formulated and passed on to those units that will execute them. Their execution comprises tactics.

Table 1 summarizes the hierarchy.

National Strategies	General plans for achieving goals and objectives of a nation with respect to its position in the world.
Organizational Strategies	General plans for attaining goals and objectives in a specific field or area.
Operational Strategies	Specific plans for acquiring and employing resources to execute the general plans of the organizational entity.
Execution Strategies	Specific plans for the employment of sub-sets of resources to execute the specific plans of the institutional entity.

Table 1. Hierarchy of Military Strategic Planning

The part of the national strategy which concerns itself with national security includes both a military and a foreign policy component. Policies (strategies) at this level are developed by the President and his National Security Council (NSC) and formalized through presidential directives (PDs) and national security decision directives (NSDDs), which are passed to cognizant executive departments to provide guidance and provoke action. The responsibility for devising military strategies in support of these national security policies (and acquiring the resources to make executing them possible) rests with the Department of Defense. Specifically, by the Defense Reorganization Act of 1986, the Chairman of the JCS is charged with "preparing strategic plans, including plans which conform with [projected] resource levels."[6]

The Planning, Programming, Budgeting System (PPBS) in place in the Department of Defense since 1961, is the structure within which the planning has been accomplished. From the strategy development perspective, it is the first "P," the planning part of the system, which is of interest here. That phase, which, in theory, begins the process, should include

> ...the definition and examination of alternative defense strategies, the analysis of exogenous conditions and trends, threat and technology assessment, and any other tasks associated with looking forward either to anticipate change or to understand the long-term implications of current choices....[7]

The principal objectives here are to define the national military strategy required to maintain the national security while supporting foreign policy over a period of time from two to eight years into the future, and to dimension the military forces necessary to execute the strategy at some acceptable level of risk.

The first product of this phase is the Joint Intelligence Estimate for Planning (JIEP) prepared by the Joint Staff of the JCS. This effort is intended to provide a basis for both individual service and joint, or combined service, planning. The JCS uses it along with inputs from the services and the unified and specified commanders to produce the Joint Strategic Planning Document (JSPD), which presents a military appraisal of the threats to national interests and objectives, recommended military objectives, and the military strategy for achieving them. Force levels available under various funding assumptions and an assessment of the risk to the country resulting from a particular level are also included, along with any recommendations for changes in force planning or program guidance. This document is submitted to the President, the National Security Council, and the Secretary of Defense.

After considering this and other more "unofficial" inputs, the Secretary of Defense formulates a draft Defense Planning Guidance (DPG) in which defense policy and strategy as well as forces and resource planning guidelines are detailed. The draft is distributed to various DOD organizations (including operational commmanders) and other departments, as appropriate, for comment. After responses are received and reviewed, the final version of the DPG is issued. It will contain all the relevant assumptions and direction needed for continuing the development process at the next level in the planning structure. Although the entire PPBS works on a two-year cycle, under the provisions of the Defense Reorganization Act of 1986, the DPG is to be issued annually.

At this point the Department of Defense planning phase is essentially over and the programming phase begins, followed in due course by budget preparation and submission. Planning continues at the other tiers in the hierarchy. The JCS provides a Joint Strategic Capabilities Plan (JSCP), developed from the guidance in the DPG, to the Unified and Specified commanders. This document directs the development of formal plans (which will include strategies) to guide military operations under certain conditions and against certain countries. The plan development directed by the JSCP encompasses the use of both conventional and theater nuclear weapons, where appropriate.

Unified commander plans developed in response to this direction contain operational strategies peculiar to the conditions specified or relevant to their geographical theater of operations. Once these operational strategies are formulated, they are passed down to the next level of the chain of command, the component Joint Task Force or sub-area commander, where execution strategies are developed. From here on down, where entities would actually engage enemy forces, activities are considered tactical, although some may have strategic effects.

As might be expected, the strategies generated at the lower rungs on the hierarchical ladder narrow in scope because more detail and focus are needed the closer one gets to the executing force. The products of all levels in each geographic theater constitute the body of military strategy. As shown in Figure 4, that body may be conceptualized as having three dimensions. One dimension encompasses various political conditions or states of the world that can exist. From a military point of view, these conditions range from peace to crisis, war, and post-war. The second dimension describes specific countries, or geographical areas of the world of interest (theaters or sub-theaters). These need not be fixed, but can be added to or subtracted from as conditions warrant. The third dimension accounts for the level in the chain of command responsible for the development and execution of the strategy for that world state in that geographical area.

In theory, each combination of area and political condition should have a strategy which will differ in content and specificity depending on the command levels involved. In practice, of course, not all combinations receive the same amount of attention; indeed, some will get none at all. Those areas and conditions specified for planning in the JSCP will be fully developed with multiple commands participating.

Figure 5 depicts this vertical development where one cell of the cube

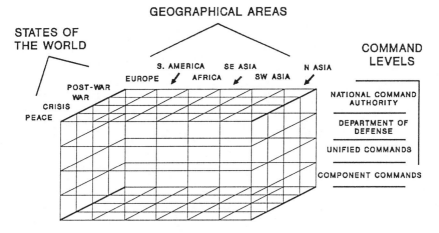

Figure 4. The Strategy Paradigm

has been isolated to display the hierarchy of strategy. For this example, assume that the National Command Authority (NCA) had developed a general strategy for crisis management in an area of the Pacific Command. This strategy would have been passed to the Department of Defense, where detail would be added that tasks the theater-level commander of the area concerned, in this case the Commander-in-Chief, Pacific (USCINCPAC), with achieving specific objectives in his area. That commander would select a strategy (e.g., a show of strength) using all of the forces assigned to his command and pass it to his subordinates, the component (or service commanders), or, if applicable, a Joint Task Force Commander. These commanders, in turn, would develop strategies for their forces to execute. Each strategy developed must support the objectives of the senior commander. As shown on the figure, other Unified Commanders may be directed to develop supporting strategies in some cases.

Although it may appear in this description that military strategies are developed in isolation at each level, in truth, the process is generally an iterative one vertically and, when appropriate, horizontally as well. Unfortunately, it is often the case that all levels of the hierarchy are working with incomplete and sometimes differing information. The operational and execution level commanders are often handed only vague and general guidelines along which to develop their strategies. Finally, the process described here is largely theoretical. In practice, echelons are often skipped, and the line between strategy and tactics, poorly understood at the best of times, sometimes disappears altogether.

The class of strategies just discussed has to do with deploying and employing armed force, generally under specific sets of conditions – the classical Clausewitzian concept of military strategy, if you will. There are,

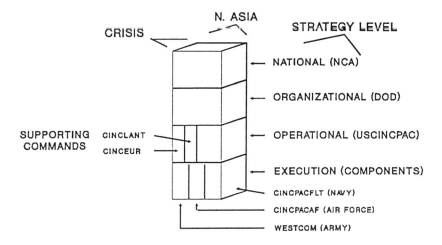

Figure 5. The Vertical Dimension of Strategy

of course, other types. There are even strategies within strategies. Employment strategies must consider numbers and types of forces; therefore, procurement strategies must be developed so that the proper resources are at the strategist's disposal, which mean budget strategies and so on.

A fairly recent categorization is called competitive strategy. Designs under this rubric are to be a combination of technological development, acquisition, and deployment strategies designed to exploit "our technological advantages . . . to cause the [enemy] to compete less efficiently or less actively . . . in military applications"[8] by rendering current Soviet (or other enemy) systems obsolete or by causing the opposing government to make dollar (or in their case, ruble) investments in new or expensive areas. For example, suppose that a new technology were available to the United States which could be developed into a novel type of weapon — one against which an enemy was unable to defend itself. If providing a defense would either be very costly or would cause the enemy to divert resources from other projects in order to develop it, use of this new technology as opposed to simply improving some current system would satisfy the competitive strategy criteria. Said another way, this theory postulates that it may be better to "hook" the mouse on a rare and expensive piece of cheese than to build another type of trap.

When all of the strategies have been developed, assessments of the manpower, money, and materials necessary to carry them out are undertaken. This leads to the final element, the acquisition of resources, whereby men and equipment are procured in the proper numbers to enable successful operations. The service secretariats and administrative organizations of the military branches (Chief of Staff of the Army, Chief of Naval

Operations, and the Chief of Staff of the Air Force and their respective staffs) bear this responsibility.

Exactly how much the unified commander gets of what he has said is needed is problematic. Although the intention of the Congress was to increase his control over at least some of the resources from a funding standpoint, there is no system in place to ensure it. The Department of Defense has required the unified commanders to prioritize their needs and the military departments to report their progress in meeting them. Experience has shown that the unified commander's needs will not be fully met until he controls his own funds, because each service uses a different procedure to attempt to balance readiness in the near term with the research and development efforts necessary to prepare for the long term within the fiscal targets provided or anticipated. Quite obviously, the individual services possess a significant amount of leverage because of the relatively large procurement budgets available, as well as the procurement authority which allows them to buy what they desire.

Theoretically, only those resources which are, or will be, useful in the execution should be procured. That is to say, strategies should drive acquisition. In the real world, however, the reverse tends to be true, because while strategies can be changed rapidly, forces and their equipment cannot.[9] Weapon systems, for example, are designed to last for a substantial period of time. Even this limitation could be overcome if it were not that costs have risen so that the investment in a specialized resource, whether it be a machine or a man, precludes an early retirement or abandonment. Given, then, that the required resources can or will not be provided in many cases, objectives must be altered to reflect what is possible. It is important that the reach not exceed the grasp.[10]

The same may be said respecting strategies. Governmental bodies in general, and the military in particular, tend to be conservative, so that each new technology is more likely to find favor if it makes the execution of existing strategies easier rather than requiring the development of novel ones, even if they might be more effective.[11] This is as true in the United States, that citadel of technological change, as it is anywhere else. The outcome, of course, has been that strategies at all levels of the strategic hierarchy tend to change only at the margin.

So long as the conditions for which the strategy was designed are not altered, no harm is done. However, when significant changes occur in the list of enemies, in their capability to threaten the United States, or in the types of conflicts anticipated, then inflexibility can be dangerous. Reducing that danger requires both thought and planning in advance of any need. Are the organization and the developmental process in place up to this challenge?

CHAPTER IX

Problems in Developing Military Strategy

In the strategically stable world of the last forty or so years, the national military strategy and the plans for implementing it have remained, for all practical purposes, the same as when they were initiated in the aftermath of World War II.[1] Fear of Soviet hegemony in a war-torn and, in many ways, helpless Europe led to the conclusion that a Sovietized Continent would pose a direct threat to the interests of a United States just rid of the Nazi threat. Out of that apprehension came the strategy of containment.

The addition of nuclear weapons to arsenals added a different dimension to the national military strategy in that its objective of deterring war with the Soviet Union to prevent the utilization of what were viewed as cataclysmic weapons became paramount. In support of the strategies of deterrence and containment, a line was drawn on the West German border and the nuclear umbrella was raised over Western Europe. The forces and type of equipment necessary to make the strategy and resultant plans work were assembled and put in place; U.S. forces were posted on the East/West border as a potential "hostage" ensuring a continuing American interest in events there, alliance relationships were cultivated so that the illusion of strength and commitment could be maintained, and the triad of nuclear response forces were aimed at specific targets in the USSR.[2]

These latter so-called strategic forces constitute both a construct of force, and weapons of war separate from all others; they are at once part of an arsenal and an arsenal apart. That is, units are staffed by members of the Navy and Air Force, and the weapons they man are procured from the same Defense budget as are conventional ones. However, strategic forces are a separate element in the budget; they are centrally controlled and exist, in most people's minds, only to deter.[3] They are forces considered most effective if they are never used. Strategic forces respond only to NCA direction, and all employment and targeting plans are developed by a staff designed and staffed specifically for that program. Weapons are currently targeted against the Soviet Union and the Warsaw Pact, but could be targeted elsewhere.

Strategy and plans for the general-purpose forces, on the other hand, are developed at the operational and execution levels, where changes in the lists of friends (or enemies), and in forces available create opportunities and demands for formal changes. For example, until the early seventies, the People's Republic of China was the subject of war plans. Once relations had been reestablished, plans were set aside. Each unified commander maintains an organization on his staff charged with creating or modifying strategies and the implementing plans of this type. This organization will have the assistance of members of the component commander's staff (either active in the development or, at least, active in the review process). Theoretically, the group follows a systematic process of formulating goals and specific objectives, analyzing the environment (including strengths and weaknesses of both enemy and its own forces), and developing strategic alternatives. These alternatives are then evaluated on the basis of suitability (does it meet the objective?), feasibility (can it be carried out?) and desirability (is the cost of achieving it acceptable?); one or several are selected.

An example of strategy alternatives at the operational level is as follows. Assume that the objective (specified by senior commanders) is the elimination of operations from one of the enemy's bases. One strategy for accomplishing this objective would be to attack the base directly with combined land- and sea-based forces. An alternative strategy would be to attempt to isolate it by denying it resupply of any kind, that is, by interdicting the land, sea, and air routes serving it. While both might meet the objective (suitability) and could be executed (feasibility), the former might accomplish the objective rapidly, but with significant losses of men and equipment, while the interdiction action might suffer fewer losses, but would take much longer. In this case, if time were not a factor, the relative costs in terms of attrition anticipated could form the basis for choosing one alternative over the other (desirability).

Once appropriate strategies are formulated and evaluated to the extent possible at the operational level, they will be forwarded up the chain of command to the organizational level for review and approval, and then down to the component commander for his use as guidance in developing the execution level strategy, if it is to be differentiated.[4] If so, the component commander will put his planning staff to work devising strategies to carry out those of his superior.

Continuing the above example, assume direct attack has been selected as the operational strategy. Alternatives available at the execution level might include attacking overtly with conventional air strikes or using clandestine operations conducted by special forces. Once a selection has been made, specific forces can be assigned and movement and logistic support directed. The task force commander who will carry out the mission would then do the tactical planning required for engagement. At these two levels, the operational and execution, the planning for force employment is military strategy in its original sense, that is, the moving of forces to checkmate the enemy or to engage him in battle.[5]

This process just described functions well in a routine mode when time for careful consideration is available and the enemy is a traditional one. It seldom is allowed to operate in crisis situations. When these occur, all or much of the strategy development and alternative selection of actions to be carried out by the component commander gets done at the highest levels of government, on the fly, with tactics sometimes being dictated directly to the commander on the scene. In the heat of action or crisis, direct intervention by senior authority is at least understandable and, perhaps even occasionally necessary in this era of extreme international sensitivity to nearly any national act.[6] The NCA obviously has the right to proceed in that fashion, but in so doing, it may well deny to itself the perspectives and input of experienced practitioners along the chain of command. While in the potential high-stakes game of nuclear confrontation, the civilian heads of government are responsible for making the agonizing, and perhaps suicidal, decisions regarding use or nonuse of their arsenals, military officers must ensure that all of the relevant and best information and military advice is available to them.

Strategy development takes place in yet another way. Individual services formulate it when they are dissatisfied with their lot or feel they are lacking in guidance. Once developed, the sponsor then attempts to "sell" it to the wider defense establishment or to the Congress, whichever seems most receptive. The Air Force was successful with this approach when it created and sold the long-range bombing strategy immediately after World War II. A more recent example of this phenomenon, and the one most discussed over the last several years, is the so-called Maritime Strategy, formally announced in 1983, which was developed entirely within the U.S. Navy. Although its specific genesis is somewhat obscure, the visibility and attention given it have ensured that it has, as the saying goes, a thousand fathers.

The Navy was sailing in stormy weather during the years immediately following World War II. It was forced to fight off an Air Force achieving dominance in the strategic role and a general attitude that nuclear weapons had made conventional forces extremely vulnerable, if not obsolete. Fortuitously, the North Koreans picked this time to attack the South. The resulting conflict, as was to be the case in Vietnam nearly twenty years later, provided a convenient showcase for the World War II-style projection of naval power ashore; amphibious landings, carrier-based aircraft attacking shore targets, and shore bombardment by surface ships again shone.[7] These opportunities showed the value of the Navy, but the argument could be made that they were isolated cases.

When the inadequacy of the massive retaliation method of deterring war was exposed and conventional forces again became popular in the early 1960s, the focus of general war planning again centered on the continent of Europe, where the Navy's role in a traditional war would require that nearly all forces be devoted to maintaining the freedom to operate on the high seas, a critical capability during the conflict which was envisaged. Controlling the sea would be necessary to maintain the flow of both strategic materials to the United States, and troops and material from there to support the conflict in Europe (movement by sea remains the only way to manage the volume envisioned). If the Navy were to be shaped for this kind of work, it would have a different appearance than it had. However, the useful life of ships, successful lobbying in Congress, and the requirement for periodic shows of force with naval units combined to ensure that the Navy of the post–Vietnam era looked very much like it did at the end of World War II (although smaller), albeit with more modern ships carrying sophisticated weapons.[8]

The Soviets, meanwhile, for reasons of their own (perhaps they rediscovered Mahan or were engaging in a "competitive" strategy themselves), had begun building a sizable fleet that, although it began life defensive in nature, appeared to be changing in such a way that it eventually might, if the direction continued, mirror the U.S. fleet in many ways. The Soviet Pacific Ocean fleet seemed to benefit most from this expansion. After decades of the Pacific being an American "lake," a genuine threat appeared to be emerging.

Despite this changing threat environment, the focus of the U.S. military planning continued to be on Europe so that, in the late 1970s, the central missions of the Navy remained as they had been. This did not suit the Commander-in-Chief, U.S. Pacific Fleet, the Navy component commander in the Pacific theater, who did not want to transfer and thus "lose" his forces to the Atlantic theater in wartime; he was convinced that there was an important role for them "at home" in the Pacific, particularly in light of the expanding Soviet fleet. Rational tasks for those forces in the event of a conventional war with the Soviet Union were needed. Several members of the Admiral's staff went to work and devised an alternative strategy which, it was felt, more usefully employed Pacific Fleet forces in the theater, with the added virtue of supporting any war in Europe, albeit indirectly. This strategy, offensive in nature as opposed to the essentially defensive one in the European theater, was first exposed within the Pacific Fleet and then to the service at large, where it generated a lot of argument.[9]

In 1979, threatened with further reductions of what seemed to be a continuously shrinking Navy, the Chief of Naval Operations (fortuitously the aforementioned Commander of the Pacific Fleet who had been elevated to the position the year before), began actively espousing the concept of "seizing the initiative" and taking the fight to the enemy, principles at the root of the Pacific Fleet strategy.[10] Shortly thereafter, the recently installed Reagan administration publicly revived the requirement for a 600-ship Navy, and the newly appointed Secretary of the Navy, John Lehman, set out to make it happen. The offensive concept of the Pacific Fleet strategy was seized upon and, with just a little more work, was extended worldwide.

The Strategy, Plans and Policy Division of the Plans, Policy and Operations directorate of the Chief of Naval Operations staff (OP-60) (not in the operational, that is, war-fighting chain of command at all, but part of the administrative chain), with assistance as required from several other quarters, developed and published the Maritime Strategy.[11] The strategy, it was declared, was not designed as a war plan, but rather "offer[ed] a global perspective . . . to operational commanders and provide[d] a foundation for advice to the National Command authorities."[12] Some specific benefits did accrue to the Navy as a result of having formulated this strategy. Foremost among those was that having such a concept allowed for rationalizing and directing programs to buy, upgrade, or develop arms and other equipment.[13] Second, such a statement served to focus and stimulate thinking among Navy leaders about methods and means for executing them. Finally, it became an important guide for training and tactical development.

The specifics of the Maritime Strategy will not be presented here, nor will its merits be argued. Suffice it to say, the Navy now had a concept with which it could justify nearly every move it made. It stirred the strategists, professional and amateur, into producing numerous articles and a book or two on both sides of the issue. Its critics, and there were (and are) many, saw it as dangerous for a number of reasons, not the least of which is that, despite words to the contrary, it was uncoordinated with the other services. However, there is no doubt that it has stimulated a strategic dialogue in the maritime arena. This saga of the Maritime Strategy is a perfect example of how uncoordinated (not to say uncontrolled) military strategy development can be. The story here is not about duplicity on the military side, but about failure on the political. Because the civilian leaders of government have been unwilling to develop a specific and explicit national strategy upon which to base long-term military and foreign policies, organizations are free (and in some ways encouraged) to interpret the world in any way they choose. Not surprisingly, most will opt to define it to their own benefit but will be careful not to rock the boat too much because stability in plans is important as well.

For example, national military strategy relative to the Soviet Union remained static for nearly twenty-five years in the relative stability of the Cold War years; changes at all levels tended to be minor and the creative side of the development process went largely unstimulated. Those tweaks which occurred tended to address new methods of execution made possible by technological advances, rather than substantive change.[14] Stability was important because the armed forces were structured to carry out the containing and deterring strategies.

While a strategy could be changed almost with the stroke of a pen, it might take years to alter the force structure to one suitable for carrying it out. Therefore, strategic thought has not done much except refine techniques when adjusting the composition and armament of standing forces. The prepared defenses, forward-based troops, and forward deploying naval units established in the mid-fifties continued. This meant that the United States has been prepared to counter at least the early acts of a nuclear war, somewhat prepared to fight a general, or large-scale, conventional war, but unprepared, psychologically as well as otherwise, for conflicts of the limited or low-intensity variety. As we have seen, all signs point to these as the types of conflict in which the United States will find itself in the years ahead.[15]

If strategies predated the crises that spawn conflicts, ad-hoc responses would be reduced (if not eliminated) and the likelihood of successful action enhanced. In order for this to be, it is necessary to have strategies developed, evaluated, and available to execute when the national interests of the United States are threatened. Unfortunately, the system in place for formal strategy development does not appear up to the challenge just described. The staff of the Senate Armed Services Committee, after studying the operations of the Department of Defense, declared that its strategy development capability was "ineffective." This grade was assigned by the staff beause they found a programming and budgeting dominance, a lack of management discipline, a weak strategic planning tradition, and incomplete policy and planning guidance working through inadequate planning "machinery."[16]

Similar criticisms of the organizational structure and processes in the Department of Defense have appeared before. Indeed, numbers of reviews, both external (the Packard Commission) and internal (most recently the Defense Management Review, or DMR, called for by the Packard report and the Goldwater-Nichols Defense Reorganization Act of 1986) have focused on these elements (among others). Some changes have been made in procedures over the years, often for the better, but, somehow, processes seldom seem to improve over the long haul. It may be that the problem lies less with the procedures than with the people charged with carrying them out because "the strategy process ... is vulnerable at every stage to the variables of human perversity. There is no adequate or structural safeguard."[17]

Strategy development typically requires an ability to look ahead. Indeed, if strategies are to be readied in advance, the range of plausible world conditions that might require action must, in some way, be anticipated. This would require studying dozens, perhaps hundreds, of possible world states rather than the handful, generally of the "worst-case variety," typically available. Humans may not be up to the task.

Developers, like all humans, are susceptible to the vagaries of cognitive processes which may block or interfere with their ability to plan. There are, for example, tendencies to reduce the complexity of a situation by systematically eliminating factors until only some skeleton remains, then doggedly maintaining that simplified view, even in the face of contradictory information. Another tendency is to seek historical precedents with such single-mindedness that exact analogies end up being drawn without any consideration of variations, or outright change in the context or environment. Various types of bias also creep in. Here, an individual tends to see reality as he needs to, not necessarily the way it actually is. This may be done to satisfy personal interests or may simply be done to understand or accept complicated situations.

Beyond all these human and personal foibles, developers are immersed in the larger American strategic culture discussed in preceding chapters. This immersion creates further distortion as reality is interpreted through the cultural structure. That is, since the individual conceives of the world in a specific way, real events are anticipated, perceived, and evaluated within that context. A prime example would be the crediting of others with a propensity for doing the same as we do, sometimes called mirror-imaging. Seeing an opponent in this way may well be convenient, but it is invariably inaccurate and may, in the final analysis, prove dangerous.[18] Not every culture shares our particular values or our view of the propriety of certain actions.

After the conclusion of World War II, Admiral Chester Nimitz, who had been the Commander-in-Chief in the Pacific, stated that because war with the Japanese had been so extensively war-gamed beforehand, the only surprise had been the kamikaze attacks. In that same theater, the Japanese Army conducted what became known as the Bataan "death march" during which several thousand Americans and more Filipinos were killed or left to die along the route. Viewed through our cultural prisms, the fanaticism exhibited by the Japanese pilots who were trained to, and did, deliberately crash into U.S. ships was inexplicable, while the treatment of men and women during the march who were, by our definition, prisoners of war, barbaric. Yet the actions of the Japanese in both instances should not have been particularly surprising in the light of their culture. While the specific events may not have been foretold, the commitment to country and culture and the disdain for the act of surrender could have been.[19]

Finally, there is the simple matter of frame of reference. Because all humans tend to be slaves to their own experience, recommendations they develop will reflect institutional biases. That is, military people will most often promote military solutions, while diplomats will favor diplomatic ones. This is not to say that either, or both, would be necessarily inappropriate. Rather, it is to note that with this condition operating, it may be difficult to figure out a solution which covers all the dimensions of a problem.

These blocks and biases working on strategists steeped in the strategic culture all shape the individual's "rational" assessment of the manner in which goals, technology, geography, the balance of forces, and uncertainty interact in various situations. They also affect his or her ability to "imagine" the full range of enemy actions possible or successful countering responses to them.[20] As if these strategic filters were not enough, the output of any one strategist is typically reviewed by a series of seniors who bring more (and perhaps different) perspectives (and biases) to the problem.

In the midst of a technological revolution of sorts, the basic processes by which man solves problems have remained pretty much the same. In a world changing in serious ways those techniques need to be challenged. Communications are nearly instantaneous; little need escape notice, if not attention. In this sort of environment, the ability to postulate and prepare for alternative futures to protect and defend the interests of the United States is a necessary quality. It would seem that some help is needed.

CHAPTER X

Selecting Strategies

Simply developing strategies will not be enough; their effectiveness in achieving the desired objective(s) must be evaluated before they are accepted, not after they are in place.[1] These assessments should not be one-time activities; rather, they should be accomplished on a continuing basis to ensure that strategies remain viable in the face of changing conditions. Currently, evaluation is spotty at best. Whereas what passes for national security strategy has been critiqued almost continually in books, periodicals and in the opinion and editorial (OpEd) sections of newspapers, its constituent parts, the national military strategy and foreign policy, have been evaluated only in the wake of some disaster or debacle.[2] Theater and area strategies are looked at more routinely.

The method chosen and the depth and breadth of examination of each case should be dictated by the type of the strategy in question and influenced by the level of specificity in statements of objectives and of detail in employment concepts. National military strategy objectives, for example, tend to be abstract (deter, defend, etc.), and the directions for employing forces, to the extent they exist at all, will be very general. At the next lower level, the organizational, objectives remain intangible (destroy, neutralize), but may contain specific directions (invade country X, etc.); and, although forces will be aggregated, they will be recognizable entities (specific fleets, armies, etc.). At the succeeding two levels, statements of objectives and employment of forces become better defined. Because the specificity has increased, the level of evaluative activity can also increase because there are tools available to assist at these levels.

However, there are none for evaluating high-level strategies. Typical quantitative analytic techniques are not well suited to handling the large combinations and permutations resulting from the variety of geographic, social, and military force issues which tend to dominate, particularly at the national strategy level. In addition to the paucity of tools, a lack of evaluative prowess may exist at these levels because today's strategist "tends to be conversant with the arithmetic of a counterforce duel but not with the politics, culture, or history of particular societies," all of which can be meaningful in the success or failure of any particular strategy.[3] Strategies are more analytically tractable at the lower levels in the strategic hierarchy; operational and execution level ones are amenable to some evaluation. The methods of evaluation available here include exercises, simulations, games and analytic models. The relative merits of each are depicted in Figure 6.[4]

Evaluative Tools

Exercises are the most realistic of the methods because forces are actually moving and maneuvering while vulnerable to malfunction, misdirection, mishandling, and chance. At the same time, the scope of the strategy or issue being examined must be limited precisely because of these elements. It takes time to move between points geographically and to prepare and execute other actions. Actually carrying out the movements involved in many strategies could take days, perhaps weeks, and be very costly in the bargain. For example, the movement of a carrier battle group from the West Coast of the United States to the Indian Ocean as part of a strategy would take more than two weeks if the group did nothing but sail directly there. In other words, there are some real limits to the use of personnel and the logistic support of the force.

Simulations can be considered fairly realistic mainly because the treatment of forces or units incorporated typically ensures that they behave quite realistically. Aircraft simulators, for instance, are remarkably like the real thing. At the same time, units can be moved around rapidly, and data bases appropriate to nearly any geographic position are available. Contemporary simulations are nearly all computer-driven and are made up of an assortment of models of interactions of all types: forces with forces, forces with the weather, and so on. They are capable of being designed so as to be used for analysis.

Games typically are unrealistic to only moderately realistic. Some games are entirely theoretical. In others, like war games, attempts are often made to duplicate environmental (converting ordinary rooms to appear like command centers, providing genuine communications equipment, etc.) and operational conditions (using actual war plans in the examination, ensuring force models move and maneuver in a realistic fashion, etc.) experienced in real life, but there are limits. There need be none on the geography of the problem or on force movement. Forces may be jumped around anywhere, maneuvered for a time, then jumped again. However, they do not generally produce data suitable for rigorous statistical analysis. While problems can, in many instances, be easily stopped, reset, and played again (repeated), it is extremely difficult to replicate a game because of the

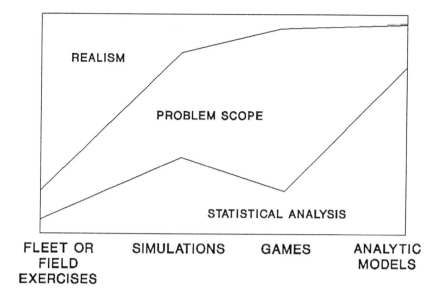

Figure 6. Relative Advantages of Evaluative Methods

myriad of variables to be considered, particularly those associated with human decision making.

Reality is represented in most analytic models only in the context or problem environment and in the characteristics of platforms, although even these may not be exact. The problem scope could be larger than in exercises, but would typically be more restrained than in simulations or games. One can usually pick any spot on the globe, or any interaction set (so long as the model can accommodate the number of entities) and run them. These models are designed to accommodate replication and statistical treatment, thus are particularly appropriate for mathematical analysis. Combinations of these methods, such as war gaming incorporating analytic assessment models, accounting for other activities via simulations or models in the middle of an exercise, all enhance the examination, but none are able to treat it fully.

Exercises range in scope and complexity from command post exercises (CPXs) which, as the name implies, involve only personnel normally in the centers where largely communications and decision systems are flexed (these are very similar to many war games), to major field and fleet exercises where troops, ships, and aircraft move and ordnance is delivered against practice targets. In the latter type, as many forces as possible are assembled and tasked to proceed as though executing all or some part of the strategy. Friendly forces are often used to portray the enemy and carry out mock attacks on the main force. There is no live firing (unless at a practice target) and no forces are lost (except through accidents). There are often complex data collection plans with subsequent efforts made to "reconstruct" the exercise in order to provide a record of events for postexercise analysis.

The difficulties encountered in evaluating strategy in this way include achieving the proper scale of warfare, ensuring sufficient realism, and avoiding compromise. As regards the first, rounding up the actual forces—not only in number but type—that would execute, for example, theater-level strategies, and making these ships, aircraft, and men all available at a specific time and place would be a daunting, if not impossible, task. Further, the cost in time, money, and opportunity would not be worth the effort, particularly since the level of realism is still not likely to be very high.[5] Determining the outcome of "engagements," for example, is very messy. Since no live firing takes place, giving proper credit for accuracy and timeliness in the mock battle is difficult and often contentious. Arbitrary decisions concerning who shot first and to what effect must be made continually, resulting in some units being forced to the "sideline" (simulating out of action due to battle damage) for a specified period of time to enforce consequences that would have occurred in real battle. Unfortunately, since the number of forces (see scale above) would quickly dwindle, the "damaged" must be returned to the problem, often rapidly and without much regard for positional probability. For example, an "enemy ship" may be reactivated within weapons range of an exercise ship.

Reconstruction in practice turns out to be a very difficult undertaking, since differences in geographical positions, reconciliation of the varying levels of knowledge of participants at specific times, and the necessity for documentation of the decision process in real time pose formidable obstacles. Finally, it may not be desirable to test a strategy in the field for fear of exposing its intricacies to an enemy in advance.[6] Exercises are useful for training personnel and for practicing skills. Whatever evaluative potential exists lies more in examining the outcome of issues involved in a battle than in a campaign. For all of these reasons, exercises are seldom, if ever, designed solely for strategy evaluation purposes.

The expense and effort of organizing an exercise may be foregone by resorting to one or more of the other methods of evaluation; simulations, games, or analytic models. The three are interleaved to a certain extent. Generally speaking, a game always involves simulation (although a simulation need not be a game), and both utilize analytic models where possible. All are attempting to simulate reality using basic models, which are representations of an object, process, or situation within which as many of the important features or properties of the original as possible are included. As we have seen, these methods are arrayed along the reality spectrum downstream from live exercises. Whereas in real war forces routinely maneuver, fire, attrite, and suffer attrition, all the while enduring the vagaries of human conduct, mechanical error, and pure chance, in the necessarily structured environment of simulation, modeling, and gaming there is often little, if any, representation of these imponderables of conflict, what Clausewitz called the "friction" of war.[7]

Simulations, games, and analytic models run the gamut from unstructured verbal or written interchanges to complex mathematically based formulations performed manually, either with computational assistance or solely on a computer. While there are similarities among these applications, there are also significant differences. However, all are

> efforts to represent a system or organization in such a way that it can be studied precisely to yield data for which general relations can be declared, or from which a greater detail or level of comprehension is afforded the analyst in his efforts to uncover parametric interactions.[8]

Most incorporate basic models of systems, concepts, or processes which may be verbal, analytic, or mathematical, as simple as a picture or diagram or as complex as a large analog or digital simulation. The verbal model is strongest in handling nuances, subtleties, and details, but often is weak in precision and logic; on the other hand, mathematical models are precise, logical, and concise, but describe poorly. Mathematical models attempt to represent structures and events in mathematical forms. They are used to represent and then analyze hypothetical and real processes, systems or events over time. The first attempts at using mathematical models in a military environment employed the Lanchester equations drawn from Frederick Lanchester's work, *Aircraft in Warfare*, published in 1916. Lanchester was a British engineer who developed algebraic equations to calculate the "fighting value" of units, which were then used in Lanchester's "law" to represent the combat strength of a force. Unit "strengths" were compared to determine the likely victor in any contest between units.[9] Picture or diagram models are often used to describe or provide a context. Maps and flow charts, for example, add to games and simulations and to post-event analysis. Analog models reproduce the significant characteristics of the real thing in three dimensions (wind tunnels and scale models are examples), or are real situations sufficiently similar to others so as to sustain analogies. Digital models use numerical descriptions of the processes and are based on and executed by computers.

Simulations

A simulation is the representation of a system or object by another system or object which behaves or can be made to behave like the original.

Simulations (particularly computer simulations) grew in importance in the analytical community during the 1950s and 1960s. They are best used in examining complex situations when direct, first-hand observation is not possible. A good simulation is the result of identifying critical factors and obtaining accurate estimates of their values. By using computer simulations, experience may be gained while making mistakes without having to bear the cost entailed if these errors occurred in the real world. Only a few simulations are capable of handling the breadth of most strategies, although there are many pretenders.

Games

Games involve humans playing roles, including themselves, in a situation (context) that can be either simulated or genuine. For our purposes, there are only two forms of games, the mathematical one based on game theory, and the more traditional war game. Game theory, which originated with mathematician John von Neumann and economist Oskar Morgenstern in 1944, is based on the concept that since games contain many of the elements present in all conflicts, studying the participants while they are playing may help in understanding strategic interactions. For example, poker is much like military conflict. Players have opposed interests (each wants to win); some elements are under the individual's control while others are not, and information available is not complete nor necessarily accurate (if it is, it is called "perfect"). The structured games which grew out of applying game theory treated broad classes of events according to fairly abstract models which follow very precise rules. In game theory, for example, a "strategy" is a plan so perfect that nothing (including enemy action) can upset it. Game theory supposes two types of games, the zero-sum, two-sided game (representing pure conflict) where the gains of one side are the losses of the other (e.g., chess), and the non-zero-sum game where decisions are required which will not result in an absolute win or loss, but where players attempt to gain as much as they can (or lose as little). This type of game may be terminated or resolved by enforceable agreement. In 1960 Thomas Schelling raised the possibility of applying game theory to strategic analysis. Critics worry about the assumption of player rationality, upon which the game rests. Each actor is assumed to "know what he wants, know what actions are available to him, [and be] able to calculate without passion or other distraction."[10] Game theory has only been used sparingly and generally only in an academic setting.

The second form, the war game, is better known and much more widely used. It has been defined as "a simulation, by whatever means, of a military operation involving two or more opposing forces, using rules, data and procedures designed to depict an actual or real life situation."[11] The earliest war games, reportedly invented by the Prussians in 1811, were played on sand tables with miniature cannon and lead soldiers. They were tactical games which became very structured the more the developers strove to make them realistic. In fact, they became so patterned and were encumbered with so many rules that the effort to learn how to play exceeded that expended playing. By 1876 a "free" game had been constructed that relaxed the rules and encouraged freedom of movement and play.

Around 1848, the Prussians used war gaming strategically by playing through a hypothetical war with Austria. Nearly all major nations were employing war gaming in the early decades of the twentieth century. Russia gamed its campaign plan designed for use against the Germans in 1914, uncovering some weaknesses in the plan in the process. Unfortunately, they went uncorrected; when the Russians attacked, the disaster which had occurred during the gaming unfolded in much the same way in real life. War gaming was used extensively for examining plans by the German Army and Navy prior to and during both world wars. Unlike the Russians, however, the Germans generally made adjustments where indicated. Japan's military also used this technique in the 1930s and early 1940s prior to attacking Pearl Harbor, the Philippines, and other locations in the Far East.

War gaming in the United States began at the Navy's War College at Newport, Rhode Island, in 1866 and in the Army at nearly the same time. Army games in the 1880s used maps with colored blocks for troops and included the use of attrition formulas to judge losses. This more engaging form was brought to the Naval War College in 1889, where it was quickly adapted and replaced the cardboard ships being moved across paper. Gaming quickly gained acceptance and the annual "problem" (exercise) of the Navy soon became a war game. Manual games continued to be played at Newport until the late 1950s when it became clear that the complexity of operations had surpassed the ability of the nonautomated game to represent them. Electronic assistance was added and systematically upgraded, as technology and funds permitted.

War gaming remains much in vogue in the U.S. military, particularly in the Navy where, at the Naval War College, it is a year-round activity. Officers travel from the fleets and the Washington area to participate in strategy and weapon system evaluations. Gaming is also conducted in the other services and at the joint level, including at the unified commander's headquarters in the Pacific (USCINCPAC) where operational level strategy is "gamed." Some games remain manual and relatively unsophisticated. However, the general direction is toward computer-based games in which many fairly detailed interactions can occur and the outcome on many variables can be tracked and recorded as events occur.

Analytic Models

Yet another method for strategy analysis is the analytic model. The models used in this technique would be those best suited for examining quantifiable issues, that is, those which include elements that can be represented numerically and for which some measures of effectiveness can be developed. Measures of effectiveness (MOE) are specific variables chosen to represent an action because outcomes can be quantified in some way. The relative "worth" of one action over another may be judged by comparing the values achieved by each on some MOE (numbers of towns captured, number of ships sunk, etc.).

Selecting MOEs is not always an easy task because strategies, particularly those at high levels, are often developed to make possible the achievement of some abstraction (peace, for example, or freedom) seldom capable of direct measurement. When this is the case, the choice of outcome to represent the abstraction is of utmost importance, for it must be unambiguous. For example, if the absence of war is to be used as an indirect measure of the existence of peace in the world, the term "war" must be rigorously defined. Are only declared wars to be counted? Should any contest of arms be considered? What about wars of words? Economic wars? The difficulty is clear, and using the wrong MOE, such as body count in the Vietnam War, can be misleading to others and, more significantly, may be misleading to the users of the information as well.

The validity of the model and its appropriateness to the issue at hand are both fundamental to its effectiveness as an analytic or evaluative tool. Each is important in assessing the significance to be attached to any outcome. Validity of a model, a measure of the extent to which the model truly represents what it was designed to represent, allows the user to calibrate the level of credence he or she should place in the results obtained. The higher the validity, the more believable the outcome. The appropriateness issue is concerned with whether a model chosen actually treats enough of the variables of interest. Clearly, a model may have high validity, but if its elements are not the same as those of the problem, the model is wrong for the task. For example, if the problem was one of calculating the effectiveness of a specific maneuver using a tracked vehicle and the model did not account for environmental factors which might affect the performance, such as snow, ice, or mud, then an assessment based solely on the results obtained from that model would not be credible.

This is more of a problem than one might think. Since creating models is a time-consuming, demanding, and often expensive process, the temptation is always present to add, change, or delete something from a model that already exists. Quite often a model originally developed to examine one particular system or aspect of a system is modified to be used to analyze additional dimensions of a system or problem, as part of an ever-widening series of applications, or even ending up grouped with others to form a larger model or simulation. The theory, one supposes, is that it is always better to start with something other than a clean sheet of paper. The danger, of course, is that after many changes it may no longer be clear exactly what the model represents. While this occurs quite often, the practice of developing new models that vary only slightly (if at all) from some already in existence is even more prevalent. In this case, many dollars and more hours are wasted in unnecessary duplication. In fairness to those who do this, however, it should be noted that in many cases it is done because there is no documentation to explain the inner workings of the extant model preventing potential users from assessing its validity.

In addition to these difficulties, the lack of precise information complicates evaluation. Many characteristics of a situation or elements of a problem are only known approximately. To compensate for this lack of accurate or complete information, the evaluator is forced to assign probabilities of occurrence to reduce uncertainty. In some cases these probabilities can be empirically derived; in others they must be estimated. Yet another method for accommodating uncertainty is to simply assume it away. This technique, a common one in almost all research, is acceptable provided that the relevant assumptions are clearly stated. The virtue of assuming is that it reduces uncertainty totally, at least with respect to that aspect of the problem, which may help in assessing other elements. For example, in a problem area where there may be ten variables, assuming a specific condition for five of them allows for closer examination of the remaining five. The danger here, of course, is that with each assumption made, any outcome or result only holds when that assumption is, in fact, true. Reducing uncertainty by assumption is used to a greater or lesser extent in nearly every evaluation or analysis, typically, to narrow, or "bound" the problem.

Finally, the issue of evaluating the achievement of desired objectives in the "real world" confounds. Probably the only true test of a strategy is to execute it under actual conditions. However appealing this might seem, the desire to validate strategic concepts would not be considered by most people as sufficient justification to start a war.

Evaluating Strategies

Simulation, analytic modeling, and war gaming are most often used in the military for technical evaluation of weapons systems, force structure, and doctrine. Little effort has been expended in evaluating high-level national military strategy where political and economic as well as military elements would be involved.[12] What has been done typically involves simple measures of force effectiveness, such as level of damage and loss of forces, outcomes selected to represent either the fulfillment of military objectives or the cost of doing so. The implicit assumption here is that the achievement of these objectives will have some effect on the war in the theater or on the war at large. For example, severing of sea lines of communication (slocs) between an enemy and its trading partners might be selected as a method for executing a strategy with the objective of isolating the opponent under the assumption that deprivation of oil and other imports would result in reduced manufacturing and, ultimately, reduced military capability (thus assumption was made vis à vis the Japanese in World War II). If, in fact, the assumption were true, the strategy (if executed properly) could be a successful one. If the assumption were false, the considerable resources expended to execute it would be wasted for little gain. Our current evaluation methods, whether in a simulation, an analytic model, or a war game, would permit examination of the capability to sever those slocs, but could do little in terms of verifying the assumption that it would mean anything to do so.

This illustration underlines the principal problem in strategy evaluation. The tools available are only capable of providing insight into the outcomes of force interactions, not what that force interaction might mean in a broader context. The effects of this limitation are exacerbated when the evaluation has been simplified as so often happens. Simplification may occur for a number of reasons, but it is generally for either administrative or technical ones. Administrative simplification happens when artificial time limits are imposed for some external reason such as availability of personnel for participation in a war game, or the allocation of time for scoping and analysis of the problem. The simplification is technical when the required data or the appropriate model is not available, so nominal data and a generic model are used. As discussed above, the more complex or abstract the problem, the more likely that simplification will be required to make it tractable. Bounding the scenario and making assumptions regarding conditions and performance are favorite techniques.

The term scenario, borrowed from the theater, found its way into formal military usage about twenty years ago. In the military application, the typical scenario includes a description of the geographical settings of a situation, identification of the participants and the military forces and other resources available to them along with an enumeration of the objectives of the participants. It usually marks the boundaries of what is in "play" and what is not, and establishes appropriate sequences of prior events in order to provide both a framework and starting point. Limiting the players' resources (or their capabilities) or the dimensions of the "playing field" drastically changes the scenario and the flow of action, potentially distorting the evaluation.

Unfortunately, there has been little study of the impact the scenario itself has on the outcome of an analysis or evaluation, but it seems likely that it is significant, since it frames both thinking and action.[13] Builder has stated, "The worth of an analytical study is more likely to be found in its scenario than in the quality of its arithmetic."[14] Generally, attempts are made to ensure that scenarios are plausible, but there is no requirement that they be so. Utilizing an unrealistic one for ease of play or analysis ill prepares the decision maker involved for operating in the real world.

Making assumptions narrows the problem in a similar fashion by artificially creating certainty where uncertainty exists. As the number of assumptions multiply, the freedom to generalize from the outcomes narrows such that, at some point, the resulting case will represent only a snapshot of one potential state of the world, perhaps at only one moment in time — one out of many. This is a dangerous and misleading situation:

> If the repeated political experience of the last twenty years have taught the military modeling and analytic community nothing else, it should be clear by now that for complex conflict situations, narrow technical analyses . . . are probably as bad as or worse than no analysis at all.[15]

Typically, those who develop and work these analytic tools on a daily basis labor in a field called Operational Analysis. Modern military operational analysis was born in the early days of World War II in England, where a group of scientists busied themselves trying to figure out the most effective use of a new technology called Radar. Operational analysis begat operations research in the United States, where the experience of the military man was combined with civilian research expertise in "think tanks." The field was given a shot in the arm in the 1960s when Secretary of Defense Robert S. MacNamara introduced the broader-based management and analytic style of systems analysis to the services.[16] The objective was to reduce uncertainty and identify the best choice under the stated circumstances through an analytic process.[17] Requirements for the use of its techniques were formalized in the Department of Defense through the installation of the Planning, Programming, Budgeting System (PPBS).

Operations or systems analysts, however, are not the sole users of all of these tools of evaluation. While they may "create" models and simulations and formulate war games, other less analytically sophisticated persons use the results or, in some cases, are participants in the evaluation itself. When this occurs, it is necessary that those in that group understand the limitations of the individual method.

Most importantly, the results obtained from using any of these tools ought not to be the *only* factor in any decision. All too often advocates of a system or a point of view drag out an execise, a simulation, a war game, or analytic results to "prove" their point, whereupon opponents produce their own, equally convincing, which proves just the opposite. Neither side is necessarily wrong. It is possible that both evaluations were correctly done, but that they consider different circumstances. On the other hand, it would be wrong to draw the conclusion that because these methods have deficiencies they are not useful. In truth, they can be of great value so long as the developer, the user, and the interpreter understand and account for both the strengths and weaknesses. For example, current simulations will be very helpful in rehearsing raids and attacks by familiarizing participants with the target area. Simulation networks will allow for the participation of many players around the world. Simulations of the future could allow for evaluations of nearly every kind.

War gaming is currently useful for working out procedures and stimulating strategic thought processes. However, because they are generally bounded so narrowly and cannot easily be replicated, specific tactical or strategic imperatives or "lessons" drawn from war games should be viewed with a healthy skepticism. When strategic planning is involved, "an inherent pessimism is a far less dangerous foe than an optimism bred of too many war games and canned exercises too far removed from the realities of actual combat."[18]

Whatever the system used for evaluation, the process should culminate in decisions. Unfortunately, although there has been a substantial amount of work in decision science over the past ten to fifteen years, little of it has been incorporated into the military decision-making process. That which has tends to suffer from some of the same vagaries found in the evaluation process. For example, contrary to some theories, real-life decision makers seldom try to maximize their gains, nor do they rely on "rigid, unchanging organizational standard operating procedures."[19] More typically, they call upon their experience and formulate their own rules based on it. This difference could be significant. In the contemporary strategic arena, there is concern over the fact that the entire concept of deterrence is based on the theory that decision makers will rationally calculate the expected outcomes of actions across the range of possibilities under all conditions. Since we do not make everyday decisions in that fashion, the concern is probably valid. Thomas Schelling observed that even responsible leaders in orderly governments are prone to imperfect decision making in crisis situations.

Another concern arises from the fact that there almost certainly will be individuals invited to advise in the decision process who were not involved in the planning process, and who have value systems, ideas about enemy intentions, and estimates of military capabilities which will differ from those who are involved on a daily basis. The appropriateness of a decision taken may well be based on who is participating in the process.

Human beings, whether in governments or out, tend to react to events in other than predictable ways. In crisis situations, the human tends to focus on "what to do" rather than on analyzing the situation itself; consequently, more emphasis is placed on doing *something* than on necessarily doing the *right* thing. Quite often the decision maker turns to the past in an attempt to shed light on the future. However,

> Man [often] fails to profit from the lessons of history because his pre-judgments prevent him from drawing the indicated conclusions, [or because] history will often capriciously take a different direction from that in which her lessons point.[20]

Moreover, relying on history as the *only* guide can result in not recognizing novel combinations of events as precursors to crisis, to conflict, or, in the extreme, to cataclysmic missile exchanges.

When choosing one strategy over another, as in all cases of choice, decisions tend to be made based on the information at hand. Unfortunately, what is available may not be the information most relevant to the decision. This is quite often the case because there has been little attempt to determine what the significant information *is*. In large measure, this is a tribute to the military (or human) propensity for doing what can, rather than what needs to, be done. For example, many information gathering (intelligence) systems have been designed to collect that which is easily collectible (generally hard data—frequencies, numbers, etc.), information which may or may not bear on any decision problem. Failing to very carefully define the needed elements of information results in support systems increasingly proficient in collecting, storing, and presenting, but containing much unused, redundant and unnecessary data. Indeed, by most accounts, there is an information overload—much more raw data exists than can be correlated and sifted for relevancy, never mind examining it for timeliness and utility.

Currently, interpretation of this plentiful data is rightly left to human beings, who will have varying levels of experience and expertise and be prone to the cognitive blocks discussed earlier as well as fatigue, anxiety, and the whole gamut of other human physical and psychological emotions and reactions, all of which may have an inhibiting effect. Moreover, human beings have a finite capacity for problem-solving which has been characterized by Herbert A. Simon, in his principle of "bounded rationality," in this way:

> The capacity of the human mind for formulating and solving complex problems is very small compared with the size of the problem whose resolution is required for objectively rational behavior in the real world—or even for a reasonable approximation to such objective reality.[21]

To counter individual human limits, a group is oftentimes made responsible for important decisions. However, groups, even those which demonstrate an ability to work well together, have their own problems.[22] Janis called their output "groupthink" because of a concurrence-seeking tendency operating in groups that interferes with critical thinking. Such gatherings also tend to stereotype and dehumanize those against whom they may be working and, very significantly, tend to be more extreme in recommending actions than would each member when acting individually.[23] Documentation on the outcomes of faulty decision making fill libraries across the land.

Not only are there problems with those who will make the decision, there are difficulties in understanding the decision to be made. Theory postulates that two conditions generally comprise the decision environment: situations where certainty exists (all of the possible outcomes are known), and those where uncertainty reigns (a variety of outcomes are possible). Clearly, decisions made under conditions of certainty are fairly straightforward and, therefore, relatively easy to make. Where uncertainty exists, the alternatives are less well defined and the range of possible outcomes much wider. Most decision problems in the area of strategy fall into this latter category.

In a perfect world, decisions would be made absolutely objectively. The world is not perfect, and neither are the decision makers. Decisions invariably involve a liking for one outcome over others (establishing a relative "value" of outcomes). Further, each decision maker brings an attitude toward risk to the weighing which is a product of individual experience, self-image, and the importance he attaches to the opinion of others.

Decision models are available and could be helpful in addressing these elements. There are two types useful under conditions of uncertainty, those which are deterministic or those which are probabilistic. Deterministic models are designed to represent a single state of the world where the values for the variables and constraints are treated as being known and the outcomes therefore predictable with statistical confidence. Probabilistic models address uncertainty by treating variations in both probability and the consequences of occurrence directly. This latter type is of interest to us in the evaluation of strategy. Many models require that the element assessed be represented by some measure which is unitary and quantitative (dollars are often used), forcing the user to reduce the variables under consideration to only that one measure. This trivializes the decision process to a large degree by artificially eliminating other, perhaps more significant, dimensions. Since most decisions are rarely based on the consideration of only one variable, and since military strategy seldom rests on dollars, a model which allows for the simultaneous consideration of multiple variables at the same time is more desirable.[24]

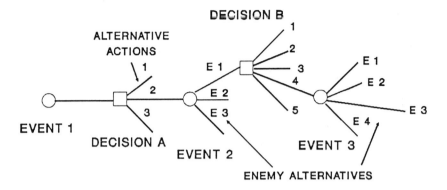

Figure 7. Decision Flow Diagram

A single decision will seldom result in the desired outcome. In warfare, the enemy will react to your action either in expected ways, or else his action will surprise and pose a completely novel situation. Surprises in warfare are not welcome and may well be disastrous, so consideration must be given to the series of decisions which typically follow because the first one was made. An event/decision stream emanates from that initial choice. Selecting and initiating an action from whatever range of options available (or thought of in the heat of the moment), evoke a reaction from those affected by the action which, in turn, creates yet another decision point, and so on. To avoid surprises to the extent possible, and to aid in selecting the alternatives most likely to bring about the desired outcome, a preliminary assessment of possible reactions to a decision can be made and an entire event/decision stream concocted. Figure 7 is a diagrammatic model of the process where circles represent events and squares decision points.

In Figure 7, precipitating event 1 has provoked decision point A. Three alternative courses of action are available as choices, any one of which will evoke some reaction from the enemy. Alternative 2 is selected, and the enemy's potential reactions postulated. A judgment is made that of the three imagined, enemy alternative E1 is the most likely for him to choose. The resulting action constitutes event 2 and presents you with the necessity for making decision B. Of the five alternatives here, number 4 will be tested, and so on. One such event/decision stream represents just one possible scenario. Selecting alternative 1 instead of 2 at decision point A and working through it in the same way would develop another possible scenario, alternative 3 yet another. As can be imagined, manually working through just one scenario normally requires the participation of several experts for an extensive period of time. Even then, given what we know about individual limitations (which may be exacerbated in a group), the confining imperatives of our strategic culture, and our mirror-imaging proclivities, the results are unlikely to account for novel courses of action on our own part, or consideration of the full range of potential outcomes from whatever the option selection might be. In lieu of having worked through the full spectrum of alternatives, serious questions arise. Has the decision maker identified all of the options available? Upon what data or information is the decision based?

Because there has been little change in strategies over time, the inadequacies in evaluation and decision-making techniques recounted here have not been a major concern. As the world order evolves, however, new plans of action must be devised which will require evaluation and, ultimately, selection of one or more for implementation. Clearly, systems superior to those in place must be ready. The consequences of choosing poorly could be serious.

CHAPTER XI

Answering the Call

Even the most casual perusal of the daily newspapers or weekly news magazines confirms the suspicion that the U.S. ship of state is sailing into uncharted waters. The political upheaval in Eastern Europe, the pending economic union of Western Europe and the continued growth of an already economically powerful Asia ensure that the shape of the world past will not be that of the future. Although it is almost certain that the United States and the Soviet Union will remain the centers of military power for some time to come, others, particularly Third World countries, are increasing their martial capabilities. At the same time, the relative significance of various elements of national power seem to be changing such that a nation's economic base will surely be most important in the long run. As economic power and the political power that flows from it continue to become more diffused, if history is any guide, that combination will beget military buildups, followed by the emergence of new superpowers, probably in both Europe and Asia.

In this more economically competitive world of the future, the uneven distribution of raw materials and natural resources may well provoke confrontations over access to them. The eight-year Iran-Iraq war provides an excellent example. World attention was focused on the two states only because of the oil in the region. In the absence of that vital resource, few would have cared. More recently, Iraq's attempted "annexation" of Kuwait and the world's collective reaction to it suggest that moving to seize control of more than one's share of an essential resource is likely to generate widespread opposition, particularly if others believe that control may be exercised to their detriment. Added to this witch's brew of potential instability will be nationalistic and ethnic movements, certain to erupt as populations attempt to shake off perceived oppression, whether by outsiders or by those within. As this is being written, ethnic forces are pulling at the seams of various Eastern European nations recently free of the Communist yoke, and forcing the formation of new entities in what was once the Soviet Union. The role the United States might play should violence break out is not clear.

Despite the alacrity with which the United States confronted Iraq, readiness to sustain an interventionist foreign policy around the globe is not in evidence. First, the cost of doing so would almost surely be prohibitive unless the armed forces essentially became mercenaries to be funded by others, as was done during the U.N.-Iraq War. However, it would not be long before those paying the bills decided that they should have some say in what gets done. Second, fear of "foreign entanglements" remains very much in the forefront of American minds despite the brevity and relative cleanliness of the most recent experience. Justifications for becoming involved anywhere will be examined in more detail each time the subject arises. In order not to squander limited material and psychological resources on causes in inappropriate places, a clarity of understanding with respect to goals and strategies for achieving them is mandatory. At the end of Chapter VIII, the question was posed whether the organization and process for developing strategy in the United States were up to the task of preparing for the next decades. Chapters IX and X lead us to the conclusion that the answer is probably no.

The Politicization of Military Planning

Preparing for the future, at least in the field of national security, does not come easily to Americans; reacting to the actions of others is much more natural. This predilection is part and parcel of the "impatient, optimistic and anti-intellectual" culture which underlies a political system based on a separation of powers and a division between "military and political authority."[1] Since the Vietnam War, the executive and legislative bodies of the federal government have been locked in a struggle over who decides what is best for the country with regard to national security. On the sidelines, each of the armed services, nominally a part of the executive, lobbies both sides with a good deal of vigor and an independent conviction that it, in any case, knows what is best.[2]

The President, the senior officer of the executive branch, the titular (if not active) head of the Armed Forces, and, arguably, the opinion leader in the country, and the Vice President are the only members of the executive branch who are elected to office. What this means, of course, is that the other principal members of the executive branch owe their allegiance not to the people, but to the President. In the legislative body, on the other hand, each member is a representative of the people by virtue of election. Getting these two power centers (not to mention the other lesser, but still powerful, concentrations of opinion sprinkled around) to agree on almost anything, particularly over the last forty or so years when one branch or the other has often been controlled by the opposing political party, is a major challenge. Political proclivities and cultural imperatives have left the country with nonspecific national interests, inadequate guidance respecting objectives, and little progress in planning for the future.

The real problem here, as in many other activities of government, is that, at bottom, all issues have become political ones, stakes in the never-ending contest for power. Each serious question to be decided generally has not only an operational and fiscal dimension, but an ideological one as well, an area where compromise is all too often viewed as surrender. In this environment where various groups are effectively serving their constituencies, the identity of the group looking out for the best interests of the country as a whole is not clear. The rule of the people was supplanted by the rule of the party long ago. That is, a single political party gets to try its hand at governing for four years, aided or obstructed (depending on your point of view) by the bicameral legislature, each chamber of which is also controlled by a party. In general, minority opinions are irrelevant. If the people are unhappy with the policies of the party in power in any one of the entities, their only defense is to vote them out as their time in office expires.[3] This should motivate incumbents to give governance their best shot (recall the belief in competition so much a part of the American culture). Unfortunately, this rarely seems the case. In practice, most spend much of their time trying to ensure reelection. Each elected member of government seems to calibrate his or her position on an issue on how it will look in a reelection campaign. This sort of arrangement makes for risk-averse, conforming behavior when the subject might be contentious, and active avocation when the issue is a popular one. This makes for near-paralysis on many important issues because officials are loath to commit themselves one way or another.[4]

One can only hope that the future will bring change. Almost half of a century after the conclusion of World War II, a new generation of leaders is waiting to assume responsibility. This cohort has grown up in a United States which has not shunned, but shouldered, its international responsibilities. Members have matured in a world thought by many to be, because of nuclear weapons, hostage to its own technology, but one which has, to date, faced that challenge responsibly. This new generation has seen a world interdependence begin to emerge, perhaps even the first stirrings of a true world community, while paradoxically, its own country has, if anything, become more polarized domestically. Even this politically sensitized leadership, however, will have difficulty in preparing the country for the future since no means is currently in place to allow for a systematic, rational, and objective assessment of what might be needed.

But all is not lost; opportunity beckons. Simply stated, the chance exists to once and, hopefully, for all, get the horse before the cart, that is, get national interests, objectives, and the supporting national and military strategy ahead of force structure and procurement. This window of opportunity is open because the disintegration of the Communist bloc in Europe has lowered the threat of superpower conflict. Although each country will surely maintain some military capability, the willingness of governments to wield it in the same way has been altered — at least temporarily, perhaps permanently.[5] Current arms negotiations, assuming they are even moderately successful, will provide more insurance. Thus, the danger of a major worldwide conflict does not seem high. There will, however, almost certainly be other crises which will occasion a national response, like the recent conflict with Iraq.

That episode illuminated many of the shortcomings of American strategic planning. First, there had been little or no preparation. Although U.S. forces had operated almost continuously in the area since the late 1970s, there were no plans to counter anyone's moves other than those of the Soviet Union. In retrospect, this seems even more surprising considering the basic instability of the general area and the historic tension between Kuwait and Iraq over borders. Second, although the term "vital interest" of the United States was bandied about, there was no explanation of what it might be. Third, the U.S. dominated what should have been a United Nations show. Fourth, the military option became the favored one in a hurry, leaving the economic blockade to be evaluated on another day. There was little debate about alternatives, the nonviolent economic sanctions were given little time to work, and attempts to resolve the issue through diplomacy were given short shrift. Finally, the long-term effects of action were not considered. It was, in short, superpowerism at its finest.

Doing strategy development differently means not only planning a route, but describing a destination. It means planning far enough ahead that one can make an orderly alteration of force levels and equipment to support what is to be done so as not to waste the investment already made. That is to say, a national security strategy for the United States must be described first, followed by a strategy for restructuring and acquisition, should any be required, and, finally, one for positioning forces to make the basic strategy work. If you pick up the problem by the force structure end of the stick, the ultimate strategy will be driven by what can be done instead of what should or needs to be done.

Restructuring Strategic Planning

The first step in the process is to form a coherent view of the world and the position of the United States in it. Once that is accomplished, a vision of the future can be developed. To complete this chore, a nonpartisan group of interested citizens should be formed to identify (using experts in particular fields as needed) specific near-, mid-, and long-term national interests and objectives, and to propose a general high-level strategy for maintaining and achieving them. This august body should be a permanent fixture (although individual members might change) and should periodically review and amend the work already done as conditions change. The entire undertaking will be contentious and need patience and cooperation on all sides, but the payoff will be worth it.[6] The hierarchy of national interests, objectives, and strategy developed by the group, after approval by both the executive and legislative bodies, should be used as a yardstick against which changing world and theater conditions are measured to determine if action by the United States is warranted. The implication here is that unless U.S. interests are being jeopardized or objectives being thwarted, events should be allowed to run their course. If there is a threat, measures appropriate to the situation should be taken.

The importance of this effort cannot be overstated. Without identification of these interests and objectives, there can be no coherent national strategy nor the military and foreign relations strategies based on it. Admittedly, the responsibility for developing a national strategy based on national interests lies with either the executive branch or with both the executive and legislative branches (depending on your position on the debate about Constitutional powers), but neither has shown themselves to be particularly adept at living up to it. Expecting the Defense Department to develop viable long-term military strategies without providing it clear objectives is an exercise in futility.[7] Once simply the nation's defense force, the military is now an integral part of both the economic and political base of the country. Its ability, under the best of circumstances, to objectively formulate the nation's strategic direction is suspect.

Once the country's needs are described, the action levels in the national security apparatus can develop their plans and identify the resources required. From the military point of view, this would involve the Department of Defense. The same sort of bipartisanship required at the national level is needed here among the Secretariat and the individual services. Military strategies should be formulated and coordinated with those of other executive departments to support objectives at the national level. The force structure and equipment needed to execute those strategies could then be identified and plans drawn to orchestrate their acquisition and maintenance.

This is not to say that strategy should be the sole dictator of what and when to "buy," because, as Francis Spinney has noted,

[S]trategy is not a separate event in an idealized sequence of discrete events; it is a way of thinking that neutralizes threats to our interests while remaining consistent with our financial, cultural, and physical limitations.[8]

Military strategy should provide the framework for the give and take of planning and procurement of military forces and equipment within the resources determined to be needed and available.[9] These requirements should be developed as far in advance of employment as possible to ensure time for proper planning and the acquisition of the specific resources. In order to ensure the proper equipment is being acquired, its need must be anticipated by predicting where and under what conditions military forces are likely to be operating in the future. Unfortunately, as discussed earlier, it will be difficult, if not impossible, for human planners to systematically and thoroughly create a representative range of alternative futures for consideration. As in many other cases, employing technology will help.

Computer systems have been available to support planning and decision processes for a number of years, but have been used simply to manipulate data, when used at all. Few decision makers have heeded the advice that

> Because the individual's information processing capabilities are limited, no responsible leader ... ought to make a policy decision without using a computer to spell out all the probable benefits and costs of each alternative under consideration.[10]

Yesterday's technology can support the decision maker by storing, recalling, manipulating, organizing, and displaying data or information tirelessly and unemotionally. Today's can give him more; systems that reason and learn.[11]

Far too little attention has been paid to that branch of computer technology called artificial intelligence (AI), which can bring these "intelligent" systems to the fray. Although research in AI has been underway since the late 1950s, the number of practical systems in any field remain relatively small and most of these "expert systems"[12] were designed to accommodate very narrowly bounded problems.[13] Such systems provide the opportunity to capture and thus retain expertise which might be lost when the individual possessing it died, was killed, or just plain was not available when it was needed. Much more seems possible. Azad Madni, an AI practitioner, visualized a time when artificial intelligence technology might provide for not only "machine-aided man," but, ultimately, "man-aided machine."[14] The state of the art is beyond the computer as memory jogger and prompter-prodder; some developmental systems are able to function as an assistant, that is, able to be used to help in doing work. The ultimate functioning will be as an associate, that is, sharing the work load, not simply assisting. Strategy developers will need this functionality.

A conceptual system to be used in strategy development would be configured to generate a set of world conditions based on various perturbations of the steady state. Each of these "event/streams," representing one alternative future, would be played out to some predetermined point (perhaps where the United States must take action). These scenarios could then be compared to identify significant commonalities and differences so that truly unique sets of potential states of the world could be isolated. This family of scenarios would benefit the developer of strategy, the strategic analyst, the systems analyst, the simulator, and the war gamer alike. Having in hand a number of alternative futures, the system would go on to develop candidate strategies which would then be evaluated by measuring their contribution toward objective achievement. One exciting aspect of generating strategies in this way would be the likelihood of producing novel ones, that is, strategies never thought of before. The result of these efforts could be catalogued in a library of alternative world states and associated strategies ready for use in crises or threat situations. This system could also be used for real-time crisis support. Here, actual events could be inserted as they occur, allowing the generation of a variety of event/streams which might eventuate. People would continue to make decisions, but at each decision point or deviation in form, the AI system could be used to examine options before action is taken.[15]

An AI system capable of such work is just over the horizon. While some developmental work would be necessary, much of the technology exists; only priorities impede its production. And therein lies the rub. In reality, it is not only the "how many" part of the Department of Defense budget request that is important, but the "what" as well. As it now stands, those systems which actually deliver ordnance against the enemy are much preferred over those which can only provide support. This may readily be seen when comparing the size, strength, and capability of the inventory of hardware (aircraft, ships, tanks, etc.) with the robustness of the command-and-control systems designed to support their use. A case can be made that this is not only short-sighted, but potentially dangerous. In this era of narrow decision "windows" caused by the proliferation of sophisticated weapons systems, commanders should have state-of-the-art reliable planning, communications, and decision support systems immediately at hand.

Until the "total" planning outlined above can be accomplished, there is absolutely no rational way to integrate the myriad needs of organizations charged with national security responsibilities. All decisions will continue to be made on the basis of individual preference, influence or cost — dubious criteria for determining the character and posture of national security forces under any conditions. More importantly, without such planning, each unusual combination of world events is likely to come as a surprise. Valuable reaction time may be lost as decision-makers grope for appropriate and possible responses. Time wasted, in this case, may be directly translated into lives, territory, or opportunities lost. Emphasizing the strategic planning process could produce a road map usable under almost any set of circumstances and a blueprint for the resources best suited for employment under each.

While there can be no doubt of the need, the likelihood of such an initiative being undertaken is close to zero. At bottom, changes in attitudes as well as behavior would be needed to pull it off—and attitudes are extremely difficult to change. In truth, there is no real constituency for looking ahead, imagining alternative futures, and assessing capabilities for meeting the challenges found there. In fact, conventional wisdom holds that events seldom conform to those upon which plans are based. There is a feeling in the military that the proper thing to do with a plan when action is required is to throw it away. It has been said that

> Operations plans, staff studies, wargame scenarios and their solutions all suffer from the same inherent weaknesses; i.e., they are all minutely conjectural. They must assume an exact sequence of future events that may never, indeed probably will never, take place.[16]

It is fair to say that, based on the discussion in previous pages, the fault may well lie with the planner, the assumer of the event sequence, not the plan. Providing the planner with an automated assistant as described above would open the opportunity to examine a multitude of sequences of events. It is likely that some would, in fact, take place. Given the uncertainty which lies ahead in this changing world, the idiosyncrasies of our strategic culture and the limitations of human planners, turning to technology for help in this important area may be the only way to conserve precious resources.

CHAPTER XII

Summing Up

The world military environment has changed drastically, from the earliest days of warfare when one warrior-king might lead a small army of his subjects against another just like him, to a time when two contemporary warrior-kings preside over a capability to eliminate each other's society, if not all those in the world. The path linking these eras is littered with obsolete weapons and antiquated ideas.

A series of revolutions have brought us to this place: a political one which resulted in massive citizen armies; an industrial one, which made possible untold numbers of weapons and equipment; and an organizational one, which promoted the use of the products of the other two. For both better and worse, these reformations have altered the world and those in it. They have, on the one hand, brought peoples and nations closer together through shared political values, rapid communications, and economic interdependence, among other things. At the same time, they have made possible the proliferation of arms throughout the world and, by so doing, helped raise genocide and fratricide to art forms. Entire populations have become inured to the violence which almost continually surrounds them.

The specter of conflict between or among those nations possessing nuclear weapons has receded to a constant, if somewhat muted, tension that provides a false sense of security to many. The availability of sophisticated, highly accurate, and extremely lethal weapons to anyone with the correct change is quickly making the world an infinitely more dangerous place for the people of all nations, large and small.

In the shadow of these menaces, truly significant changes have taken place in the world political and physical environment in just the last year. The antagonisms between East and West are ebbing as the political grip of the Communist party is loosened throughout Eastern Europe and in Russia itself. The West European states grow in strength and confidence and look forward to their economic union scheduled in 1992. Even as internal tensions continue in the People's Republic of China, the spirit of democracy lives on.

On the down side, the environment continues to be abused, resources continue to be devoured, and the gap between the haves and the have-nots continues to grow despite heightened expectations of a better life everywhere. While the superpowers work diligently toward arms control agreements of some sort, the trade in sophisticated weapons continues largely unabated, and Third World countries blithely arm themselves. In other words, all the conditions which have traditionally fostered conflict between and among states still flourish.

This brave new world finds the United States at a strategic crossroads of sorts. For the past forty-six years, the Soviet Union has been the target at which the U.S. military establishment was aimed. With this threat diminished and no adequate substitute at hand, the justification for the large military establishment erected to counter it rings hollow. However, there is danger in peremptorily applying the wrecking ball, as evidenced by the U.N.–Iraq War.

The patterns of power and influence which will emerge in the world over the next several years are shrouded in mystery. Those who are allies today may well be enemies tomorrow, and vice versa. As the world becomes an integrated marketplace, it will be very difficult to distinguish between friend and foe; in a military sense, even more so. In what surely is a sign of the coming times, a U.S. company has received a contract to upgrade five Egyptian submarines with U.S. fire control and navigation systems. The work is being done in Egypt financed by the U.S. government under the Foreign Military Sales (FMS) program. The submarines themselves are of Soviet design built by the People's Republic of China, and once refitted, will carry antiship missiles purchased from the U.S. The potential for being attacked by an enemy you took for a friend or attacking a friend you took for an enemy is increasing rapidly.[1]

Further, more nations are sporting sophisticated and deadly arms than ever before. When and in what circumstances they might be used cannot be foretold. As this continues, the margin between the military haves and have-nots will decrease, and the leverage which military forces promise with it. The balance of power between the rival alliances which developed in the decades after World War II provided a stability which underwrote such antiwar overtures as the renunciation of violence in the United Nations Charter. Today, with the demise of the Warsaw Pact and the need for a military NATO being questioned, renegade states may feel fewer inhibitions respecting the use of their militaries. While there is no possibility of these states inflicting a mortal wound to the United States, they could, nevertheless, do damage and take lives.

The making and distributing of the tools of conflict continue to be big business. Some nations are developing significant arms production industries while others, currently outside the nuclear "club," are known to be seeking either technology or materials for the development of such weapons.[2] The Soviet Union, or its successor state(s), will, despite arms control limitations, retain a substantial arsenal (as will the British, French, and Chinese), and many more nations will soon have the technical capability to acquire a modest one.[3]

If national security forces, including the military, are prepared for most eventualities, the inevitable "dithering" that typically follows the onset of crisis, or a surprise, will not put the country at a disadvantage. Although the need to prepare for a future where the direction, the type, and the magnitude of any threat to the United States or its interests may not be as plain as it has been during the past forty-plus years, it is, nevertheless, clear. The period of uncertainty ahead should give impetus to establishing a national security system effective against all comers by mandating the coordinated planning in military and foreign policy needed to ensure it. Our strategic culture, however, even under threat, does not support much advanced planning. In an environment where threats are not so obvious, it may well be viewed as an absolute waste of time. Yet it is in anticipating that true security lies.[4] Bringing about change in the strategic culture will not be a simple task.

The first step will be to face the realities of power, particularly with respect to the place of the United States in the world community. By most accounts, American power is declining, at least in relative terms. That is not to say that the United States is no longer an economic and military superpower, but other nations are developing resources and capabilities, thus increasing their ability to influence actions, economically if not always militarily. Kennedy made the case that this is a natural adjustment necessary because the status of the United States was achieved under conditions particularly favorable to its growth.[5]

The next step is to develop a tolerance for ambiguity because situations usually are neither as simple nor as complex as they are made out to be. They are seldom black and white, as we would like them to be, and, all too often, have no definable beginning or end. Every indication is that world affairs have gotten more involved, not less. Despite increased communications and voluminous information, human beings still make the decisions.

Finally, citizens must once again get involved in debates about the pressing issues of the times, and throw off the "involuntary servitude" imposed by leaders who placate rather than challenge, pacify rather than lead. Elected officials need to work toward establishing bipartisan and enduring definitions of national interests and objectives, methodologies for identifying true threats to national security and foreign policies, and national military strategies that counter these threats and meet the stated objectives. They must do this in a dialogue with the electorate.

From the warfighting perspective, the long standing preference for massing large numbers of men and equipment in an effort to annihilate an enemy must be replaced by the notion of anticipating and outsmarting him. Experience gained during the past forty years has shown that, in the types of conflict most likely to occur, massing of resources is likely to be ineffective, or what is worse, irrelevant. Adjusting to play "smart" will require developing and fielding robust strategic planning tools and command and control systems instead of more airplanes, missiles, and ships. Very expensive weapon systems may well be abused rather than used properly because an effective strategy does not exist.

Finally, it must be accepted that no one system, idea, or strategy will make the nation safe. With dozens of salesmen, each hawking his "widget" as *the* answer, the allure of the panacea exerts a powerful influence. We should have learned that there is no one answer; harnessing the atom did not do it for us!

Clearly, there is much which can be done to prepare for the years ahead. Since opportunity is the correlate of risk, making those preparations should position the United States to continue to provide leadership in an always maturing world. Unfortunately, experience tells us that, left to its own devices, the national security establishment, like its parent the federal government, is unlikely to change the way it does business without powerful incentives to do so.

Since ensuring the security of the nation is, in the United States at least, a political issue first, some leverage is available to each citizen through the electoral process. Hopefully, it will not be necessary to resort to this final refuge of a dismayed constituency. Calling representatives' attention to the inadequacies in perspective and preparation should be enough.

Let us begin with that.

Chapter Notes

Introduction

1. Quoted in Raymond Aron, *Clausewitz: Philosopher of War*, tr. Christine Booker and Norman Stone (Englewood Cliffs, NJ: Prentice-Hall, 1985), 43. The French translation is "of cannon" instead "of vision."

2. Early evidence of the deliberate use of strategy can be dated back to Alexander the Great and his campaigns of ca. 334 B.C.

3. In more recent times, its use has broadened so that, today, the word is part of the vocabulary of most disciplines and generally means a scheme or design for action to achieve high-level objectives over some, usually long, period of time. There are business, economic and political as well as military strategies.

4. *Department of Defense Dictionary of Military and Associated Terms*, JCS Pub 1 (Washington, DC: Joint Chiefs of Staff, January 1986).

5. There are several definitions of the term *strategic*. Most typically it is used to describe a global or "big picture" view, indefinite time spans, a futuristic orientation, or a "national" rather than a "local" frame of reference. That will be the use in this book. Urs Schwarz and Laszlo Hadik in *Strategic Terminology: A Trilingual Glossary* (New York: Praeger, 1966), p. 104, defined the term as "pertaining to strategy as scientifically defined" and also, in American and British use, "a journalistic term to designate any tactically dominating, or otherwise important point, object or plan." It is also used to categorize targets which have to do with the war-making capability of an enemy, and to describe long range, usually nuclear, weapons system. Friedman wrote about an "abhorrence of elaborately expressed theoretical approaches to war in the U.S." which "...may explain the devaluation of the word 'strategic' from a description of the highest form of military thinking to a description of a particular class of weapon." In Friedman, Norman, "U.S. Maritime Strategy," *International Defense Review*, vol. 18, no. 7, 1071-5.

6. Robert E. Osgood, "American Grand Strategy: Patterns, Problems and Prescriptions," *Naval War College Review*, vol. 36, no. 5 (Sept./Oct. 1983), 13.

7. United States Department of State, Bureau of Public Affairs, *Atlas of United States Foreign Relations* (Washington, DC, December 1985), 17.

8. Richard A. Stubbing with Richard A. Mendel, *The Defense Game* (New York: Harper and Row, 1986), xii.

9. *Statistical Abstract of the United States 1989*, U.S. Department of Commerce, Washington, DC, January 1989.

10. Dennis M. Drew, LTCOL, USAF, "Trends for Future Policy Consideration," in *Nuclear Winter and National Security: Implications for Future Policy* (Maxwell Air Force Base, AL: Air University Press, July 1986), 75.

11. J. C. Wylie, RADM, USN, *Military Strategy: A General Theory of Power* (New Brunswick, NJ: Rutgers University Press, 1967), iii.

Chapter I: Living in an Uncertain World

1. Resources used for this chapter include: Raymond Aron, *Clausewitz: Philosopher of War*, translated by Christine Booker and Norman Stone (Englewood Cliffs, NJ: Prentice-Hall, 1985); Robert Bigelow, *The Dawn Warriors* (Boston: Little, Brown and Company, 1969); Alastair Bushan, ed., *Problems of Modern Strategy* (New York: Praeger, 1970); Ken Booth, *Strategy and Ethnocentrism* (London: Croom Helm, 1979); Gérard Chaliand and Jean-Paul Rageau, *Strategic Atlas: A Comparative Geopolitics of the World's Powers* (New York: Harper and Row, 1985); John M. Collins, *Grand Strategy: Principles and Practices* (Annapolis, MD: Naval Institute Press, 1973); David J. Dean, LTCOL, USAF, ed., *Low-Intensity Conflict and Modern Technology* (Maxwell Air Force Base, AL: Air University Press, June 1986); Dennis M. Drew, LTCOL, USAF, Study Director, *Nuclear Winter and National Security: Implications for Future Policy* (Maxwell Air Force Base, AL: Air University Press, July 1986); Paul Kennedy, *The Rise and Fall of the Great Powers* (New York: Random House, 1987); Peter Paret, ed., *Makers of Modern Strategy: From Machiavelli to the Nuclear Age* (Princeton, NJ: Princeton University Press, 1986); Anatol Rapaport, ed., Carl von Clausewitz, *On War* (Baltimore: Penguin Books, 1968); Commission on Integrated Long Term Strategy, *Discriminate Deterrence* (Washington, DC, January 1988); Charles Alexander Robinson, Jr., *Ancient History from Prehistoric Times to the Death of Justinian* (New York: Macmillan, 1951); Joseph R. Strayer and Dana Carleton Munro, *The Middle Ages 395–1500* (New York: Appleton-Century-Crofts, Inc., 1942); Harry Summers, Jr., COL, USA, *On Strategy: The Vietnam War in Context* (Carlisle Barracks, PA: Strategic Studies Institute, U.S. Army War College, 1981); Martin Van Creveld, *Command in War* (Cambridge, MA: Harvard University Press, 1985).

2. Unfortunately, the effect on a battle of changes in any of these elements was seldom anticipated. Advances in strategic and tactical expertise were almost always the result of on-the-job training.

3. Raymond Aron, "The Evolution of Modern Strategic Thought," in Bushan, p. 25.

4. A desire to end the drain on the treasury sometimes resulted in a negotiated peace.

5. This issue is of particular interest, since it raises the matter as one of concern to all nations of the world, not just any combatants. Carl Sagan, Paul Ehrlich, and others have postulated that as few as 300 small to medium detonations might plunge the earth into a "nuclear winter" such as is described. See Sagan *et al.*, *The Cold and the Dark: The World After Nuclear War* (New York: Norton, 1984).

6. In the UN-Iraq War of 1991, Iraq set over 500 Kuwaiti oil wells afire. Some argued that the resulting heavy smoke might have the same effect. It did not.

7. The nuclear winter phenomenon has been discounted by other scientists (Dr. Edward Teller, for one) and has gotten relatively short shrift from the Department of Defense, at least in the open. To gain insight into what nuclear winter might mean see Drew, *op. cit.*

8. This may have as much to do with those in power as it does with the system in place—that is, those in power generally want to stay there. People do not make wars, governments do.

9. By U.S. definition, these are the weapons ticketed for use primarily deep inside the borders of an enemy, to be delivered by ballistic missile or Strategic Air Command bomber.

10. President Bush added the protection of American citizens and the establishment of regional stability to the list.

11. Some systems may be capable of participation in more than one type of conflict. For example, B-52 bombers, nominally strategic assets, carried and dropped conventional "iron" bombs during the Vietnam and UN-Iraq wars. This was a tactical use of the weapon system.

12. Harry Summers, Jr., COL, USA, attributed this neglect to the government's preemptive conclusion that support for the propping up of the South Vietnamese would not materialize in any case. See Summers, *op. cit.*

13. One gets the sense that the public was wary of its possible reaction to a drawn-out conflict. A collective sigh of relief was expelled when victory was declared.

14. Unconventional in this case means out of the ordinary and includes guerrilla warfare, subversion, sabotage, evasion and escape, and the gathering of intelligence in denied areas.

15. The outcomes of the invasions of Grenada and Panama by U.S. forces are not included here because they were one-time, U.S. initiated events.

16. See Chaliand and Rageau, *op. cit.*

Chapter II: The Strategic Heritage
of the United States from the Beginning to 1945

1. Resources used for this chapter include: Raymond Aron, *op. cit.*; Alastair Bushan, ed., *op. cit.*; James Chace and Caleb Carr, *America Invulnerable* (New York: Summit Books, 1988); Kent Roberts Greenfield, *American Strategy in World War II: A Reconsideration* (Baltimore: Johns Hopkins University Press, 1963); Don Higginbotham, *The War of American Independence* (New York: Macmillan, 1971); Walter Millis, *Arms and Men* (New York: Putman, 1956); Allan R. Millett and Peter Maslowski, *For the Common Defense* (New York: The Free Press, 1984); Andrew P. O'Meara, Jr., COL, USA, "Strategy and the Military Professional, Part I," *Military Review*, vol. LX, no. 1 (Jan. 1980), 38–45; Peter Paret, ed., *op. cit.*; Geoffrey Perret, *A Country Made by War* (New York: Random House, 1989); Anatol Rapoport, ed., Carl von Clausewitz, *op. cit.*; John F. Reichart and Steven R. Sturm, eds., *American Defense Policy*, 5th ed. (Baltimore: Johns Hopkins University Press, 1982); Urs Schwarz, *American Strategy: A New Perspective* (Garden City, NJ: Doubleday, 1966); Russell F. Weigley, *The American Way of War* (New York: Macmillan, 1973); T. Harry Williams, *The History of American Wars from 1745 to 1918* (New York: Alfred A. Knopf, 1981); Martin Van Creveld, *op. cit.*

2. After the French Revolution in 1789, nonprofessional armies became even more prevalent, and, from the American Civil War on, most were raised through some sort of conscription.

3. All the colonies except one had such compulsory laws. Service was voluntary in Quaker Pennsylvania.

4. Higginbotham, 7.

5. In the absence of any unifying or central agency, each colony assumed the responsibility for raising and supporting its own troops.

6. The Congress had no legal standing until the Articles of Confederation were drafted in 1781.

7. There is speculation that the principal motivation for such an act was to gain assistance from European countries who would not aid in healing a breach between Great Britain and her colonies, but might well if permanent separation were the goal.

8. The British commanders, at the same time, were proceeding slowly. A defeat would puncture their carefully nurtured mystique of invincibility and, equally important, their forces could not sustain the attrition sure to occur if they were too bold. The British adhered to the dictum that a general should fight only when forced to, or if the odds were heavily in his favor. A sort of slow dance ensued. See Higginbotham, 76.

9. See Weigley, 43.

10. Peter Paret, "Frederick the Great, Guibert, Bulow: From Dynasties to National War," in Paret, ed., 91.

11. In John Shay, "Jomini," in Paret, ed., 179. Jomini's influence was long lasting and pervasive; his prescriptions were employed in the American Civil War, in the First World War, and warmed over in the strategic bombing thesis of the air power enthusiasts in the 1920s. Indeed, Jomini's construct of war as a sort of chess game and his support for military control of warfare remain persuasive in some circles today.

12. Clausewitz has survived the years in better fashion than has Jomini, although the writings of both have been used to justify all manner of activity. The same is true of the works of Alfred Thayer Mahan, who expanded the strategic equation by taking it to sea.

13. Clausewitz (Rapoport), 119.

14. This philosophy persisted through the war with Mexico in 1848 principally because General Winfield Scott, the general-in-chief of the Army who planned and led the decisive invasion, was of this school.

15. The Academy had been established in 1802 but was supported in a meaningful way only after the poor performance of Army troops in the War of 1812.

16. General Scott, regarded as the premier strategist in the United States during the first half of the nineteenth century, was 75 years old when the war began. He was a soldier of the old school.

17. Seizing the enemy's capital would, in Jomini's terms, end the war since the enemy's will and morale would be broken.

18. Annihilation would typically be the strategy of choice for the side with large quantities of resources, while a strategy of attrition is pretty much forced on the weaker side. For example, in the American War of Independence, the "stronger" British sought to bring the Continental Army to a decisive battle, while Washington fought so as to tire the enemy. In the battle for control and land in the American West, the U.S. Army used a strategy of annihilation in fighting the Indians.

19. This line of thinking was particularly pleasing to those in the budding arms and ship-building industries, who wanted to keep people working and plants and yards producing even in the absence of a genuine threat.

20. Perhaps the most illuminating example is found in the mobilization plan for the German Army. The orders for it were so intricately devised that when Kaiser Wilhelm II, perhaps in a prescient mood, ordered mobilization stopped, his chief of staff, General Helmuth von Moltke, aghast at the chaos he imagined would result, avowed that it could not be reversed. See Barbara W. Tuchman, *The Guns of August*, New York: Macmillan, 1972, 99.

21. Chace and Carr, 161.

22. Although strategic bombardment was added to the missions of the U.S. Army Air Corps in 1926, the number of bombers required to carry out Douhet's prescription literally was so large that it was decided target analysis was needed to make the number more palatable. It was said at the time that the Air Corps thus defined strategy as a targeting problem.

23. The Germans did just that thus introducing *Blitzkrieg*, or "lightning war," to the world.

24. It continued to be staffed, updated, and war-gamed through 1938. Weapons systems acquisition and tactics evaluations were based on it.

25. When war broke out and France quickly fell, President Roosevelt found himself leading a nation where some 80 percent of the population were opposed to going to war. However, about the same percentage were anxious to help Britain.

26. This tradition of separating political and military responsibilities during war had remained fairly consistent through the years. During the War for Independence, strategy was left to General Washington after some initial attempts at controlling it by members of the Continental Congress. Although presidents Polk, Lincoln, and McKinley had all taken active, personal roles in military strategy development and execution as part of their duties as commander-in-chief, political considerations had been largely ignored, and other civilian members of the government generally had little to no impact on strategy. In fact, it has been argued that the number of casualties in World War I could be at least partially attributed to the abdication of responsibility for military operations by the civilian leaders of the protagonists. Clausewitz would not have approved!

27. When the Japanese began flexing their imperialistic muscles in the 1930s, American attention was focused in the Pacific and Asia, areas toward which, for complicated reasons, isolationist feelings never seemed to apply. The bulk of the U.S. fleet, still considered the first line of defense, was in the Pacific.

28. It was certainly possible that the strength of the personalities involved (Nimitz and MacArthur), personifications of Army-Navy rivalry, contributed as much as anything else to the continued attention the Asian theater received.

29. There was yet another strategy of warfare being executed in the Far East, but one which would not be recognized in the West for a decade or more. The guerrilla strategy, with origins in Sun Tzu's *The Art of War* written around 400 B.C., whose foremost contemporary proponent was Mao Ze-dong, required a group of dedicated "peasant" believers to conduct political, social, and economic warfare against an incumbent regime and its forces.

Chapter III: The Strategic Heritage of the United States from World War II to the Present

1. Resources used for this chapter include: Bevin Alexander, *Korea: The First War We Lost* (New York: Hippocrene Books, 1986); *Annual Report to the Congress, Fiscal Year 1988, Casper W. Weinberger, Secretary of Defense* (Washington, DC: U.S. Government Printing Office, January 12, 1987); Robert W. Ginsburg, COL, USAF, *U.S. Military Strategy in the Sixties* (New York: W. W. Norton & Co., 1965); *Goldwater-Nichols Department of Defense Reorganization Act of 1986*, P.L. 99-433 (October 1, 1986); Walter Isaacson and Evan Thomas, *The Wise Men* (New York: Simon and Schuster, 1986); Walter Laqueur and Brad Roberts, ed., *America in the World 1962–1987* (New York: St. Martin's Press, 1987); Allan R. Millett and Peter Maslowski, *op. cit.*; Walter Millis, *op. cit.*; John Norton Moore and Robert F. Turner, *The Legal Structure of Defense Organization*, memorandum prepared for President's Blue Ribbon Commission on Defense Management (Washington, DC, January 15, 1986); Peter Paret, ed., *op. cit.*; Geoffrey Perret, *op. cit.*; Urs Schwarz, *op. cit.*; Harry G. Summers, Jr., COL, USA, *op. cit.*; Jeffrey Record, *Revising U.S. Military Strategy* (Washington, DC: Pergamon-Bassey's, 1984); *U.S. Codes Congressional and Administrative News*, vol. 4, Legislative History, 99th Congress, 2nd Session (Washington, DC, 1986); John E. Tashjean, "The Transatlantic Clausewitz, 1952–1982," *Naval War College Review*, vol. 35, no. 6 (Nov–Dec 1982), 69–86; Russell F. Weigley, *op. cit.*; T. Harry Williams, *op. cit.*; H. P. Willmott, *Empires in the Balance* (Annapolis, MD: U.S. Naval Institute Press, 1982).

2. Kennedy, 361.

3. Millett and Maslowski, 474.

4. That same act created a general staff corps that was to be a planning body and a Chief of Staff who "supervised" the Army. The position was later reaffirmed in the National Defense Act of 1916.

5. All of the services conducted extensive lobbying campaigns against unification; thus a sort of "federated" military system much like that employed during World War II was established.

6. Millett and Maslowski, 473.

7. Isaacson and Thomas, 220.

8. Isaacson and Thomas, 498.

9. The Soviet Union and North Korea share about twelve miles of border.

10. And so they did. Fifteen nations contributed some thirty-nine thousand troops to operations there. The bulk of the forces, however, were American and Republic of Korean. See Summers, 101.

11. Alexander, 1.

12. Tashjean, 72.

13. The issue was not of great moment to the United States, so that there was little real justification for the use of nuclear weapons. The French would not give assurances that they would continue the fight even if the situation at Dien Bien Phu could be turned around. There was also concern about a Chinese response. See Weigley, 405.

14. This abdication on the part of the military may have been because nuclear munitions were thought to be more political than military weapons.

15. As it turned out, NATO formally adopted flexible response in 1967, and it remains in essence operable strategy today, although no country has ever provided the support in troops and equipment required to make it truly viable. What it is called and which aspect of the response is highlighted depend on the perception of the threat and who is enunciating its latest version. It remains attractive because it provides the United States with the greatest latitude in any particular confrontation.

16. The U.S. Army Special Forces (the Green Berets) were formed during these years.

17. The Rapid Deployment Force.

18. The theory behind horizontal escalation is that the enemy (the Soviet Union) will not be permitted to fight on only one front where he could conceivably concentrate his forces. Rather, the United States would open hostilities on other fronts to force them to spread their forces. Of course, this means that U.S. forces would also be spread thin.

19. The Secretary of Defense's *Annual Report to the Congress Fiscal Year 1988*, 46.
20. The North Vietnamese Army overran South Vietnam shortly thereafter.
21. *Los Angeles Times*, August 2, 1990, p. 1.
22. The vaunted Iraqi Air Force remained mostly invisible.
23. Millis, 78.

Chapter IV: The Contemporary Strategic Environment

1. *President's Blue Ribbon Commission on Defense Management: An Interim Report to the President* (February 23, 1986), p. 5.
2. Richard J. Barnet, "Looking to a Post-Cold War World," *Los Angeles Times*, June 6, 1988, 7.
3. The former can only be altered relatively slowly, while intentions may rapidly change.
4. Low-intensity conflict, for instance, requires coordinated political, military, and economic planning, but has received little.
5. Henry Kissinger once said, "What passes for planning is frequently the projection of the familiar into the future." Quoted in Jerrold P. Allen, "Institutionalizing Long-Range Planning," in Perry M. Smith, Jerrold P. Allen, John H. Stewart II, and F. Douglas Whitehouse, *Creating Strategic Vision* (Washington, DC: National Defense University Press, 1987), 28–29.
6. There have also been groups, in some cases large groups, of Americans aching to get involved in more crises than are available.
7. Not surprisingly, they ended up deceiving each other in the bargain.
8. Carnes Lord, "American Strategic Culture," *Comparative Strategy*, vol. 5, no. 3, 273.
9. The positive outcome of this national pattern has been the availability for industry of men and women who might otherwise be in the service.
10. The four multilateral treaties are the North Atlantic Treaty (NATO), the Inter-American Treaty of Reciprocal Assistance (Rio Treaty), the Australia, New Zealand, U.S. Pact (ANZUS), and the Southeast Asia Collective Defense Treaty (the organization, SEATO, was disbanded in 1975, but the obligations remain). The bilateral treaties are with the Philippines, Korea, and Japan.
11. Donald E. Nuechterlein, *United States National Interests in the 1980's* (Lexington: University Press of Kentucky, 1985), 7.
12. Harry G. Summers, Jr., COL, USA, "On Joint Doctrine for Low-Intensity Conflict," in David J. Dean, LTCOL, USAF, 369.
13. William V. Kennedy, "Why America's National Security Planning Process Went Awry," *Christian Science Monitor*, January 12, 1987, 7.
14. Occasionally the incumbent administration is charged with being overly bellicose or providing "too much defense."
15. Samuel P. Huntington, "The Defense Policy of the Reagan Administration, 1981–1982," in Fred I. Greenstein, *The Reagan Presidency: An Early Assessment* (Baltimore, MD: Johns Hopkins University Press, 1983), 82–83.
16. There was, however, no coherent strategy guiding the spending of the budgeted dollars. Some assessments conclude that there was only a marginal gain in defense capability despite all the dollars spent.
17. Richard J. Barnet, *Rockets' Red Glare*, (New York: Simon and Schuster, 1990), 399–400.
18. The armed services receive sophisticated equipment, politicians bring (or retain) jobs in their states or districts, and the industry profits (or should).
19. See Richard A. Stubbing, *op. cit.*
20. A current example of this phenomenon is the V-22 Osprey program. The Secretary of Defense decreed that the V-22, a tiltrotor aircraft originally proposed for the Army and Marines as a helicopter replacement, was not going to be pursued further because of its cost. Proponents in the Congress, particularly those worthies who represent areas where the aircraft

would be built, along with the building contractors and interested parties in the service involved (now only the Marines) who feed them data, continue to press for carrying the program further. Studies are continually ordered by Congress to examine the V-22's utility; the Secretary ignores them. One of the interesting aspects of this contest of wills is that while Secretaries come and go, members of Congress generally remain for years.

21. "Which Weapons Will Work?" *U.S. News & World Report*, January 19, 1987, 19.

22. The Staff of the Senate Armed Forces Committee quoted an earlier Defense Resource Management Study that concluded, "...each service has its own global military strategy which permits it to justify its programs and is primarily driven by resource competition." Quoted in *Defense Organization: The Need for Change*, Staff Report to the Committee on Armed Services, United States Senate (Washington, DC, October 16, 1985), 488.

23. Some think this perspective may arise from the attitude that this intramural competition is, in reality, the sport—that to "win" the most resources is the point of the game.

24. This is equally true of the very senior military officers. Prior to the Korean War, the military was reasonably apolitical. During the relatively austere years of the Eisenhower administration, the Joint Chiefs of Staff were invited by Ike to go along with his defense plans or to quit. That policy, for all practical purposes, continues today. See Perret, Millet, and Maslowski and others.

25. Many members of Congress are veterans with at least emotional ties to their service branch; others have installations or facilities in their districts or states. The optimum situation for a service (or a defense contractor) is to propose acquisition of a weapons system in which all 50 states have a piece of action, either manufacture, assembly, or basing.

26. There are many—still—who maintain that what is best for their service *is* best for the country.

27. Executive Order 11905 of February 18, 1976, specifies the statutory members of the Council to be the President, Vice President, Secretary of State, and Secretary of Defense. Others are invited.

28. Per Goldwater-Nichols, the Chairman of the Joint Chiefs of Staff may be inserted into the chain of command by the Secretary of Defense. If he is, the operational chain of command runs from the NCA, through the Chairman to the Unified and Specified Commanders.

29. The current Chairman of the JCS, General Colin Powell, has proposed a radical restructuring of the Unified Commands. As currently understood, under this plan there would be only four commands with combat forces, a Strategic Command, an Atlantic Command, a Pacific Command, and a Contingency Command. The need for support of the forces assigned (e.g., transportation) might require the establishment of several others as well. While not much detail about the plan is known at this writing, it can be said with assurance that getting it approved will be most difficult because there are so many oxen being gored. In particular, the grouping of forces directly challenges some deeply held positions of the individual military services.

30. The House and Senate Armed Services, Budget, and Appropriations committees.

31. *White Paper on the Department of Defense and the Congress*, A report to the President by the Secretary of Defense, January 1990. The paper identifies problems from the Department of Defense perspective and provides some recommendations for resolving differences and smoothing out operations.

32. From an editorial in *Aviation Week & Space Technology*, April 9, 1990, 7.

33. Ibid.

34. Quoted in Strobe Talbott, "America Abroad," *Time*, December 11, 1989, 40.

Chapter V: Elements of the
Strategic Culture: Geography and Politics

1. Resources for this chapter include: James Chace and Caleb Carr, *America Invulnerable* (New York: Summit Books, 1988); Paul Kennedy, *op. cit.*, (New York: Random House, 1987); Robert H. Ferrell, *American Diplomacy* (New York: W. W. Norton and Co., 1969);

Colin Gray, "National Style in Strategy," *International Security* (Fall 1981), 21–47; Howard Jones, *The Course of American Diplomacy from the Revolution to the Present* (New York: Franklin Watts, Inc., 1985); Carnes Lord, *op. cit.*; W. H. McNeill, *The Pursuit of Power* (Chicago: University of Chicago Press, 1982); Samuel Eliot Morrison, Henry Steele Commager, and William E. Leuchtenburg, *The Growth of the American Republic* (New York: Oxford University Press, 1980); Geoffrey Perret, *op. cit.*

2. The doctrine also pledged that Americans would remain out of European quarrels.

3. Regulating immigration was done by the individual states until 1982, when the Congress was forced to act. State policies in New York, Massachusetts, and Pennsylvania, where most of the immigrants entered, tried to keep out the diseased, the poor, and criminals with some success. After the federal govenment assumed the load, policies became more and more restrictive. See Morrison, Commager, and Leuchtenburg, *op. cit.*

4. Initially the Continental Congress attempted to control strategy, but soon gave that up.

5. The Constitution was ratified by the ninth state, New Hampshire, and took effect on June 21, 1788.

6. Moore and Turner, 81–82.

7. The Department of the Navy was added nine years later.

8. A general less principled than George Washington might well have taken advantage of the prestige and acclaim he was accorded during and after the war, but he did not. Washington was respectful and subservient to the Congress to the end of his assignment.

9. Schwarz, 5.

Chapter VI: Elements of the Strategic Culture: The American Military Experience

1. Resources used for this chapter include: R. Ernest Dupuy, COL, USA (Ret) and Trevor N. Dupuy, COL, USA, *The Military Heritage of America* (Fairfax, VA: Hero Books, 1984); R. Ernest Dupuy, COL, USA, and William H. Baumer, MAJGEN, USA, *The Little Wars of the U.S.* (New York: Hawthorne Books, 1968); Robert W. Ginsburg, COL, USAF, *op. cit.*; Kent Roberts Greenfield, *op. cit.*; Walter Laqueur and Brad Roberts, ed., *op. cit.*; Robert Leckie, *The Wars of America* (New York: Harper and Row, 1968); Allan R. Millett and Peter Maslowski, *op. cit.*; Walter Millis, *op. cit.*; Peter Paret, ed., *op. cit.*; Geoffrey Perret, *op. cit.*; Urs Schwarz, *op. cit.*; T. Harry Williams, *op. cit.*; H. P. Willmott, *op. cit.*

2. This sort of experience later influenced George Washington, who had participated in two expeditions with the British, the last as a colonel in the Virginia militia in action on the Virginia frontier in 1758.

3. Unfortunately, the Continental Congress continually underestimated the enlistment period required, ensuring that, at regular intervals, one army was being discharged as another was being recruited.

4. This phenomenon, enlistments of short duration, first felt here on the windswept plains before Quebec City, was to plague the Continental Army for some time to come.

5. The Continental Navy played absolutely no part in this naval action. By 1780, only five ships were still commissioned and they were off conducting raids on commercial shipping.

6. The Naval Act of 1794. In 1798, the creation of an executive-level Navy Department equal in rank to that of the Army finished the job.

7. This "demobilization" set a precedent for action that was to be taken after every conflict—the Army and Navy were cut back drastically until the next threat arose.

8. The Army numbered about 2,800 men and the Navy had a total of 16 ships, of which only seven were truly battle-capable frigates. In contrast, the Royal Navy had some 600 ships.

9. One such penetration did occur. British troops, freed from European battles, were landed near the capital city of Washington, whereupon they marched into and set fire to it.

10. In the sense intended here, the Confederate States of America are considered to have been a nation. As pointed out earlier, before this time a nation-state's participation in war, no matter the scale, was most often carried out by a "professional" military. In addition, prior to the Civil War, conflict was seldom, if ever, about the survival of a way of life.

11. West Point men led both sides in 55 of the 60 largest battles.

12. The term "yellow press" was applied to those employing sensationalist journalism for the purpose of selling more papers.

13. More contemporary analysis suggests that the *Maine* suffered an explosion caused by an engine-room fire which spread to an adjacent ammunition storage area. See Perret, p. 280.

14. Trains were so scarce and the desire to get to Cuba was apparently so strong that troops fought each other over the transport. See Leckie, *op. cit.*

15. This was a time when the Monroe Doctrine was interpreted in such a way as to justify U.S. preemptive intervention to ensure "order." Sound familiar? See T. Harry Williams, 355.

16. The Mexican expedition's commander, General Pershing, went into Mexico with six obsolete observation aircraft. Within 30 days, all had crashed.

17. Not only had the Germans taken their toll, but the French Army was in mutiny.

18. Dupuy and Dupuy, 364.

19. The total displacement of all the battleships possessed could not exceed 500,000 tons for Great Britain and the United States, and 300,000 for Japan. France and Italy were each limited to 175,000 tons.

20. The draft was to last for only one year. The following year, despite the conflict in Europe, extension of the law passed the Senate by the margin of one vote!

21. It was to be a come-as-you-are war for a while. By the end of 1943, however, there were 300 new construction and 222 conversion and repair shipyards operating; the massive efforts to produce and repair ships resulted in an armada unlike any the world had ever seen.

22. This situation was not unlike one early in the First World War. When the Foreign Minister of France was asked to name the minimum force required to assist the French, he replied, "A single British soldier — and we will see to it that he is killed." In Barbara W. Tuchman, *The Guns of August* (New York: Macmillan, 1972), 49.

23. An interesting sidenote is that in this time of paring back defense budgets, another Navy–Air Force mission argument is simmering over who should be the lead service in today's environment. The arguments are still being marshaled.

24. The North Korean action was, in one sense, a boon. It provided a pretext not only for mobilizing and rearming to fight the incursion into South Korea, but, almost in the same motion, would allow for strengthening, without a lot of fanfare, military capabilities in Europe as called for in NSC-68.

25. It is likely that the domestic political situation in the United States played a significant part in the decision. The Democrats, stung by charges that they had "lost" China and were "soft" on communism, may have seen this as an opportunity to demonstrate their toughness.

26. A permanent arrangement for peace, however, still eludes the participants and probably will continue to do so; it seems that it is necessary for at least the North Koreans to have an enemy.

27. A conventional bombing mission was added later.

28. The addition of submarines capable of launching ballistic missiles, which were (and are) nearly invulnerable to destruction before they have fulfilled their mission, incalculably added to the credibility of the nation's deterrent posture.

29. Geoffrey Perret, 530.

30. An all-volunteer force had been established, pay schedules adjusted, the military justice system overhauled, and training had been improved. Morale was generally high.

Chapter VII: Elements of the Strategic Culture: Values

1. Resources used for this chapter include: Richard J. Barnet, *The Rocket's Red Glare*; John Bayliss, Ken Booth, John Garnett, Phil Williams, *Contemporary Strategy* (New York: Holmes and Meier, 1975); Barry Berzan, *People, States and Fear: The National Security Problem and International Relations* (Chapel Hill: University of North Carolina Press, 1983); Ken Booth, *op. cit.*; Inis L. Claude, Jr., *Swords Into Plowshares*, revised 3d ed. (New York: Random House, 1964); Colin S. Gray, "National Style in Strategy," *International Security* (Fall

1981), 21–47; Thomas Owens Mackubbin, *op. cit.*; James Oliver Robertson, *American Myth, American Reality* (New York: Hill and Wong, 1980).

2. Participation as measured by the percent of the population of voting age who do vote in presidential elections has ranged between 51 and 63 percent for the last fifty-some years. See *The World Almanac and Book of Facts* (New York: Pharos Books, 1984) and *1989 Statistical Abstract of the United States* (Washington, DC: U.S. Department of Commerce, Washington, January 1989).

3. Indeed, many of the "in group" would confuse the two.

4. Barnet, *Rocket's Red Glare*, 400.

5. From a speech to the National Strategy Forum as reported in the *Hawaii Navy News*, September 25, 1986.

6. For example, the national interest and objective satisfied by the invasion of the small island nation of Grenada continues to elude many, despite the postevent rhetoric.

7. Kenneth Keniston, quoted by Douglas H. Rosenberg in "Arms and the American Way: The Ideological Dimension of Military Growth," in Bruce M. Russett and Alfred Stepan, eds., *Military Forces and American Society* (New York: Harper and Row, 1973), 145.

8. Editorial in *Aviation Week and Space Technology*, February 1, 1988, 9.

9. Klaus Knorr quoted in Ken Booth, p. 130.

10. Claude, p. 88.

11. Even the name of the Panama invasion, Operation "Just Cause," has a wonderfully moral ring to it.

12. It is not clear how many citizens are aware of the aggressive lobbying of Congress and the administrations by agents of foreign powers.

13. War Plan Red, devised in the early 1900s on the premise that Great Britain might be the enemy, was maintained and updated into the 1930s.

14. Fear of the British seemed to be based on the notion that they wanted to take what we had, whereas the Soviets are feared because they wanted to give us something (communism).

15. Strobe Talbott, "America Abroad," *Time*, September 3, 1990, 40.

16. Recent examples include President Reagan's characterization of the Soviet Union as an "evil empire," and the vilification of Panama's General Noriega and Iraq's Saddam Hussein, characterizations which were fairly rapid reversals from more charitable earlier ones.

17. These interventions have often occurred in Central and South America, most recently in El Salvador, Nicaragua, and Panama. There seems to be little consideration of the possibility that the United States may be the only place on earth where such a government can take root because of the unique mix of people, space, climate, and natural resources.

18. Which American does not believe, for instance, that, given an opportunity to learn about life in the United States, a Soviet (or anyone else, for that matter) would choose it over his own.

19. The Korean and Vietnam wars can be contrasted with invasions of Grenada, Panama, and Iraq in considering how we characterize our enemies, and the extent to which most Americans are aware of the contributions of the British and the Russians in World Wars I and II can serve as an example of our attitudes toward our allies.

20. This is one of the frightening aspects of a war of any kind with the Soviets. They might be more willing to tolerate setbacks than we will. The United States may be the one who ups the ante by escalating to nuclear weapons.

21. As an example, it was said that President George Bush considered his decision for U.S. intervention when Iraq invaded Kuwait as "the moment for which he had spent a lifetime preparing, the epochal event that would bear out his campaign slogan, 'ready to be a great President from Day 1'." Dan Goodgame, "What If We Do Nothing," *Time*, January 7, 1991, 22.

22. The Army is not permitted to operate fixed-wing combat aircraft or it would probably have been involved as well.

23. See Thomas Schilling, *op. cit.*

24. Considering time in this way is fundamental to the decision-making approach taught by Richard Neustadt and Ernest May. See Neustadt and May, *Thinking in Time: The Uses of History for Decision Makers* (New York: The Free Press, 1986).

25. One problem associated with this issue centers on the believability of the leadership. Unfortunately,

> Since the beginning of history, kings, chieftains, and priests have been simplifying reality for their followers, supplying them with soothing cover stories, and turning the enemies they want to mark for destruction into subhuman hate figures. (Barnet, *Rocket's Red Glare*, 220)

Presidents have been among those who manipulated the news, and, thus opinion.
26. Thomas Owens Mackubbin, p. 57.
27. Carnes Lord, p. 280.

Chapter VIII: Developing Military Strategy

1. Resources used for this chapter include: C. W. Borklund, *The Department of Defense* (New York: Praeger, 1968); Department of the Air Force, *BPPBS Primer* (Washington, January 1989); Glenn A. Kent, *A Framework for Defense Planning* (Santa Monica, CA: Rand, 1989); Thomas Owens Mackubbin, *op. cit.*; Richard A. Stubbing with Richard A. Mendel, *op. cit.*; *U.S. Codes and Administrative News*, vol. 4, Legislative History, 99th Congress, 2nd Session (Washington, DC, 1986).
2. B. H. Liddell-Hart, *Strategy* (New York: Praeger, 1967), p. 335.
3. Definition from the *Department of Defense Dictionary of Military and Associated Terms*, JCS Pub 1, p. 240.
4. *National Security Strategy of the United States*, The White House, March 1990, pp. 2, 3.
5. Ibid.
6. Defense Reorganization Act of 1986, Section 153.
7. From the *Defense Resource Management Study*, quoted in *Defense Organization: The Need For Change*, p. 488.
8. *National Security Strategy of the United States*, p. 20.
9. Another factor is that large dollar amounts mean that business and political interests are an important part of the acquisition process.
10. What is more typical, however, is that nothing is changed, and, therefore, little or no chance exists that an execution would be successful.
11. "The Defense Department has evolved into a grouping of large rigid bureaucracies ... which embrace the past and adapt new technology to fit traditional missions and methods." General David Jones, former Chief of Staff of the U.S. Air Force and Chairman of the JCS, quoted in Stubbing, p. 87.

Chapter IX: Problems in Developing Military Strategy

1. Resources used for this chapter include: Albert Clarkson, *Toward Effective Strategic Analysis: New Applications of Information Technology* (Boulder, CO: Westview Press, 1981); Keith A. Dunn and William O. Staundenmaier, "Strategy for Survival," *Foreign Policy* (Fall 1983), pp. 22–41; Stephen Majeski, "A Recommendation Model of War Initiation: The Plausibility and Generalizability of General Cultural Rules," in Cimbala, *op. cit.*; Lawrence Martin, "Is Military Force Losing Its Utility?" in John Reichart and Steven R. Sturm, eds., *op. cit.*; Richard E. Neustadt and Ernest R. May, *op. cit.*; Thomas C. Schelling, *op. cit.*; Jack Snyder, *The Ideology of the Offensive: Military Decision Making and the Disaster of 1914* (Ithaca, NY: Cornell University Press, 1984); Staff Report to the Committee on Armed Services, United States Senate, *Defense Organization: The Need for Change*, *op. cit.*; William O. Staudenmaier, COL, USA, *Military Strategy in Transition*, Military Issues Research Memorandum, Strategic Studies Institute, U.S. Army War College (Carlisle Barracks, PA, November 20, 1978); John D. Steinbrunner, "The Doubtful Presumption of Rationality," in John Reichart and Steven R. Sturm, eds., *op. cit.*; William J. Taylor, Jr., Steven A.

Maasaner, and Gerrit W. Gong, *Strategic Responses to Conflict in the 80's* (Lexington, MA: Lexington Books, 1984); Stansfield Turner and George Thibault, "Preparing for the Unexpected: The Need for a New Military Strategy," *Foreign Affairs*, 61 (Fall 1982), pp. 122–132; James D. Watkins, ADM, USN, *The Maritime Strategy*, U.S. Naval Institute, January 1986.

2. The triad is made up of land- and sea-based missiles and manned aircraft.

3. There has been little thought of actually fighting a nuclear war, despite occasional analysis of the effects of doing so, until the recent past.

4. Strategy which requires single service (e.g., Army, Navy, etc.) forces for execution will have had, in all likelihood, the participation of the component commander of the involved service in the development process. The specifics of the strategy chosen may well be applicable at both levels, leaving only tactical planning to be done.

5. Liddell-Hart wrote, "[the strategist's] true aim is not so much to seek battle as to seek a strategic situation so advantageous that if it does not of itself produce the decision, its continuation by a battle is sure to achieve this." In Basil Liddell-Hart, p. 339.

6. Part of the motivation for intervening directly may be that it always seems easier to direct than to plan action.

7. Indeed, a battleship was brought out of mothballs to serve once again off Vietnam.

8. Ballistic missile submarines (SSBNs) were an addition to the traditional force structure.

9. The strategy eventually entered into the formal planning process through the unified commander, USCINCPAC, who endorsed it, accepted it as his own, and forwarded it on to the JCS.

10. See Norman Polmar and Dr. Scott C. Truver, "The Maritime Strategy," in *Air Force Magazine* (November 1987), pp. 70–79.

11. The U.S. Naval Institute published an unclassified version as a supplement to its January 1986 issue of *Proceedings*.

12. Watkins, p. 4.

13. Not a few cynics aver that this is *the* reason for the existence of the maritime strategy. Even if that is true, at least it is a rationale for spending the enormous amounts requested.

14. The swings between counterforce (attacking the other's missiles) and countervalue (attacking the other's economic base, cities, etc.) targeting over the years, driven the one way by increased accuracy and multiple warhead development and the other way by advances on the Soviet side, have been typical of the extremes of movement.

15. Korea, Vietnam, Lebanon, and Iraq are testaments to this assertion.

16. *Defense Organization: The Need for Change.*

17. William V. Kennedy, "Why America's National Security Planning Process Went Awry," p. 7.

18. Recall that one of the principal assumptions of modern-day strategic analysis is that all leaders will behave "rationally" in times of crisis. Will that be our rationality or his?

19. A sense of the Japanese perspective may be gained by reading John Toland's *The Rising Sun* (New York: Random House, 1970).

20. Groups may help ameliorate but do not eliminate these inhibitors. Experts cloistered in "think tanks" while engaged in speculative study on what the future might bring, like ad-hoc groups and commissions gathered to consider a specific problem or event, are as prone to these effects as is the lone strategist.

Chapter X: Selecting Strategies

1. Resources used for this chapter include: Thomas B. Allen, *War Games* (New York: McGraw-Hill, 1987); Bruce F. Baird, *Introduction to Decision Analysis* (North Scituate, MA: Duxbury Press, 1978); Garry D. Brewer and Martin Shubik, *The War Game: A Critique of Military Problem Solving* (Cambridge: Harvard University Press, 1979); Colin S. Gray, *Strategic Studies and Public Policy: The American Experience* (Lexington: University of Kentucky Press, 1982); Alfred H. Hausrath, *Venture Simulation in War, Business and Politics* (New York: McGraw-Hill, 1971); Robert G. Hendrickson, *Pro's and Con's of War Gaming and Simulation* (Washington, DC: Research Analysis Corporation, 1961); David B. Hertz

and Howard Thomas, *Risk Analysis and Its Applications* (New York: John Wiley and Sons, 1983); Irving L. Janis, *Victims of Groupthink*, 2d ed. (Boston: Houghton Mifflin, 1982); Robert M. Krone, *Systems Analysis and Policy Science: Theory and Practice* (New York: John Wiley and Sons, 1980); Bruce R. Linder, CDR, USN, "Ops Analysis: Just 'Quantitative Common Sense'" and "Naval Analysis Through the Years," *Proceedings*, U.S. Naval Institute (August 1988), pp. 98–101; *Maritime Power: Some Observations on Strategy, Tactics and Technology* (Fairfax, VA: National Security Research, 1986); Dale K. Pace, "Scenario Use in Naval System Design," *Naval Engineers Journal* (January 1986); Thomas C. Schelling, *op. cit.*; Martin Shubik, *The Uses and Limitations of Game Theoretic Methods in Defense Analysis*, Cowles Foundation Research Paper, Yale University, New Haven, CT, Oct. 9, 1985; J. D. Williams, *The Compleat Strategyst* (New York: McGraw-Hill, 1966).

2. Examples abound. The bombing of the Marine Corps barracks in Lebanon and the attack on U.S.S. *Stark* in the Persian Gulf come immediately to mind.

3. Gray, *Strategic Studies and Public Policy: The American Experience*, p. 110.

4. This depiction was inspired by a similar one in Allen, p. 4.

5. This refers to the reality of executing the strategy. There are, of course, training benefits to actually being at sea, flying, or exercising with other ground forces, as the case may be.

6. This would certainly be counterproductive were the strategy intended to be used in a real situation. In that double-think which can be a part of national strategy, however, a compromise could be part of yet another larger-scale deception strategy.

7. Simulation technology has given us quite real environments in narrow applications such as aircraft trainers; perhaps it will soon help in this arena as well.

8. Hendrickson, p. 1.

9. Lanchester's Square Law stated, "Fighting strength of a force may be broadly defined as proportional to the square of its numerical strength multiplied by the fighting value of its individual units." Quoted in Allen, p. 224.

10. Shubik, p. 11.

11. *Department of Defense Dictionary of Military Terms*, p. 389.

12. Based on a survey reported in Brewer and Shubik. The RAND Strategy Assessment System (RSAS) developed under the sponsorship of the Office of Net Assessment, Office of the Secretary of Defense is a move in this direction. It provides automated war-gaming through the application of artificial intelligence techniques, and is one of the few systems which offers the ability to integrate several levels of command or decision making. There are systems installed at the U.S. Naval Postgraduate School, the Naval War College, the National Defense University, and other DOD activities.

13. Brewer and Shubik.

14. Carl H. Builder, quoted in Pace, p. 59.

15. Brewer and Shubik, p. 74.

16. Those who are devoted to more mystical methods of decision making would say that the needle was applied to another part of the anatomy.

17. Systems analysis has been defined as "a systematic approach to helping a decision-maker choose a course of action by investigating his full problem, searching out objectives and alternatives, and comparing them in the light of their consequences, using an appropriate framework—in so far as possible analytic—to bring expert judgement and intuition to bear on a problem." See Martin E. O'Connor, LTCOL, USMC, and Lawrence E. Probst, LCDR, USN, *Analytical Techniques for Decisionmaking* (Washington, DC: National Defense University, 1974), p. 2.

18. *Maritime Power: Some Observations on Strategy, Tactics and Technology*, p. 110.

19. Majeski, p. 74.

20. Barbara W. Tuchman, *Practicing History* (New York: Alfred A. Knopf, 1981), p. 251.

21. Quoted in Robert D. Behn and James W. Vaupel, *Quick Analysis for Busy Decision Makers* (New York: Basic Books, 1982), p. 18.

22. Those groups where members work well together are often viewed as being "successful."

23. Janis, *op. cit.*

24. Multiattribute utility models satisfy this criterion.

Chapter XI: Answering the Call

1. Jeffrey Record, *Beyond Military Reform* (New York: Pergamon-Brassey, 1988), p. 198.

2. It should not be surprising to know that the institutional belief is that what is good for the individual service *is* best for the country.

3. There are, of course, more timely remedies for malfeasance (impeachment is one), but they are seldom used.

4. The inaction and party-inspired maneuvering on the budget deficit over the past several years is only the most recent example.

5. If Eastern European governments ordered their armed forces to attack another country, it is not at all clear that the soldiers and sailors would fight. They surely would do so to repel invaders.

6. Representative Norman Dicks (Democrat, Washington) has proposed a similar idea. The bill he reportedly will offer establishes an independent commission to review U.S. defense and national security requirements and to advise the administration and the Congress on current and future policy.

7. Nevertheless, the House Armed Services Committee has done just that in the Fiscal Year 1991 authorization bill. Of course, their order has little to do with strategic direction and everything to do with budgeting.

8. Franklin C. Spinney, "A Defensive Strategy That Works," in Professional Notes, *Proceedings* of the U.S. Naval Institute (January 1990), p. 99.

9. Letting what the military wants to buy establish what the country will do in the international arena stands the problem on its head.

10. Janis, p. 2.

11. In assisting in decisions, "smart" computers are more important than large ones. See Stephen J. Cimbala, *Artificial Intelligence and National Security* (Washington, DC: Heath and Company, 1987).

12. An expert system is "a computer application that solves complicated problems that would otherwise require extensive human expertise." From David W. Rolston, *Principles of Artificial Intelligence and Expert System Development* (New York: McGraw-Hill, 1988), p. 2.

13. More complex problems are currently under attack. For example, applications to assist a pilot in maintaining awareness of his environment while fighting his aircraft are under development as this is written.

14. A more complete description may be found in Stephen J. Andriole, "AI and Strategic Intelligence Analysis and Production: Some Opportunities and the Limits to Growth" in Stephen J. Cimbala, ed., *Artificial Intelligence and National Security*, p. 32.

15. See James N. Rosenau in Stephen J. Cimbala, *op. cit.*

16. Phillip A. Crowl, "The Strategist's Short Catechism," in Reichart and Sturm, p. 88.

Chapter XII: Summing Up

1. One could reasonably ask why Egypt feels the need to own and operate submarines — or why South Korea or Saudi Arabia or Australia feels they must. Each country could provide a list of reasons. They would also proceed whether or not we would agree (unless we were financing the purchase, as we often do).

2. Pakistan is and Iraq was in this group. Reports indicate that most, if not all, of Iraq's capability was destroyed by coalition forces during the UN-Iraq War.

3. "In the next century, forty or more countries in Europe, Asia, the Middle East and elsewhere will have the technical wherewithal to build such [nuclear arsenals] within a few years." *Discriminate Deterrence*, Report of the Commission on Integrated Long-Term Strategy, Washington, DC (January 1988), p. 10.

4. Many folks do just that in their personal lives through insurance, retirement plans, Individual Retirement Accounts, and other such opportunities.

5. See Paul Kennedy, p. 533.

Bibliography

Books

Alexander, Bevin. *Korea: The First War We Lost*. New York: Hippocrene Books, 1986. Excellent coverage of the first war in a new age.

Allen, Thomas B. *War Games*. New York: McGraw-Hill, 1987. This is a must for those interested in the subject. It traces the historical derivations, the growth, and the current uses of the technique.

Andriole, Stephen J. *The Handbook of Problem Solving*. New York: Petrocelli Books, 1983. Details the basic elements of decision making and includes a discussion on tools which might help.

Aron, Raymond. *Clausewitz, Philosopher of War*. Translated by Christine Booker and Norman Stone. Englewood Cliffs, NJ: Prentice-Hall, 1985. An interpretation of Clausewitz applied to modern military history by a respected expert in strategy.

Baird, Bruce F. *Introduction to Decision Analysis*. North Scituate, MA: Duxbury Press, 1978. Excellent coverage of utility theory and its offspring.

Barnet, Richard J. *The Rocket's Red Glare*. New York: Simon and Schuster, 1990. A fascinating review of war, politics, the people, and the presidency.

Barrett, Archie D. *Reappraising Defense Organization*. Washington, DC: National Defense University Press, 1983. Familiarizes the reader with the Department as it is organized, together with problems which have been identified and some recommendations for improvement. Based on the Defense Organization Study undertaken from 1977 to 1980.

Bates, Donald L., and David L. Eldredge. *Strategy and Policy*. Dubuque, IA: Wm. C. Brown Co., 1980. Reviews the elements and suggests that a systems view of strategy must be taken because it transcends any one area.

Baylis, John, Ken Booth, John Garnett, and Phil Williams. *Contemporary Strategy: Theories and Concepts*, vol. I. New York: Holmes and Meier, 1987. An outstanding review of strategic theories and their relevancy.

Behn, Robert D., and James W. Vaupel. *Quick Analysis for Busy Decision Makers*. New York: Basic Books, 1982. Provides a straightforward methodology for analyzing the issues and making decisions.

Bigelow, Robert. *The Dawn Warrior*. Boston: Little, Brown, 1969. An interesting study of man, conflict, and cooperation.

Booth, Ken. *Strategy and Ethnocentrism*. New York: Holmes and Meier, 1979. A must for anyone interested in understanding the effects of a strategic culture.

Borklund, C. W. *The Department of Defense*. New York: Praeger, 1968. An excellent discussion of the origins and growth of the DOD, and the problems its Secretary has in exercising control over all its factions.

Brewer, Gary D., and Martin Shubik. *The War Game: A Critique of Military Problem Solving*. Cambridge: Harvard University Press, 1979. The other book (along with Allen's) to be used in exploring the development and uses (and misuses) of games and simulations by the military.

Burns, James MacGregor. *The Vineyard of Liberty*. New York: Alfred A. Knopf, 1982. The first of three volumes on the "American Experiment." An important and very readable political history of the United States by a celebrated historian and biographer.

Bushan, Alastir, ed. *Problems of Modern Strategy*. New York: Praeger, 1970. Dated but still relevant review of strategic issues.

Chace, James, and Caleb Carr. *America Invulnerable*. New York: Summit, 1988. Chronicle of the search for true national security. The wavering steps and detours are well documented and woven together in an illuminating way.

Chaliand, Gérard, and Jean-Pierre Rageau. *Strategic Atlas: A Comparative Geopolitics of the World's Powers*. New York: Harper and Row, 1985. A small, but informative book, which includes illustrations of the world as seen from different perspectives.

Cimbala, Stephen J., ed. *Artificial Intelligence and National Security*. Washington, DC: Heath and Company, 1987. Selections detail some of the ways the power of AI systems might be brought to bear on security problems.

Clarkson, Albert. *Toward Effective Strategic Analysis: New Applications of Information Technology*. Boulder, CO: Westview Press, 1981. An interesting book which calls attention to the problems intelligence analysts have in objectively interpreting data.

Claude, Inis L., Jr. *Swords Into Plowshares*. 3d rev. ed. New York: Random House, 1964. The definitive work on the value of international organizations.

Clausewitz, Carl von. *On War*. Edited by Anatol Rapoport, translated by J. J. Graham. Baltimore: Penguin Books, 1968. A very readable translation. The introduction and concluding remarks by the editor are both informative and thought-provoking.

Collins, John M. *Grand Strategy: Principles and Practices*. Annapolis: Naval Institute Press, 1973. An early appreciation of the distinctions in levels of strategy and cultural influences.

Dean, David J., LTCOL, USAF, ed. *Low-Intensity Conflict and Modern Technology*. Maxwell Air Force Base, AL: Air University Press, June 1986. A primer on low-intensity conflict, including sections on policy, technology and doctrine. The articles were originally written for a workshop on the subject.

Donald, David Herbert. *Liberty and Union*. Boston: Little, Brown, 1978. Comprehensive look at the origins, actions and aftermath of the Civil War. Explanations of the political aspects are especially good.

Drew, Dennis M., LTCOL, USAF, Study Director. *Nuclear Winter and National Security: Implications for Future Policy*. Maxwell AFB, AL: Air University Press, July 1986. Reports on a study of the policy implications which might arise when assuming the nuclear winter phenomenon will occur in one of three scenarios, differentiated by the number and yield of nuclear weapons employed.

Dupuy, R. Ernest, COL, USA, and William H. Baumer, MAJ GEN, USA. *The Little Wars of the U.S.* New York: Hawthorne Books, 1968. Excellent and detailed coverage of the unglamorous and little known military actions which are part of U.S. military history.

_____, and Trevor N. Dupuy, COL, USA. *Military Heritage of America*. Fairfax, VA: Hero Books, 1984. Straightforward account of military thought and operations from the Revolution through Korea. Contains an excellent section on concepts, definitions, and the evolution of tactical theory.

Erickson, John, Edward L. Crowley, and Nikolai Galay, eds. *The Military-Technical Revolution: Its Impact on Strategy and Foreign Policy*. New York: Praeger, 1966. A dated but still interesting review of aspects of nuclear weapons and strategy as seen from both the American and Soviet side.

Essays on Strategy III. Washington, DC: National Defense University, 1986.

Essays on Strategy IV. Washington, DC: National Defense University, 1987.

Essays on Strategy V. Washington, DC: National Defense University, 1988. These three books contain essays selected from those submitted in the yearly competition sponsored by the Chairman of the Joint Chiefs of Staff. They provide insights into the thinking of attendees at the war colleges and other senior military schools.

Ferrell, Robert H. *American Diplomacy*. New York: Norton, 1969. Engaging diplomatic history of the United States.

Ginsburgh, Robert N., COL, USAF. *U.S. Military Strategy in the Sixties*. New York: Norton, 1965. An outstanding review of strategic patterns in U.S. history, including the roles of institutions, and their relevance to the strategy of the sixties.

Gray, Colin S. *The Geopolitics of the Nuclear Era: Heartland, Rimlands and the Technological Revolution*. New York: Crane, Russak and Co., 1977. A study of the continual struggle for the control of Europe and the neighboring seas based on geopolitical imperatives.

_____. *Strategic Studies and Public Policy: The American Experience*. Lexington: University Press of Kentucky, 1982. Comprehensive review of post–World War II strategic thought and the effects of each policy.

_____. *Maritime Strategy, Geopolitics and the Defense of the West*. New York: National Strategy Information Center, 1986. A treatise on the efficacy of a maritime strategy for this maritime power. Concentrates on the design of military strategy in the context of geopolitics.

Greenfield, Kent Roberts. *American Strategy in World War II: A Reconsideration*. Baltimore: The Johns Hopkins University Press, 1963. A dated but nevertheless interesting review of the important aspects of the American and Allied strategy executed during World War II.

Greenstein, Fred I., ed. *The Reagan Presidency: An Early Assessment*. Baltimore: The Johns Hopkins University Press, 1983. Selections treat various facets of the Reagan administration's first few years. Huntington's coverage of the defense policy is excellent.

Hadley, Arthur T. *The Straw Giant*. New York: Random House, 1986. This third edition is an updated but still generally unflattering look at the United States Armed Forces. Unfortunately, much of the commentary is right on the mark.

Hammond, Kenneth R., Gary H. McClelland, and Jeryl Mumpower. *Human Judgement and Decision-Making*. New York: Praeger, 1980. Covers most of what you want to know about the structure of decisions and man's ability to make them.

Hausrath, Alfred H. *Venture Simulation in War, Business, and Politics*. New York: McGraw-Hill, 1971. A handbook of games describing their strengths, weaknesses, and uses. Dated, but still valuable. Should be read with Allen and Brewer.

Hertz, David B., and Thomas Howard. *Risk Analysis and Its Application*. New York: John Wiley and Sons, 1983. A primer on the opportunities and dangers connected with risk. Discusses some tools to be used in assessment.

Higginbotham, Don. *The War of American Independence*. New York: Macmillan, 1971. A rousing recounting of the Revolutionary War. Rich in detail.

Isaacson, Walter, and Evan Thomas. *The Wise Men*. New York: Simon and Schuster, 1986. A very readable account of six men (Robert Lovett, John McCloy, Averill Harriman, Chip Bohlen, George Kennan, and Dean Acheson) and America's vision of the world fashioned under their stewardship in the post–World War II years.

Janis, Irving L. *Victims of Groupthink*. 2d ed. Boston: Houghton-Mifflin, 1982. A fascinating and important contribution to the literature on decision making. Describes the problems encountered in making decisions in groups; includes case studies.

Jones, Archer. *The Art of War in the Western World*. Chicago: University of Illinois Press, 1987. This exhaustive study thoroughly covers the more than 2,500 years of human warfare. The liberal use of diagrams of movements and drawings of weaponry add meaning to the text. An important source for understanding the evolution of warfare.

Jones, Howard. *American Diplomacy from the Revolution to the Present*. New York: Franklin Watts, 1985. A detailed and highly readable diplomatic history, stressing the motivation behind actions.

Kennedy, Paul. *The Rise and Fall of the Great Powers*. New York: Random House, 1987. This is one of the most important books of our time. The intimate relationship between economics and warfare seldom gets such splendid treatment. A must for the student of warfare.

Krone, Robert M. *Systems Analysis and Policy Sciences Theory and Practice*. New York: John Wiley, 1980. Basic work on using analysis in policy making.

Langguth, A. J. *Patriots*. New York: Simon and Schuster, 1988. A thoroughly readable and spirited account of the War of Independence, with particular attention paid to the personalities of the best-known participants.

Laqueur, Walter, and Brad Roberts, ed. *America in the World 1962–1987*. New York: St. Martin's, 1987. Collection of articles by powerful thinkers and movers on the strategic scene reviewing where the U.S. has been and where it should be heading. An important source.

Leckie, Robert. *The Wars of America*. New York: Harper and Row, 1968. This is a two-volume history of the U.S. military in combat. Like others, the author details battles, but he also makes an effort to expose the human side of the main actors. The treatment adds more weight to the contention that there is a militaristic streak in Americans.

Liddell-Hart, Basil. *Strategy*. New York: Praeger, 1967. This is one of the classics on the subject. Strategy in war is surveyed from the fifth century B.C. through the Second World War. The author finds that attacking the enemy where he does not expect it seems to be an important ingredient of success.

Luttwak, Edward N. *On the Meaning of Victory: Essays on Strategy*. New York: Simon and Schuster, 1986. A collection of essays about strategic thinking and the economic and political elements of strategy.

————. *Strategy: The Logic of War and Peace*. Cambridge, MA: Belknap Press, 1987. The author presents a novel, albeit tortuous, approach to thinking about peace and war involving the paradoxes of strategic choices. Very difficult to follow.

McNeill, W. H. *The Pursuit of Power*. Chicago: University of Chicago Press, 1982. An excellent treatment of how military force has been employed through history to enhance the power of the state. An important resource.

Millett, Allan R., and Peter Maslowski. *For the Common Defense*. New York: The Free Press, 1984. This military history of the United States not only documents military actions, but sets them in the context of the eonomic and political pressures which are so much a part of life in this country.

Millis, Walter. *Arms and Men*. New York: G. P. Putman's Sons, 1965. This venerable military history provides some true insights on man at war.

Mittra, Sitansu. *Decision Support System, Tools and Techniques*. New York: John Wiley, 1986. Contains an excellent discussion of logic trees.

Morrison, Samuel Eliot, Henry Steele Commager, and William E. Leuchtenburg. *The Growth of the American Republic*, vol II. New York: Oxford University Press, 1980. A wonderfully readable social and political history by some old pros. This volume paints an exceptional picture of post–Civil War America.

Neustadt, Richard E., and Ernest R. May. *Thinking in Time: The Uses of History for Decision Makers*. New York: The Free Press, 1986. This book presents much of the material from a class the authors teach at Harvard. It encourages thinking of time as a stream.

Nuechterlein, Donald E. *America Overcommitted: United States National Interests in the 1980's*. Lexington: The University Press of Kentucky, 1985. A primer on how to think about U.S. interests in general, and in various parts of the world. A must for the strategist.

O'Connor, Martin E., LCOL, USMC, and Lawrence E. Probst, LCDR, USN, eds. *Analytical Techniques for Decisionmaking*. Washington, DC: National Defense University, 1971. An old, but still relevant discussion of the strengths and weaknesses of using analytical methods for decision making.

Palmer, David Richard. *The Way of the Fox: American Strategy in the War for America 1775–1783*. Westport: Greenwood Press, 1975. Spotlights General Washington as a strategist.

Paret, Peter, ed. *Makers of Modern Strategy from Machiavelli to the Nuclear Age*. Princeton: Princeton University Press, 1986. Another important book for the student of strategy. A collection of articles which discuss all the significant strategists and events in the modern era.

Perret, Geoffrey. *A Country Made By War*. New York: Random House, 1989. A book which ranks with *The Rise and Fall of the Great Powers* in significance. The author's thesis that, far from the image of a reluctant warrior never prepared for wars, the United States (as it is today) is a reflection of its militaristic tendencies, challenges the reader.

Posen, Barry R. *The Sources of Military Doctrine*. Ithaca, NY: Cornell University Press, 1984. Addresses the roots of military practices and their relationship to the nation's security needs.

Ra'anon, Uri, Robert L. Pfaltzgraff, Jr., and Geofrey Kemp, eds. *Projection of Power: Perspectives, Perceptions and Problems*. Hamden, CT: Archon Books, 1982. Selections having to do with the perceptions of power and its uses.

Record, Jeffrey. *Revising U.S. Military Strategy: Tailoring Means to Ends*. Washington, DC: Pergamon-Brassey's, 1984. Builds a rationale for adjusting the U.S. strategic overreach by reining in the military and developing a long-term strategy.

_____. *Beyond Military Reform*. New York: Pergamon-Brassey's, 1988. Places the military in the cultural spectrum and proposes actions to improve its productivity.

Reichart, John F., and Steven R. Sturm, eds. *American Defense Policy.* 5th ed. Baltimore: Johns Hopkins University Press, 1982. A collection of some important writers in the field. Articles are particularly diverse in subject matter from nuclear strategy to nonmilitary threats to national security.

Robertson, James Oliver. *American Myth, American Reality.* New York: Hill and Wang, 1980. An exploration of the stories and images Americans tell themselves and which color reality they see. An important work.

Robinson, Charles Alexander, Jr. *Ancient History from Prehistoric Times to the Death of Justinian.* New York: The MacMillan Company, 1951. A detailed chronicle of important events and people of the ancient world.

Rolston, David W. *Principles of Artificial Intelligence and Expert Systems Development.* New York: McGraw-Hill, 1988. A primer on expert systems.

Roth, John K., and Robert C. Whittemore, eds. *Ideology and American Experience.* Washington, DC: The Washington Institute Press, 1986. A collection of essays which explore the effects of ideology and philosophy on U.S. interactions in the world.

Russett, Bruce M., and Alfred Stepan, eds. *Military Forces and American Society.* New York: Harper and Row, 1973. This set of essays, although dated, document thinking near the end of the Vietnam War, a critical time in U.S. history.

Schelling, Thomas. *The Strategy of Conflict.* Cambridge: Harvard University Press, 1970. Interesting discussion of the true character of decision makers.

Schwarz, Urs. *American Strategy: A New Perspective.* Garden City, NJ: Doubleday and Co., 1966. An entertaining and informative review of American strategic thought through the Korean War.

_____, and Laszlo Hodik. *Strategic Terminology: A Trilingual Glossary.* New York: Praeger, 1966. A glossary of terms in the field.

Smith, Perry, Jerrold P. Allen, John H. Stewart, III, and F. Douglas Whitehouse. *Creating Strategic Vision.* Washington, DC: National Defense University Press, 1987. Four essays written after a year-long research seminar. Excellent treatment of the need for long-range planning, and some methods to be used in developing alternative futures.

Snyder, Jack. *The Ideology of the Offensive: Military Decision Making and the Disasters of 1914.* Ithaca, NY: Cornell University Press, 1984. Important work on strategic choice. Snyder identifies all the questions which should be asked.

Statistical Abstract of the United States 1989. Washington, DC: U.S. Department of Commerce, 1989.

Strayer, Joseph R., and Dana Carleton Munro. *The Middle Ages 395–1500.* New York: Appleton-Century-Crofts, Inc., 1942. A timeless and comprehensive treatment of an interesting and important period in European history.

Stubbing, Richard A., with Richard A. Mendel. *The Defense Game.* New York: Harper and Row, 1986. A searing critique of the defense establishment and how it operates by one who was part of it.

Toland, John. *The Rising Sun.* New York: Random House, 1970. A history, largely from the Japanese perspective, of the decline and fall of the Japanese Empire between the years 1936 and 1945.

Tuchman, Barbara W. *The Guns of August.* New York: Macmillan, 1972. A delightful and eminently readable account of the first month of World War I.

_____. *Practicing History.* New York: Alfred A. Knopf, 1981. A collection of Prof. Tuchman's essays on writing about and learning from history.

Van Creveld, Martin. *Command in War*. Cambridge: Harvard University Press, 1985. Masterful description of the evolution of command.

Webster's New World Dictionary, 2nd College Edition. New York: The World Publishing Company, 1970.

Weigley, Russell F. *The American Way of War*. New York: Macmillan, 1973. One of the basic books for the study of strategy in the United States.

Wildausky, Aaron, ed. *Beyond Containment: Alternative American Policies Toward the Soviet Union*. San Francisco: ICS Press, 1983. Selections examine the effectiveness and future of the containment policy aimed at the Soviet Union.

Williams, J. D. *The Compleat Strategyst*. New York: McGraw-Hill, 1966. An important resource on game theory.

Williams, T. Harry. *The History of American Wars from 1745 to 1918*. New York: Alfred A. Knopf, 1981. Another excellent military history by a noted historian.

Willmott, H. P. *Empires in the Balance*. Annapolis: Naval Institute Press, 1982. Excellent recounting of the origins of and the actions incident to the war in the Pacific.

Wright, Robert K., Jr. *The Continental Army*. Washington, DC: U.S. Army Center of Military History, 1986. A very detailed history of the Continental Army, including unit lineages. The last volume of a special study on the Revolutionary War.

Wylie, J. C., RADM, USN. *Military Strategy: A General Theory of Power*. New Brunswick, NJ: Rutgers University Press, 1967. An outstanding and informative book on the how and why of strategic theory and strategy development.

Yanitz, Boris, and William H. Newman. *Strategy in Action*. New York: The Free Press, 1982. Brings strategy and strategic planning to the business world.

Monographs

Annual Report to the Congress Fiscal Year 1988 by Caspar W. Weinberger, Secretary of Defense. Washington, DC: U.S. Government Printing Office, January 12, 1987. The Secretary of Defense's annual report.

Brown, Thomas A. *Potential Applications of Manual Games*. Paper from a talk given at the 1982 Joint National Meeting of the Operations Research Society of America and The Institute of Management Sciences, February 1984. If you still play manual war games, you can get some suggestions.

Carr, John W., III, Noah S. Prywes, *et al. Man-Computer Problem Solving in Real-Time Naval Duels*. Technical report. The Moore School of Electrical Engineering, University of Pennsylvania, October 1970. A research report on some early decision-aiding work.

Davis, Paul K., and James A. Winnefeld. *The RAND Strategy Assessment Center: An Overview and Interim Conclusions About Utility and Development Options*. Santa Monica: RAND, March 1983. More information on RAND's work in strategy assessment through simulation. An exciting report.

_____. *RAND's Experience in Applying Artificial Intelligence Techniques to Strategic-Level Military-Political War Gaming*. Santa Monica: RAND, April 1984. Their system is on line.

Defense Organization: The Need for Change. Washington, DC: Staff Report to the Committee on Armed Services, U.S. Senate, October 16, 1985. The report of an in-depth study of the Defense Department and all its warts, conducted by the staff of the Senate Armed Services Committee.

Department of Defense Dictionary of Military and Associated Terms. JCS Pub 1. Washington, DC: Joint Chiefs of Staff, January 1, 1986. Invaluable if you are not familiar with the jargon.

Discriminate Deterrence. Report of the Commission on Integrated Long-Term Strategy. Washington, DC, January 1988. Interesting endorsement of precision guided weapons as a panacea to strategic ills.

Hendrickson, Robert G. *Pro's and Con's of War Gaming and Simulation.* Washington, DC: Research Analysis Corp., October 1961. The questions here and those of today do not differ much.

Jones, William M. *On the Adapting of Political-Military Games for Various Purposes.* Santa Monica: RAND, March 1986. A paper on what might be gained from gaming high-level scenarios.

Kent, Glenn A. *A Framework for Defense Planning.* Santa Monica: RAND, August 1989. Very interesting work on what needs to be done to improve strategic planning.

Lambcth, Benjamin S. *On Thresholds in Soviet Military Thought.* Santa Monica: RAND, March 1983. Some of the ways the Soviets think, by an expert.

Leal, Antonio. *Evaluating the Effectiveness of Military Decision Support Systems: Theoretical Foundations, Expert System Design and Experimental Plan.* U.S. Army Research Institute for Behavioral and Social Sciences, September 1982. Some early work on what might be important to look for in an expert system decision aid.

Maritime Power: Some Observations on Strategy, Tactics and Technology. Fairfax, VA: National Security Research, March 1986. An excellent review of the strengths and weaknesses of maritime power.

The Maritime Strategy. Annapolis: U.S. Naval Institute, 1986. This is the unclassified version of the Navy's road map.

Mindset: National Styles in Warfare and the Operational Level of Planning, Conduct and Analysis. Potomac, MD: C & L Associates for the Office of Net Assessment, DOD, March 10, 1980. Interesting analysis of the effect of perceptions on planning.

Moore, John Norton, and Robert F. Turner. *The Legal Structure of Defense Organization.* Memorandum prepared for President's Blue Ribbon Commission on Defense Management, Washington, DC, January 15, 1986. Well researched and informative history of legislation affecting the defense establishment.

National Security Strategy of the United States. Washington, DC: The White House, March 1990. This is the document required by Goldwater-Nichols. It is the only document in the public view which addresses the national strategy.

Pappageorge, John G., COL, USA. *Maintaining the Geostrategic Advantage.* Military Issues Research Memorandum. Strategic Studies Institute, Carlisle Barracks, PA: U.S. Army War College, December 1977. Extremely interesting discourse on how national, military and "geostrategy" have been linked over time as well as in our times.

President's Blue Ribbon Commission on Defense Management: An Interim Report to the President. Washington, DC: February 23, 1986. The so-called Packard Report, which focused much-needed attention on some management ills.

RAND's *Experience in Applying AI Techniques to Strategic-Level Military-Political War Gaming.* Paper prepared for delivery at the Summer Computer Simulation

Conference of the Society for Computer Simulation, July 23–26, 1984, Boston, Massachusetts. A description of RAND's beginning efforts with their strategic analysis simulation.

Report of the Secretary of Defense Caspar W. Weinberger to the Congress on the FY 1986 Budget, FY 1987 Authorization Request and FY 1986–90 Defense Program. Washington, DC: U.S. Government Printing Office, February 4, 1985. The Secretary's annual report.

Reule, Fred J., LTCOL, USAF. *Dynamic Stability: A New Concept for Deterrence*. Maxwell AFB, AL: Air University Press, September 1987. Collection of essays describing a novel way of approaching deterrence wherein the United States stops implicit cooperation with the Soviets and denies them targets.

Shubik, M. *The Uses, Value and Limitations of Game Theoretic Methods in Defense Analysis*. Cowles Foundation Discussion Paper #766, Cowles Foundation for Research in Economics, Yale University, October 9, 1985. A description of the strengths and weaknesses of classes of models.

Staudenmaier, William O., COL, USA. *Military Strategy in Transition*. Military Issues Research Memorandum. Carlisle Barracks, PA: Strategic Studies Institute, U.S. Army War College, November 1978. Details the changes in strategy brought about by nuclear weapons and notes the need for more planning.

Thibault, George E., ed. *The Art and Practice of Military Strategy*. Washington, DC: National Defense University, 1984. Traces military strategy through its practitioners.

U.S. Codes and Administrative News, vol. 4. Legislative History, 99th Congress, 2nd Session, Washington, 1986. Contains a summary and complete text of Goldwater-Nichols.

Articles

Allen, Thomas B. "Sam and Ivan: Bottomline on Wargames." *Jane's Defense Weekly*, February 6, 1988, pp. 217–218. Describes the "agents" in RAND's strategy assessment system and the use to which they are being put by the U.S. military.

Brooks, Linton F., CAPT, USN. "Escalation and Naval Strategy." U.S. Naval Institute *Proceedings*, August 1984, pp. 33–37. Points out the importance of escalation control in a nuclear environment and the implications for strategy.

Brown, Harold. "A Restructuring in Search of a Strategy." *Los Angeles Times*, November 26, 1989, p. M7. Military cuts should only be done on the basis of a new strategy.

Cawood, David. "Managing Innovations: Military Strategy in Business." *Business Horizons*, 27, No. 6, Nov–Dec 1984. How the tenets of military strategy can be applied in the business world.

Friedman, Norman. "U.S. Maritime Strategy." *International Defense Review*, 18, No. 7, 1988, pp. 1071–5. A review of the historical antecedents of the maritime strategy and its utility for the Navy.

Gray, Colin S. "National Style in Strategy." *International Security*, Fall 1981, pp. 21–47. A contribution to the literature on strategic culture.

———. "Maritime Strategy." U.S. Naval Institute *Proceedings*, February 1986, pp. 34–42. Reiterates the utility of navies in support of land action.

Hughes, Wayne P., CAPT, USN (RET). "Naval Tactics and Their Influence on Strategy." *Naval War College Review*, 39, No. 1, Jan–Feb 1986, pp. 2–17. Tactical capability makes strategy possible; build from the bottom up.

Kissinger, Henry A. "Preparing a New U.S. Position to Meet the Next World Order." *Los Angeles Times*, editorial section, March 27, 1988, p. 1. An analysis of American interests and threats to them in the new world environment is a necessity.

Komer, Robert. "Maritime Strategy vs. Coalition Defense." *Foreign Affairs*, Summer 1982, pp. 1124-1144. The continental or land strategy rather than the maritime. Mr. Komer is European-minded.

Lehman, John F. "Nine Principles for the Future of American Maritime Power." U.S. Naval Institute *Proceedings*, February 1984, pp. 47-51. The ex-Secretary of the Navy on how to keep the Navy in the game.

Lenat, Douglas B. "Computer Software for Intelligent Systems." *Scientific American*, 251, No. 3, September 1984, pp. 204-213. Moving intelligent systems into the front lines.

Lord, Carnes. "American Strategic Culture." *Comparative Strategy*, 5, No. 3, 1985. An important article if you want to understand the concept of strategic culture.

McFetridge, Charles D., MAJ, USA. "Foreign Policy and Military Strategy: The Civil-Military Equation." *Military Review*, April 1986, pp. 22-30. Unless objectives are well defined, military strategy has no chance of being relevant.

MacKubin, Thomas Owen. "American Strategic Culture and Civil-Military Relations: The Case for JCS Reform." *Naval War College Review*, 39, No. 2, Mar-Apr 1986, pp. 43-59. Organizational reform is suggested because bureaucratic tendencies are preventing the development of an effective military strategy.

Mustin, Henry C., VADM, USN. "Maritime Strategy from the Deckplates." U.S. Naval Institute *Proceedings*, September 1986, p. 33. A crusty Admiral translates the maritime strategy.

O'Meara, Andrew P., Jr., LCOL, USA. "Strategy and the Military Professional, Part I." *Military Review*, LX, No. 1, January 1980, pp. 38-45. An attempt to bring a little order to the definition of strategy and how it is regarded.

Osgood, Robert E. "American Grand Strategy: Patterns, Problems and Prescriptions." *Naval War College Review*, 36, No. 5, Sept-Oct 1983, pp. 5-17. The lack of specificity regarding national interests is at the root of the strategic problem.

Pace, Dale K. "Scenario Use in Naval System Design." *Naval Engineers Journal*, January 1986, pp. 59-66. How scenarios affect technical evaluations, and how to put together useful ones.

Polmar, Norman, and Dr. Scott C. Truver. "The Maritime Strategy." *Air Force Magazine*, November 1987, pp. 70-79. How the maritime strategy came to be and what it is about.

Powers, Robert C., CAPT, USN. "Castles, Knights and Bishops in Naval Strategy." U.S. Naval Institute *Proceedings*, June 1984, pp. 30-37. Maneuvering is the key to both strategic and tactical success.

Richelson, Jeffrey. "PD 59, NSDD-13 and the Reagan Strategic Modernization Program." *Journal of Strategic Studies*, June 1983, pp. 125-146. The effect of Reagan programs on nuclear strategy.

Shelton, Michael W., CDR, CEC, USN. "Plan Orange Revisited." U.S. Naval Institute *Proceedings*, December 1984, pp. 50-56. The author finds similarities in the old Plan Orange, which was targeted at Japan, and what might work against the Soviet Navy.

Spinney, Franklin C. "A Defense Strategy That Works." In "Professional Notes,"

U.S. Naval Institute *Proceedings*, January 1990, pp. 98–99. Strategy is, in a very real sense, resource-driven. This article proposes a methodology for bringing fiscal reality to the process.

Summers, Harry G., Jr., COL, USA (RET). "War: Deter, Fight, Terminate. The Purpose of War Is a Better Peace." *Naval War College Review*, 39, No. 1, Jan–Feb 1986. Strategy and operations are simply means to an end.

Talbott, Strobe. "America Abroad." *Time*, December 11, 1989, p. 38. Commentary on developing an enemy against which to measure ourselves.

Tashjean, John E. "The Transatlantic Clausewitz, 1952–1982." *Naval War College Review*, 35, No. 6, Nov–Dec 1982, pp. 69–86. New strategic approach after Korea required different thinking and preparation.

Toth, Robert C. "U.S. Urged to Revise Security Plan for Future." *Los Angeles Times*, Monday, January 11, 1988, p. 6. A report about the results of the deliberations of the Commission on Integrated Long-Term Strategy.

Turner, Stanfield, and George Thibault. "Preparing for the Unexpected." *Foreign Affairs*, 61, Fall 1982, pp. 122–36. Two experienced naval officers call for a more flexible strategy and force structure to go with it.

Vlahos, Michael. "Wargaming, An Enforcer of Strategic Realism: 1919–1942." *Naval War College Review*, 39, No. 2, Mar–Apr 1986, pp. 7–22. How the Navy broadened its strategic view through war gaming.

Watkins, James D., ADM, USN. "The Maritime Strategy." U.S. Naval Institute *Proceedings*, special supplement, January 1986. The Chief of Naval Operations explains the maritime strategy.

"Which Weapons Will Work." *U.S. News & World Report*, January 19, 1987, p. 19. Raises the question of the appropriateness of the weapons in hand to the problem.

Index

Acheson, Dean 49
Adams, Samuel 30
Air power 38, 50, 95
Alexander, Bevin 50
Alternative futures 153, 154, 155
Ambiguity, tolerance of 158
American Civil War: casualties 35, 86; character of 35, 86; as first "modern" war 85; lessons from 35, 37, 77, 86; opposing strategies 34
American cultural makeup 109
American foreign policy 3
Analytic models: creation of 139; reality of 134; structure of 139; uses of 139; validity and appropriateness of 139
Annihilation strategy 35
Antipathy of the electorate 102
Arab-Israeli Wars 19
Arkbatov, Georgi 71
Army of the Potomac 35
Army of the Republic of Vietnam (ARVN) 54
Army of the West 35
Aron, Raymond 14
Articles of Confederation 75
Artificial intelligence: continuum of applications 153; expert systems 153
Assuming conditions 140, 142
Atom bomb 15, 43
Attrition strategy 35

Baker, Newton D. 91
Board of Engineers (1821), report of 33
Body of military strategy, elements of 120
Bonaparte, Napoleon: as change agent

in warfare 32; defeat 14; in sale of Louisiana Territory 73
Breed's Hill, Battle of 82
British army: in North America 29; strategy during War for Independence 30
Brodie, Bernard 49
Budget cutting 65
Builder, Carl 142

California Territory 74
Central Intelligence Agency 6, 47
Characterizing enemies 106
Chief of Naval Operations 128
Churchill, Winston 41
CINCPAC 121, 138
CINCPACFLT 128
Classes of strategy 121
Close air support 69
Coalition warfare 41
Cognitive processes, impediments to 130
Cold War: end 71; origins 57, 95
Colonial Wars 81
Combined Chiefs of Staff 41
Command question 46
Communication capabilities 12–13
Competition in American life 107
Competitive strategies 122
Compromising on objectives 112
Confederacy strategy 34
Confederate army 35
Confederate States of America 77
Conflict: economic factors 14, 28; evolution of 11; preparation for 25; spectrum of 6, 15; U.S. philosophy of 25; with atomic weapons 15

187